PORTFOLIO
ELEPHANTS AND CHEETAHS

Saral Mukherjee is an associate professor in the production and quantitative methods area at IIM Ahmedabad (IIMA). He specializes in Operations Management and is involved in research, teaching and consulting in the areas of supply chain redesign, operations strategy, marketing–operations interface and managing platform businesses. He is a recipient of the Marti Mannariah Gurunath Outstanding Teacher Award at IIMA for seven successive years, from 2014 to 2020, and the SRK Distinguished PGPX Faculty Award at IIMA for 2017 and 2020. A production engineer from Jadavpur University, he worked on production shop floors before joining IIM Calcutta as a doctoral student. In an academic career spanning close to two decades at IIMA, he has taught core courses on Operations, Marketing and Ethics for MBA students as well as working executives.

INDIA'S BESTSELLING BUSINESS BOOKS SERIES

IIM

AHMEDABAD
BUSINESS BOOKS

ELEPHANTS AND CHEETAHS

The Beauty of Operations

SARAL MUKHERJEE

PORTFOLIO
PENGUIN

An imprint of Penguin Random House

PORTFOLIO

USA | Canada | UK | Ireland | Australia
New Zealand | India | South Africa | China | Singapore

Portfolio is part of the Penguin Random House group of companies
whose addresses can be found at global.penguinrandomhouse.com

Published by Penguin Random House India Pvt. Ltd
4th Floor, Capital Tower 1, MG Road,
Gurugram 122 002, Haryana, India

First published in Portfolio in Penguin Random House India 2021

ISBN 9780143451730

Typeset in Sabon by Manipal Technologies Limited, Manipal

Printed at Repro India Limited

www.penguin.co.in

To my parents,
Biswanath and Abha Mukherjee

ॐ भूर्भुवः स्वः
तत्सवितुर्वरेण्यं
भर्गो देवस्य धीमहि
धियो यो नः प्रचोदयात् ॥

The eternal, earth, air, heaven
That glory, that resplendence of the sun
May we contemplate the brilliance of that light
May the sun inspire our minds.

(*Gayatri Mantra*, *Rig Veda* 3.62.10,
translation by Dr Douglas Brooks)

Contents

Acknowledgements   xi
Preface   xiii
The Beauty of My Beloved   xvii

PART I: THE WHOLE

1. Systems Have Souls   3
2. System–Constraint Duality   10
3. Are Business Organizations Autopoietic?   18
4. Autopoiesis and Innovation   28
5. Purpose   37

PART II: THE DOORS

6. Closed Doors   45
7. Decision Areas in Operations Strategy   54
8. Performance Metrics and Dimensions   61

PART III: THE PATHS

9. Cost Leadership   71
10. Time Responsiveness   105

11. Cost-Cutting   129
12. Superior Quality   145
13. Superior Design   160
14. Convenience   201
15. Risk Minimization   223
16. Flexibility   240
17. The System Designed to Fail   259
18. Multiple Paths   291

PART IV: THE BEAUTY

19. The Beauty of Operations   309
20. Consciousness of Systems   327

Appendix A: Case Analysis
    A1. McDonald's Corporation   339
    A2. ZARA: Fast Fashion   350
    A3. Jiro Dreams of Sushi   366
Appendix B: Course Outline
Elephants and Cheetahs: Systems, Strategy
and Bottlenecks   385
Bibliography   391

Acknowledgements

THIS BOOK WOULD not have been possible without my students. While I have written this book *for* my students, they too have brought this book into existence by actively questioning me in the classroom and outside it, educating me, introducing me to concepts and case studies, encouraging me and writing to me years after the course is over. It is the students who have been pushing me to write down my thoughts and publish them as a book. I owe the biggest gratitude to my graduate students and the participants in the various executive education programmes that I have taught at IIMA over the years.

I am grateful to students, friends and faculty colleagues who have reviewed the book and given me suggestions for improvement. I would like to thank Sumit Tripathi, Darshit Jaju, Kishore Warrier, Santanu Ghosh, Sudarshan Jain, Prof. Amit Karna, Prof. N. Ravichandran and Prof. M.R. Dixit for taking time to provide me valuable feedback on the draft of the book. I thank my doctoral student Harit Joshi for reviewing the draft as well as helping me with some of the exhibits. I thank my friend Kaustubh Ray, whom I had the privilege of teaching photography during my student days, for help with the design of the book cover. I thank Radhika Marwah, Shreya Chakravertty, Antra K. and the team at Penguin Random House India for the editorial support.

The biggest support for writing this book has been my family. My wife, Parna, has been a critic of my lethargy in writing the book and encouraged me through the entire process. Together with my daughter, Upasana, and my sister, Pratiti, the three beautiful women in my life have provided me the inspiration to talk about the beauty of my beloved. Thank you.

Preface

THIS BOOK IS not about biology or the animal kingdom; this book is about Operations Strategy. This book is about the beauty inherent in business models seen from an Operations perspective. This book is about systems. It uses metaphors inspired by nature only as a means to arrive at a better appreciation of the system being studied.

The origin of this book can be traced to my sessions in the core courses of Operations Management I and Operations Management II in the PGP first-year curriculum, and the difficulties I faced in explaining the notion of operational trade-offs. Students would learn about how time-based competition differed from competing on costs and yet come back and ask why we can't have both. The metaphor of the Cheetah was a very powerful tool to intuitively explain the differences in strategic choice, and the students could immediately grasp that an elephant is not structured to run as a cheetah, and we cannot have both cost efficiency and time responsiveness beyond a point. The first case study where I used the Elephant and Cheetah metaphors was the Harvard Business School case study on Benetton, around 2002. The response was magical. I started using the metaphors in executive education classes. The response was euphoric.

Over the years, the metaphors multiplied. So too, the students meeting me after several years and telling me, 'I have forgotten everything other than Elephants and Cheetahs.' I didn't know whether to laugh or cry. In 2010, I made a leap of faith and started teaching core courses in Marketing as I believed that the Marketing–Operations interface was a neglected area in management education. In 2013, I returned to teaching Operations, but instead of teaching core courses, offered an elective on Operations Strategy titled 'Elephants and Cheetahs: Systems, Strategy and Bottlenecks'. When the course outline underwent peer review, a colleague suggested I rename the course as 'Operations Strategy'. Obstinate as always, I argued that a rose by any other name should smell as sweet.

The Elephants and Cheetahs elective was offered in Term 4 (June–August), 2013, and I expected about twenty to thirty students to register. I was pleasantly surprised when seventy-six students enrolled for the course. The initial registrations had been even higher, but predictably, several students ran away after the first class when I started discussing the concept of autopoiesis. After the course ended, I received a request from the student body to offer the course a second time in a subsequent term. The registrations continued to swell, and by 2019 I was teaching four sections across programmes, all packed with more than a hundred students in each class. We frequently ran out of chairs in the classroom, with students sitting in the aisles.

You might find the above boastful. I mention it because I know in my heart that the students are not thronging the classroom for hearing me; they are there for my beloved. I know my capabilities as a teacher; they are average at best. The students are not dazzled by my non-existent intellectual brilliance; they are starting to see meaning in their existence as managers, to see beauty in the workplace, to fall in love with the subject, to find a purpose in life.

The purpose of writing this book is to reach out to a larger set of students, to enable them to see beauty in Operations. The word 'beauty' is conspicuous by its absence in Operations texts; my purpose is to make you open your eyes to it. If you fail to see this beauty after reading this book, it does not mean there is no beauty; it means I have not been able to communicate it over the medium of the written word. I pray for forgiveness for wasting your time. In my defence, I would like to say just one thing. I tried.

I tried to bring back systems orientation in teaching Operations. I tried to bring aesthetics into a field obsessed with quantification. I tried to appreciate Operations systems and see parallels in nature. I tried to connect them with literature, with music, with arts. I tried to dig deeper into the case studies of organizations to identify the core set of tensions which ran through them. I tried to see meaning in an otherwise meaningless existence. I tried.

The Beauty of My Beloved

I WANT YOU to fall in love with my beloved. My beloved is everywhere but has chosen to reveal herself to me through, of all things, Operations Management. Fortunate are those to whom she reveals herself through the arts. An engineer by training, a management science academic by profession, I am the least likely person to have had a glimpse of her. The world of commerce and business are far away from romanticism, and are the least likely places for falling in love with my beloved. Yet, is there a place where she cannot be found? If you can fall in love with my beloved, nay, our beloved, in the din and bustle of the marketplace and the factory, you can fall in love with her anywhere. Take a chance on her through managing organizations; if you fail to grasp her, you might as well go home rich.

Have you seen her different faces? Have you ever wondered how many different types of organizations there are in the world? Look around you, you can see establishments of all sizes and shapes. There are private firms, public sector organizations, non-governmental organizations and governments. I am sure you would have encountered quite a few organizations in your daily life. In fact, unless you are living alone on an island, it would be quite difficult for any ordinary person not to have transacted with any such entity. You may be an employee of an organization, engaged in activities related to serving consumers, businesses and governments. But familiarity with organizations does not mean you understand them. And managing an organization without understanding it is a recipe for disaster. Understanding rarely comes without appreciating the beauty lying hidden in plain sight.

My students want to understand businesses so as to manage them. A classification of businesses based on ownership (private, public sector, etc.) or sector (consumer durables, fashion, heavy industries, software, banking, etc.) or market structure (monopoly, duopoly, perfect competition, etc.) or regulation (regulated, informal, etc.) or type (manufacturing, service, etc.) is very helpful in telling us *what* the firm is. Such classification provides little insight on *how* to manage them. Understanding the beauty of Operations helps us classify businesses in a way which connects to how they are structured internally to produce and deliver goods and services.

As an academic, it has been my job to understand businesses so that I can share my knowledge with my students. My understanding of businesses is tinged with the disciplinary background I come from. I trained as a production engineer, worked on the shop floor, completed my doctoral thesis on Operations Management, and I have been teaching, training and consulting in the domain of Operations and Supply Chain Management. The world of business that I perceive is through the lens of Operations. Hence, the beauty I perceive in business is the beauty of Operations. I do not claim that this beauty is superior to the beauty of businesses perceived through any other disciplinary lens. I do claim that there is a beauty in Operations and my mission is to make you open your eyes to that beauty so that you can perceive a whole new world hidden in plain sight.

A whole new world hidden in plain sight! Surely you have seen enough businesses, and they all seem the same after some time. The world we perceive is based on our sensory organs. Human beings do not have the keen sense of smell of a dog or the night vision capability of an owl or the echolocation capabilities of a bat. The reality we perceive may be different from that of a dog, owl or bat. Is there an absolute reality out there or are there multiple realities?

One day, when I was working on the factory shop floor, I had to visit the corporate office next door. As I hurried through the shop floor, a colleague asked where I was going. He then prophetically warned me, 'You will slip out of corporate office.' I had no idea what he meant. Did he mean that I was more suited to a factory shop floor rather than a corporate office? I realized the truth when I started walking on the smooth marble flooring of the office and my feet slid around. As it turns out, the soles of the shoes you wear on the shop floor soak in oil over a long duration. When you wear the same shoes into the relatively much smoother floor of an office, it's hard to maintain solid footing. You need to take extra care and walk slowly, lest you fall. None of the other denizens of the office or visitors experience this reality. The shop floor worker experiences a walk through the corporate office in a manner different from any other corporate employee or visitor.

I have worn the Operations shoes for such a long time and walked through so many factories and service facilities that the Operations oil has soaked into my skin. I see the corporate world through this Operations-soaked lens. I cannot help it. What I can do is to lend you these shoes so that you experience business models from the Operations viewpoint.

Review the shoes you have worn. If you have worn Human Resource (HR) shoes, you may perceive an organization differently from a person who has worn Finance shoes all along. Each one is a different reality, each one is beautiful, each one incomparable. To be a general manager, you need to wear all kinds of shoes. Change your lens of inquiry and you can perceive a whole new world. If you haven't tried on an Operations Strategy lens before, try looking at businesses from that viewpoint and you will be surprised at how much you missed.

If you are daunted by the prospect of learning the rigour of Operations, fret not. I will gift you my Operations shoes so that you can perceive the beauty of my beloved. The objective of writing this book is to bring this unconventional treatment of Operations Strategy to a wider audience. I would consider my efforts fruitful if you are able to catch a glimpse of my beloved and fall in love with her.

PART I: THE WHOLE

CHAPTER 1

Systems Have Souls

YES, YOU READ it right, systems have souls. And that single sentence has the potential to have me excommunicated from my academic discipline. Not a single textbook on Operations Management mentions this statement. Operations Management has its roots in management science, and science demands proof for any statement. Where is the proof that a system has a soul? But wait, before you think about proof, first define soul.

I offer no definitions; I offer no proof. I offer only the scientific temper of questioning: Does a system have a soul? The statement 'systems have souls' is thus a hypothesis that we would want to prove or disprove. I myself have not been able to prove or disprove this statement. But that does not mean others cannot. What worries me is not the proof either for or against this statement, nor the absence of proof, but the complete silence on this question in the Operations Management domain. It is as if this question is irrelevant. I beg to differ. I do not know of any question more fundamental to Operations Management than this one.

In the absence of proof or a counter example, one approach towards progress is to raise the question at a metaphysical level. A philosophical treatment of this question is not meant to provide definite answers but to expound alternate viewpoints. I do not claim my viewpoint as superior, let alone infallible. In my view, systems have souls. It does not matter what my view is; what matters is your own viewpoint. What do you think? Do systems have souls? The question is highly philosophical since you first need to ask yourself, do you have a soul?

If your answer to this question is affirmative, stay with me and question my viewpoint. If the answer is negative, stay with me and question my viewpoint rigorously, and question your viewpoint too. If you have never been bothered by such questions, read no further.

But why are the two questions related? It is because the human observer and the organization being observed are both systems. Have you ever thought of yourself as a system? What is a system anyway?

A System Is Greater Than the Sum of Its Parts

This conception of a system mirrors the statement 'The whole is greater than the sum of its parts', attributed to Aristotle. Do you have parts in your body? Of course you do. Your body has sub-systems, like the circulatory system, nervous system, digestive system, etc., which are themselves made up of smaller parts like individual cells. Each cell is itself a system made up of even smaller parts, and we can go on like this to sub-atomic particles. Similarly, a car can be disassembled into sub-assemblies like the engine, transmission, chassis, etc., and further into individual parts made up of molecules. An organization is made up of departments and factories with machines and workers. It is very easy to see that a system has parts. But a mere collection of the parts is not a system. A system is *greater* than the sum of its parts.

The quality which makes a system a 'system' is thus inherent in that word 'greater'. If I disassemble a car and put all the parts in a box and give it to you, would you call it a car? Surely something is missing. The parts of the car need to interact with each other. In the process of this interaction, certain parts, like fuel, may get transformed. It is worthwhile to think of a system as being composed of a set of components, a set of interactions and a set of transformations. When the parts interact with each other flawlessly and the transformations are as planned, the system exhibits synergy. It is this synergy which is the difference between the sum of the parts and the whole. Note that synergy is not a part of the system, nor is it an interaction or transformation. This synergy is a result, not a physical or logical input. Synergy has to be attained; it cannot be guaranteed by providing a set of inputs.

Figure 1: A System Is Not Just the Sum of Parts

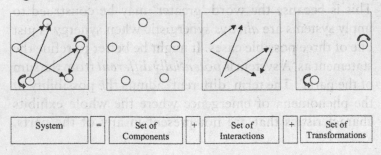

| System | = | Set of Components | + | Set of Interactions | + | Set of Transformations |

A system which is just a collection of parts is more of an apology of a system as it involves no interactions or transformations of the parts constituting the whole. The value of this collection is just the sum of the values of individual parts. Worse still is the situation where the collection's value is destroyed if the parts are disharmonious in the union. How much is 2 + 2? It is 4 only under the assumption that there exists no cross-interaction effect between the parts being added. The sum may be more than 4 or less than 4 if the cross-interaction effect is positive or negative respectively. It is precisely the job of the management to create and nurture an organization where 2 + 2 > 4. The management can create value for shareholders through a merger between two firms if the merged entity achieves synergy. The management can also create value for shareholders by demerging a large conflict-ridden firm into its constituents when the constituents are working at cross purposes and fighting against each other rather than fighting competition. A system is greater than the sum of its parts since the system includes not just the parts but also the interaction effects between the parts; the interaction effect being potentially conflicting, non-existent or synergistic.

The gestalt statement that 'a system is greater than the sum of its parts' thus needs to be used with caution. This is because the word 'greater' may be construed to imply systems are *always* synergistic when synergy is just one of three possible cases. It might be better to refine the statement as 'A system is *potentially different* from the sum of the parts'. The term 'different' admits the possibility of the phenomena of emergence where the whole exhibits characteristics that are not present in any of the parts.

The term 'potential' refers to the *potential* existence of a non-material gap between the whole and the sum of the parts arising from conflicts or synergy between parts. The potential to be different extends to situations where the parts *behave differently* when they are part of different wholes. On first thought, this seems fantastic—think of a situation where the same fuel behaves differently if it is poured into a car versus a truck. Yet, in socio-technical systems like organizations, the behaviour of the same person may change when the person is aware of the norms that the system expects everyone to adhere to.

A system admits the possibility of a difference or gap between itself and the aggregation of its constituents. This difference is non-material and beyond quantification and scientific measurement, yet something that can be sensed! It belongs to the realm of poetry. You can call this gap anything—X or Y or Z or synergy or essence or soul. The name does not matter, the potential existence of the difference matters. I am comfortable with the word 'soul'; if you are not, you could perhaps use the word 'synergy' or 'essence' or any other word you are comfortable with.

Our search for systems is thus inherently linked to our search for soul. In fact, I want you to embark on not one but two parallel searches. One search is in the realm of the organization. Look at the organizations around you and ask whether they are systems, and if so, what is their soul like? This realm is the domain of your professional world. If you are managing an organization, ask yourself what is the soul of the organization you are managing. If you are leading your organization, ask yourself what is the soul of the organization you are building. Simultaneously, ask yourself, 'Who am I? Do I have a soul? If I do not have a soul then who is this person who is asking?'

Philosophical questions about existence have been dealt with by illustrious philosophers. I do not have any delusions of grandeur. I don't know who I am but I have a fair idea of who I am not. The meagre knowledge I have is related to the study of Operations Management in organizations. So I would restrict myself to the organizational domain rather than venture into the domain of philosophy and religion. However, if you are able to develop an insight into the essence of organizations, nothing can stop you from turning the search inwards and questioning yourself. I do it myself and recommend that you do it too. It is one way in which the distance between professional and personal lives can be bridged.

Managers like you have an advantage that philosophers do not. Remember that synergy is not automatic, it has to be attained. Thus, there is a possibility that under your leadership the organization can be turned around from being a mere collection of parts to a whole, from being soulless (or the soul of a collection) to one with a distinct soul. Better still, there is a possibility that under your leadership the organization can be turned around from one characterized by organization silos, infighting and a departmental 'we vs they' mentality to a purpose-driven outfit where employees in different roles support and depend on each other; a transformation from a soul-sapping work environment to a soulful one. And even more aspirational is the possibility that under your leadership the organization can create and nurture in employees an understanding of 'Who are we? Why do we exist? How do we do things?' which leads to a unique culture where the parts behave *differently* within your organizational system because they understand the unique system and their role in it. Think about the implications of these statements. You can actually nurture the organizational soul. You can feel the ebb and flow of the organizational soul, celebrate its flowering, witness its transformations and mourn its decay. You can guide its development and witness how the organizational soul transforms who you are. What a privilege to be a manager!

CHAPTER 2

System–Constraint Duality

'Constraints are of high importance in cybernetics because *when a constraint exists advantage can usually be taken of it.*'

—Ross Ashby

A CAR, A human being and an organization are all systems, but at different levels. To understand the classification of systems, you need to first understand the fundamental connection between systems and constraints. We are indebted to cybernetics pioneer Ross Ashby for showing the ubiquitous nature of constraints, since every law of nature, every object, every prediction, every learning and every machine is a constraint. While he did not explicitly state it, his analysis hints at a system–constraint duality.

> There Cannot Exist a System Without a Constraint

A constraint exists when the set of all possible outcomes is restricted. For example, consider a chair with four legs. Each of these legs separately can have six degrees of freedom, and thus the collection of four legs has a total of twenty-four degrees of freedom. However, when these legs are joined together to form the chair, the chair has six degrees of freedom. Thus, what makes a chair a 'chair' is the existence of a constraint which removes eighteen degrees of freedom. Similarly, consider a system of weather forecasting. If all weather outcomes are equally likely then a forecast has no meaning. A forecast of sunny weather implies a constraint which removes the possibility of thunderstorms. Ross Ashby showed us the world as constraints. For example, every object is a constraint, every law in physics implies the existence of constraints (for instance, $E = mc^2$ implies that for a specific value of m only a specific value of E is possible, cutting off the infinitely many other values of E), every information system is a constraint (for instance, a traffic light system where all possible combinations of red, yellow and green are allowed is simply chaos), etc.

The equivalence of systems and constraints allows us to classify systems based on the type of constraint, as elucidated by John Mingers. Level 1 systems are those which are defined by spatial constraints. For example, a crystal is defined by the spatial arrangement of its constituent atoms, a chair is defined by the spatial constraints on the movement of its constituent legs, etc. Level 2 systems are defined by temporal constraints in addition to spatial constraints. For example, a clock is defined by specific angular velocities (temporal constraints) of the minute hand and the second hand as well as the relative positions

Table 1: A Hierarchy of Complexity

Level	Description	Characteristic	Type of relations	Example
1	Structures and frameworks	Static, spatial patterns	Topology (where)	Bridge, mountain, table, crystal
2	Single mechanistic systems	Dynamic, predetermined changes, processes	Order (when)	Solar system, clock, tune, computer
3	Control mechanisms, cybernetic systems	Error-controlled feedback, information	Specification (what)	Thermostat, body temperature system, auto-catalytic system
4	Living systems	Continuous self-production	Autopoietic relations	Cell, amoeba, single-celled bacteria
5	Multicellular systems	Functional differentiation	Structural coupling between cells (second-order autopoiesis)	Plants, fungi, moulds, algae
6	Organisms with nervous systems	Interaction with relations	Symbolic, abstract relations	Most animals (except, e.g., sponges)
7	Observing systems	Language, self-consciousness	Recursive, self-referential relations	Humans
8	Social systems	Rules, meanings, norms, power	Structural coupling between organisms (third-order autopoiesis)	Families, organizations
9	Transcendental systems			

Source: Mingers, J. (1997). Systems Typologies in the Light of Autopoiesis: A Reconceptualization of Boulding's Hierarchy, and a Typology of Self-Referential Systems. *Systems Research and Behavioral Science,* 14, 303–13.

of those hands (spatial constraints) at a particular instant. Level 3 systems include temporal and spatial constraints as well as a specific variable or set of variables which are kept constant or within a range. An example of a Level 3 system is the thermostat in an air conditioner which keeps the temperature constant by disconnecting the circuit when the temperature drops below a range and reconnecting the circuit when it increases beyond the set range. Note that each higher level includes the characteristics of the lower levels.

At Level 4, a crucial distinction arises. Till Level 3, all systems are non-living. At Level 4, the living cell makes its appearance. But what is the connection of a living cell to a constraint? We owe it to two Chilean biologists, Humberto Maturana and Francesco Varela, for introducing the concept of autopoiesis.

Maturana and Varela were concerned about the question 'What makes a living system living?' Is it the characteristic of autonomy, the ability to reproduce, or something else? A computer virus is a non-living entity and yet it can reproduce. On the other hand, a mule is a living creature but it cannot reproduce. To Maturana and Varela, the defining characteristic of a living organism is not its ability to *re*produce but its ability to *self*-produce, which they called autopoiesis (auto = self, poiesis = production). Autopoiesis is a necessary and sufficient condition for a system to be living. A single cell is a living system as it maintains the set of interactions and transformations needed to continually regenerate the components and the set of interactions and transformations. To understand autopoiesis you need to remember the characteristic of a homeostatic machine introduced in Level 3 earlier. A homeostatic machine keeps a variable or a set of variables constant or within a range. Instead of a set of variables, the autopoietic machine keeps the set of interactions and transformations constant. This small change makes a big difference. Note that among the three sets of components, interactions and transformations constituting a system, two of the sets are kept constant under autopoiesis. The crucial set which is left out is the set of components. This results in a very interesting situation. The cell is made up of a set of components which some time ago was outside the boundary of the cell, currently is inside the cell and sometime later would cease to be a part of the cell. Yet it is this set of components which maintains the set of interactions and transformations. An autopoietic system is thus relation-static rather than component-static. The components do not matter *as long as* the set of interactions and transformations is kept unchanged.

An allopoietic system, like a car or a man-made toy or machine, differs from an autopoietic one in that the car does not produce the car while the living cell produces itself. The most striking feature of autopoiesis is that components do not matter *as long as* relations of interactions and transformations are kept constant. The controversial nature of this statement will become apparent when we discuss Level 8 systems later on. At this point, you need to note that autopoiesis is a constraint since certain things are being held constant. Hence the system–constraint duality applies as much to non-living systems (Level 1–3) as well as living systems (Level 4–7).

Level 5 systems are where there exists structural coupling between Level 4 systems. Examples are multicellular plants. Structural coupling implies that in addition to the autopoietic constraints applicable for each of the individual cells, the interactions between Level 4 systems are not random and follow certain constraints. A Level 5 system thus exemplifies loose coupling between two or more sub-systems, referred to as second-order autopoiesis.

Organisms at Level 6 develop a central nervous system and are able to differentiate between abstract concepts like hot and cold, before and after. Most animals belong to this level. The big jump comes when, at Level 7, an organism like a human being is able to reflect on not just external objects but also itself. It can make self-referential statements like 'I think, therefore I am'. The emergence of language is a cornerstone of Level 7 systems. Note that Levels 5, 6 and 7 are all second-order autopoietic systems and hence the system–constraint duality holds.

At Level 8, we have the emergence of third-order autopoietic systems like social institutions (families, clans, clubs), national institutions (Parliament, courts, army) and business institutions (corporates, partnership firms). The components of these institutions include Level 7 human beings who are themselves second-order autopoietic systems.

Finally, at Level 9, John Mingers tantalizingly mentioned transcendental systems but refrained from making any observations on them. Yet, the very mention of the transcendental within a scientific classification of systems keeps open the possibility of an integrative framework that encompasses a human being (Level 7), her social and professional contexts (Level 8) and her spiritual experiences (Level 9).

What is common to all levels up to Level 8 is that their existence is contingent on the existence of specific constraints. Perhaps Level 9 too has constraints, but our scientific inquiry is too feeble to comprehend that stage yet. Perhaps Level 9 is all about the lack of constraints. What constraint does the formless have? In contrast, the world of form is the world of constraints.

At this stage, I want you to look around you at the world in wonder. The whole world is made up of constraints! Think for once of a world without constraints—would it be worth living? Tell me frankly, does not the word 'constraint' have a negative connotation in your mind? The time has come for you to remove this negativity.

A constraint is beautiful. It allows a whole world to come into existence.

That whole world includes you as a component of social systems as well as you as a system by yourself. Look at yourself and see the constraints that define you. These constraints include not just the autopoietic constraint related to your physical body but also the constraints that society has imposed on you and the constraints that you have voluntarily imposed on yourself. Unless you are a slave and under duress, the social constraints exist because you allow them to be imposed on you. Thus, a free human being is free not from constraints but from constraints imposed by others. But this freedom may impinge on the freedom of others and hence the need for ethics and morality. Ethical codes may be social or religious in origin, and hence constraints imposed by others, or they may be like the Categorical Imperative of Immanuel Kant which is self-given. You are free to choose between constraints imposed by others or your own constraints. You just cannot escape constraints. Neither can business organizations.

CHAPTER 3

Are Business Organizations Autopoietic?

'You cannot step twice into the same river.'

—Heraclitus

AS A MANAGER, your focus is on systems at Level 8. The crucial question is whether Level 8 systems are autopoietic in nature. Why is this question so crucial? As per Maturana and Varela, autopoiesis is a necessary and sufficient condition for a system to be living. Thus, if an organization at Level 8 can be shown to be autopoietic, it implies that it is living. Conversely, if something is living, it must be autopoietic.

Is the firm you are working for a living firm? Is it autopoietic?

Whether Level 8 organizations are autopoietic or not is a highly debated topic. Maturana himself remained opposed to claiming Level 8 organizations as autopoietic. In his view, a Level 8 organization acts as a *medium* for the autopoiesis of Level 7 human beings. A main hurdle for claiming a Level 8 system as autopoietic is the question of domain. An autopoietic system would continuously produce the components which would themselves become part of interactions and transformations and help produce, maintain and remove other components. If we admit the human being as the component of a Level 8 system like a business organization, it is easy to see that the business does not create the human being. From this viewpoint, a business organization is a collection of Level 7 systems but is not autopoietic in itself. The immediate implication of this viewpoint is that business organizations are non-living.

Yet, we use so much imagery and terminology related to life when we discuss business organizations. Businesses are born, they grow, mature and die. They are treated as a distinct legal entity which has a date of incorporation and a date of dissolution. They have a separate identity different from their founders or managers and employees. Businesses strive to create and nurture brands which allow customers and others to refer to them, similar to individuals. The brands communicate with customers and stakeholders. Each of these brands strives to create an individuality which allows customer intimacy and the ability to refer to businesses by name. The businesses are valued as going concerns which may be substantially higher than the replacement cost of the assets. Employees create a vibrant culture inside the organization and managers nurture the workplace environment. Organizations are not just workplaces where you go to earn your daily bread. You laugh, cry, aspire, despair, compete and celebrate life along with your co-workers. It is difficult to think of all this as emanating from a non-living system.

A business organization is just one kind of Level 8 system. The field of sociology has long been concerned with other kinds of Level 8 systems like families and political systems. Sociology is thus the field of study which has been most concerned with the question of whether Level 8 systems are autopoietic or not. Niklas Luhmann, a well-respected and established sociologist, adopted and adapted the concept of autopoiesis to the field of sociology. In his view, Level 8 systems are autopoietic in the domain of communication. Communication is not just the act of speaking, it involves utterance and understanding. In Luhmann's view, communication gives rise to more communication and hence serves as the domain of autopoiesis. This crucial choice of domain was very controversial since he chose communication rather than the communicator. Critics argued that such a system means that the communicator does not matter, a step which dehumanizes communication. Luhmann held on to his views and later specifically addressed the question of domain in organizations. He believed that the domain of autopoiesis for organizations is decisions. Decisions create more decisions. Note again the criticism that follows that such an autopoietic system favours the decision over the decision-maker. While Luhmann's views have been well studied in sociology, it is interesting to note that management science has taken little note of them.

From the management science point of view, the choice of decision as the domain is appealing. A manager makes decisions; management science is the science of decision-making. But an organization constitutes not just of managers and their decision-making function.

What about the workers who are told what to do? What about the machines which need to be operated? To convert an organization into only a decision-making one takes away not just the field of emotion but also the field of work. Decision-making is the preserve of higher ranks in an army, for example. The work of the soldier who takes orders would thus be neglected under such an autopoietic system.

In my experience of organizations, I find both communication and decision as the choice of domain to be unsatisfactory. Yet to throw away the concept of autopoiesis just because our choice of domain is not satisfactory is like throwing out the baby with the bathwater. Management science needs to question if there are alternate choices of domains which would allow the constitution of an autopoietic system at Level 8. To date, there has not been much effort in this direction.

In my view, business organizations are Level 8 autopoietic systems in the domain of roles. Look inside an organization and you would find a variety of roles, from the janitor to the chairman of the board of directors. Each of these roles is important for the proper functioning of the organization. Employees are hired to fit these roles. As the employee grows in her career, she is groomed to take on other roles. In the process, the employee is always in the process of fitting into new roles and relinquishing previous ones. Sometimes a role may be designed to fit an employee in a process known as job-crafting. When a candidate is not hired, the rejected candidate is often informed that they do not fit the role. This is to allay any qualitative judgement of the capability of the candidate—the candidate may not fit a specific role but be the absolutely right fit for another. An employee can be assigned more than one role at a time.

Thus, we can look at the organization not as a collection of Level 7 human beings but a collection of different roles. The concept of roles can be extended even to inanimate systems like machines. For example, different machines on a factory shop floor perform different roles. Machine operation thus entails the machine playing its role and the operator playing her role.

Roles are not static but evolving over time. In the start-up stage, the team size may be small, resulting in lesser need for elaborate roles for coordination across multiple departments. The roles in a start-up could also be fluid and informal, compared to very formal and hierarchical roles in a bureaucracy.

An organization is not just a collection of roles. The roles interact among themselves to create synergy. Functional managers coordinate the interaction between roles within a department or function. The general management role in an organization differs from functional management roles in the need for coordination across departments. These roles also transform other roles through the process of performance evaluations, feedback and mentoring. The senior leadership role has a transformative role by acting as an exemplar or by inspiring others.

The most crucial test of the appropriateness of role as the domain of autopoiesis is how roles create roles and perpetuate the process of regeneration. The HR role in an organization involves the roles of recruiting, training, learning and development and retrenchment. This HR role can be performed by specialist managers with HR designations or by any employee. There is a need to thus distinguish between roles and designations. An employee mentoring another employee is performing an HR role, whatever be the designation.

It is interesting to see in detail how a person moves across the boundaries of the organization. Consider a student in a business school applying for the post of management trainee in an organization. The student is outside the boundary of the organization and may be evaluating several other alternative organizations to join. It is the job of the person in the HR role to build a strong campus brand so as to attract the right kind of talent. Recruiting is a two-sided process of matching candidate to organization. Once the graduate is recruited, she goes through induction training and is assigned a role in the organization. Through this process, a person who just a few months ago was an outsider now starts to perform roles within the organization. Sometimes, the person may not feel comfortable with the assigned role and hence start a dialogue with the HR role for finding a better fit. If such a fit is not possible or if the person is found incapable of delivering the role requirements then the person may be asked to leave the organization. Over a period of time, the graduate becomes so much a part of the organization that the firm sends her back to recruit more people from her alma mater. She is now performing a dual role, the role of recruiter as well as the role of alumna. She conveys a picture of the future self to a candidate who is considering joining this organization. 'She is from my own school and if I join this organization then in a few years I could be performing the roles that she is performing now.' The new candidate thus begins her own journey of selection and absorption through the organizational boundary and then taking up roles and perhaps returning several years later in the role of the recruiter herself.

You can frequently hear HR managers stating 'People are our biggest assets'. This statement is only partially true. The biggest asset of a firm are the people who are able to perform the roles assigned to them and even create and design new roles for themselves and other employees as the environment demands. The primacy is to the performance of roles rather than the people per se. Would an organization continue to employ a wonderful human being who has been a stellar performer in the past but has unfortunately become incapable of performing any role, perhaps due to a medical reason? The HR role may first try to reassign the person to a less demanding role and try to retrain them. But if all such efforts fail, would the person be employed if they are not fit to perform any role? Most probably, the person would be asked to leave. If the organization is very considerate, it might provide outplacement service and try to rehabilitate the person in another organization. In most cases, the person would be given a severance package which might be just one month's salary.

This is the ugly truth, and the earlier we accept this truth the better. Do not despise the HR manager for this action. The role of the HR manager includes not just compassion towards fellow employees but also a fiduciary duty towards the interests of the shareholders of the company. Most employees may even take the same action if they are performing the HR role themselves. However, there is a sense of hypocrisy in trumpeting that 'People are our biggest assets' without adding 'as long as they perform their roles'. Components (human beings) do not matter in an autopoietic system (business organization) *as long as* the interactions and transformation roles are performed.

The statement 'components do not matter' is thus very shocking once we realize the implication of it for human beings employed by organizations. It is as shocking as a sociologist reading Niklas Luhmann and stumbling upon the implication that communication matters, not the communicator. It is through these shocking statements that we realize the significance of the concept of autopoiesis of a living cell introduced by Maturana and Varela. The molecules that constitute the cell come inside the cell through a process of ingestion, become part of intercellular processes, regulate the ingestion and excretion processes, and one fine day exit the cell boundary through the cellular process of excretion. What makes the cell living is not the quality of the molecules constituting it. The type of molecules is important only so far as to keep the cellular processes of interactions and transformations constant. Life is not reducible to any component; life is autopoiesis itself.

The dilemma of whether components matter or not can be traced back to the Greek philosophers' Ship of Theseus paradox. Consider a ship which is periodically repaired through a process of replacing the individual wooden planks making up the ship, till one day all the original planks have been replaced. Is this repaired ship the original ship? A component orientation would provide a negative answer while the system orientation would state otherwise. Just like the Ship of Theseus, organizations are in a state of constant flux with employees entering the organization boundary, moving across different departmental boundaries and then exiting the organization. Unlike the Ship of Theseus, which was repaired when it returned to dock, this modern organizational ship is repaired while fighting competitors and facing environmental turbulence. It is a wonder that the modern organization with a high attrition rate can maintain its identity through the process of autopoiesis.

It is easy to think of a system and list its components. The naive view of systems assigns the good or bad performance of the system to the existence of good and bad quality components. So, to obtain a high-performance organization, you just need to recruit high-quality employees. Nothing can be further from the truth. A collection of extremely talented employees under a bureaucratic dysfunctional management may wither away, while a collection of ordinary mortals may perform extraordinarily as a team. The visible hand of the management is the crucial difference in enabling a high-performance organization to evolve. Note that this visible hand of management may not be evident or present in all types of Level 8 social organizations. So, while it is still an open question whether Level 8 systems in general are autopoietic, organizations which have a formal management role have the *potential* to be autopoietic and hence living.

Take your learning from life. Life is brutal, life is sweet. Look around in your organization and marvel at the diversity of the roles, the process of role creation and role dissolution. Watch how people transition from the outside to the inside, become a loyal part of the organization, and how one day they leave the organization to play a loyal part somewhere else. Know the truth that components do not matter *as long as* roles are performed. Serve the organization with dedication and loyalty, knowing fully well you will one day be replaced. The higher you reach in the organizational hierarchy, the more you should strive to have a business continuity plan and nurture your successor so that the show goes on when you leave. And if, unfortunately, one day, your role asks you to terminate a colleague, do so with empathy. Long live the organization.

CHAPTER 4

Autopoiesis and Innovation

'Plus ça change, plus c'est la même chose.'

—Jean-Baptiste Alphonse Karr

IF A SYSTEM is autopoietic, it would maintain its interactions and transformations. If so, how does it change and evolve over time? Here we must differentiate between two kinds of change processes. One is pre-programmed, the other depends on random and emergent causes. A caterpillar transforms into a larva and then into a butterfly, a toddler grows into an adolescent and then into a mature adult. These kinds of changes are driven by the genetic code of the organism.

A different kind of change entails change in the genetic code itself due to mutation. Mutations are random events and are caused by triggers external to the system. All mutations do not result in a new species. A lot of mutations may not be viable as an organism and may die out; others may be infertile. Genetic variations are common in the natural environment due to the existence of mutation. The birth of a new species depends on the workings of natural selection. When there is a change in environment (like the onset of the Ice Age), it may so happen that the phenotype (greater ability to withstand cold) possessed by a genetic variant is better suited than the base population. The base population may die out in the changed environment, leaving the variant to thrive.

It is an absolute wonder to look at the diverse species on the face of the earth and realize how they have been shaped by natural selection. It is an absolute wonder to look at the diversity of business organizations and realize how they have been shaped by market forces. Just as the natural environment has always been in a state of flux, market dynamics and technological change too are unpredictable and volatile. Survival of the fittest in the changed environment is the brutal test of sustainability of the species as well as business models.

To understand change processes, we need to start from the basics of cybernetics. A change in one variable may either increase or decrease the value of another variable. An arrow with a positive (negative) polarity is used to characterize a situation when an increase in value of the independent variable leads to an increase (decrease) in value of a dependent variable. A feedback loop is formed when there is a path from one variable to itself. The polarity of the feedback loop is considered to be positive if the number of negative arrows is zero or even. If there are an odd number of negative polarity arrows in a loop then the overall loop polarity is negative. A system may have multiple positive or negative feedback loops but some of them may lie latent, and their presence may not be reflected in system behaviour. The latent feedback loops may become dominant at a later stage due to changes in other parts of the system or environment.

Negative feedback loops are an essential part of control systems as they allow a variable to be kept constant or within a range of values. Homeostasis, or the regulation of the core body temperature, is an example of the negative feedback loop, the thermostat in the air conditioner is another. If a system is autopoietic then it must maintain the set of interactions and transformations and hence there must be a set of negative feedback loops in operation.

Negative feedback loops are easily found in business organizations. They are seen in variance analysis to identify and correct the deviation between the plan and actual outcome. They are thus an integral part of organizational life, ranging from a shareholder's evaluation of management performance based on earlier guidance, a sales executive striving to reach sales targets, and a production manager worrying about monthly volume targets. Negative feedback loops are in operation when a root cause analysis is done to identify why a quality characteristic has fallen outside control limits, when a manager orders the requisite amount to bring the inventory position up to a specified level in a periodic review inventory system.

The initial years of cybernetics were so devoted to the study of negative feedback loops that cybernetics was seen as a science related to the control of systems. Indeed, the term 'feedback loop' referred to the negative feedback loop as the concept of a positive feedback loop was alien. The concept of positive feedback loops was introduced by Magoroh Maruyama in 1963. He used the term 'deviation-amplifying mutual causal processes' to explain systems with positive feedback while using the term 'deviation-counteracting mutual causal processes' to describe systems with negative feedback loops. This change in nomenclature signifies a shift from focus on structure (the presence of a feedback loop) to the effect (deviation amplifying or counteracting).

Look around you to identify deviation-amplifying mutual causal processes. Finance professionals are well aware of the value of compounding. The interest earned in a period is added to the principal at the end of the period. The interest earned in the next period is on the new principal which includes the interest earned in the earlier period. Thus, there exists a positive feedback loop, and the deviation (interest) is amplified in each subsequent period. The causality is mutual since there is a circularity (the feedback loop) between the principal and the interest. The more the principal increases, the effect on the interest is even more, which again causes the principal to increase in the next period. The result is exponential growth. This kind of deviation-amplifying process can be hard to control. Indeed, the viewpoint of control is not the right viewpoint when the system in a sense spirals out of control. The relevant viewpoint is the viewpoint of change and innovation. This change in viewpoint is so fundamental that Maruyama titled his work *The Second Cybernetics*. In today's parlance, he might as well have used the term Cybernetics 2.0.

Maruyama used the concept of deviation-amplifying mutual causal processes to explain the process of evolution.

Two things are required for evolution: (i) a mutation and (ii) deviation-amplifying mutual causal processes. The mere occurrence of mutation is not sufficient; there must be processes which build on this initial kick, as Maruyama put it. He identified three main types of deviation-amplifying processes: (i) intra-species (ii) inter-species and (iii) environment, based on whether the causal loop passed through only the species or involved other species or involved the environment. If the members of a species prefer a specific physical characteristic in their choice of mates then the causal loops are intra-species. An inter-species evolution could occur if the change in one species (the prey becomes better camouflaged) effects a change in another species (those predators that are better equipped to see through the camouflage thrive through natural selection). The environment-related evolution occurs when the mutation allows those individuals to survive in an adverse environment while the base population is weeded out.

I want you to see the parallel between the concepts of mutation and evolution and that of creativity and innovation. Creativity is akin to mutation while innovation is akin to the evolution of the species. Mere creativity is not innovation. Creativity is the spark which ignites innovation. Without that spark, no innovation is possible. But just having a creative spark does not necessarily result in innovation. Innovation requires an enabling environment where the initial spark starts a chain reaction and mutual causal processes fan the fire. The insight of one person regarding consumer behaviour, technology or process may lead to discussions within small teams across the department or firm boundaries which may inspire others to review assumptions and make changes. Then another person may get an insight to completely remodel the architecture of the solution to create something which no one could have anticipated earlier.

Creativity resides in the individual while innovation resides in the system. A collection of highly creative people may not necessarily mean a highly innovative organization. In the same vein, a collection of ordinary mortals with reasonable levels of creativity can be highly innovative if deviation-amplifying mutual causal processes are active in the organization. A brilliant idea in an environment of 'not invented here' would die a quick death. A creative idea related to miniaturization would flower in a society like Japan which sees beauty in a bonsai plant. The same idea is likely to be overlooked in a country where bigger is better.

The deviation-amplifying loop can lie entirely inside a specific firm, like when an idea related to increasing the efficiency of a particular machine is acted on by engineers in the production, maintenance, design and industrial engineering departments. Inter-species innovation can occur if the causal loop includes collaborators in the upstream or downstream firms in the supply chain or even customers. Changes in environment like regulations, technology or customer behaviour may fuel innovation ideas within the firm. Firms may either adapt to a new environment or create the technological breakthrough for a completely new environment. Next time you observe an innovation in a firm, focus on the extent to which the positive feedback loop encompasses internal departments, outside collaborators and the environment. Each of these intra-species, inter-species and environment innovations may require different kinds of stakeholders to be managed and hence a different set of competencies. A firm focused on process innovations to achieve higher internal efficiency and a firm focused on product innovation and working with external collaborators to bring about a change in society are both innovative firms, but their natures are different.

The system view of innovation allows us to understand why it is so difficult for some managers to handle an innovative firm. Most managers are exposed to deviation-counteracting mutual causal processes as they climb the organization hierarchy. They start by executing the decisions of top and senior managers, and are held accountable to adhering to an implementation plan. What these managers understand very well are the deviation-counteracting mutual causal processes of a command and control system. And one day, as the same manager adept at handling negative feedback loops reaches senior management, the requirement changes to making the firm more innovative. The manager enthusiastically brings the toolkit of control orientation into a situation which requires a different toolkit related to managing deviation-amplifying loops. The manager may hire or train creative personnel but the culture of the firm may not allow causal interactions which amplify creativity. The inevitable failure of the manager in handling an innovative project is also the failure of top management in understanding innovation as a system.

Managing an innovative firm thus requires mastery of both kinds of feedback loops. The management needs to improve processes, introduce new technologies, products and services and simultaneously deliver the quarterly targets. Future-oriented change processes need to be handled along with present-oriented adherence to the annual plan and shareholder guidance. The successful firm not just reports the financial numbers exceeding shareholder expectations but also improves the percentage of revenue or profit derived from products or services introduced in the last few years. This is not an easy task by any stretch of the imagination.

The inherent tension between the two kinds of feedback loops comes to a flashpoint in firms attempting business model innovations. Product and process innovations require deviation-amplifying loops, but the loops may be in localized structures inside the firm. For example, certain process innovations may require interactions between the quality and production departments without involving any other team. Product innovations may be localized between the design, engineering and marketing departments. A firm may handle these kinds of innovations by creating a loose coupling between those parts which are involved in innovation and the rest that need to be governed differently. However, a business model innovation may require rewiring the entire organizational circuitry, changing the nature, quantum and quality of interactions, and transformations across departmental boundaries. Frequently, the firm attempting a business model innovation finds it very difficult to disrupt itself. The enormity of this disruption challenge become apparent when we understand what exactly is being disrupted.

Autopoiesis involves maintaining as constant the interaction and transformation processes. Disruptive innovation involves rearranging those same interactions and transformations. Successful autopoiesis will kill business model disruption, and successful disruption of the business model would mean an altered autopoiesis. Since the system is autopoietic, it implies that the change process is self-inflicted. An autopoietic firm attempting a business model disruption is thus a sight to behold for an academic researcher, a potential multi-bagger or an unmitigated value destroyer for the shareholder, a state of confusion for employees, an opportunity for change agents in middle and junior management to earn their stripes, a challenge to learn new tricks for old hands and a test of transformative leadership for the top management. The stronger the autopoiesis of the firm, stronger the resistance to change. It may be much easier to build from scratch a firm with a new business model than to transition an existing firm to a new business model. For once, think of this resistance to change as a blessing rather than a curse. Such resistance, inside big organizations, allows start-ups a chance to prove themselves against Goliaths.

Autopoiesis is thus more than a constraint, it allows the possibility of a *changing constraint*. The autopoietic system is not cast in stone, it has the *potential* to evolve while maintaining itself. The secret behind this seemingly contradictory characteristic is the simultaneous operation of both deviation-amplifying and deviation-counteracting mutual causal processes. It is an absolute wonder to watch an organization as an evolving constraint. It is like the Ship of Theseus deciding to become a yacht in mid sea by rearranging its wooden planks, yet striving to reach its destination in time while the winds howl, the waves roll and competitors attack. Is the ship which left the port the same as the yacht that arrives? The more things change, the more they stay the same!

CHAPTER 5

Purpose

'It happens that the stage sets collapse. Rising, streetcar, four hours in the office or the factory, meal, streetcar, four hours of work, meal, sleep, and Monday Tuesday Wednesday Thursday Friday and Saturday according to the same rhythm—this path is easily followed most of the time. But one day the "why" arises and everything begins in that weariness tinged with amazement.'

—Albert Camus, *The Myth of Sisyphus*

Is there a purpose for a Level 8 system like a business organization? Is there a purpose for Level 7 systems like you and me? Have you ever wondered what is the purpose of your existence? Most people go through the daily grind of life without ever asking this question. Yet the question lurks around, waiting to pounce on us when we least expect it. When it arises, the feeling of meaninglessness can be nauseating. It overwhelms the individual and can drive the person to commit suicide, embrace religion or, as Camus suggests, revel in the life of Sisyphus.

At first glance, the existential angst related to purpose seems highly philosophical and far removed from the world of business. Business, by its very nature, conjures up images of materialistic men going about their jobs. There are innovations to be developed, capital to be raised, products to be lunched, production to be arranged, markets to be created, customers to be serviced and money to be made. This is not the world of search for meaning sitting under a tree in the Himalayas. Yet, lo and behold, the question of purpose raises its head in the din and bustle of the modern fast-paced corporate life. It can raise its head suddenly in the middle of a presentation in the conference room, while waiting in the airport lounge, or on firming up next quarter's sales targets and production volumes. Presentations after presentations, flights after flights, quarters after quarters—even grown-ups cry silently when they see infinity stretching out before them. To what end are we striving?

The severity of this question lies in the identity of the questioner. There is a world of difference between asking someone 'What is the purpose of your life', and asking oneself the same question. There is a world of difference between analysing another firm and asking 'What is the purpose of our existence as a business?' For a business, the question of purpose can be felt by any employee but must be settled by the top management.

The default answer to the question of purpose for a business is quite simple. A business exists to create profit for shareholders, a theory passionately argued by American economist Milton Friedman in 1970. It is a money-making machine. Month after month, quarter after quarter, year after year, decade after decade, it should not just make money, but more of it, every time. At one extreme, this orientation may collapse every performance characteristic into money, thereby becoming insensitive to the colour of the money—black or white or grey or tinged with the blood of employees, customers and future generations. Such a capitalist purpose of business would either culminate in a revolutionary uprising or an environmental catastrophe.

An employee in a money-making machine who does not work for money but for lofty ideals of serving society is an anomaly. Statements like 'work is worship' are mere platitudes to an employee whose main reason for continuing in a soul-sapping workplace is the expectation of payday. The purpose of work for this employee is not related to the organization but to the money earned by them. The meaning of selling one's soul to a money-making machine is to be found in the meals the bread-earner can place before the hungry family, the medical care that the son can arrange for parents, the education the employee can provide for their children, or the luxurious lifestyle that the employee aspires to. Such a money-making machine exists to serve the money needs of its workers, managers and shareholders. It has no other purpose for existence. Its purpose is externally given rather than derived from itself.

Whether a purpose is externally imposed or internally derived is of prime importance in differentiating between allopoietic and autopoietic systems. An allopoietic system is designed for a purpose by a creator. In contrast, an autopoietic system has no external creator and no intrinsic

purpose other than maintaining its autopoiesis. As per
Maturana and Varela, purpose belongs to the realm of
the observer, not the autopoietic system. When Rene
Descartes states, 'I think therefore I am', the causality of
existence is internal to the system. The Level 7 autopoietic
human being is able to reflect on itself. The serpent eating
its own tail. The observer, observing, is observed.

When you ask, 'What is the purpose of my existence?',
you as an observer observe your own system. You can
start to peel away the different layers of purpose. Some
of these purposes are imposed by society, some by family
and some by your inclination. None of these purposes
are hard-coded into the autopoiesis of your system. You
choose to have those purposes and tomorrow you can
choose to change your purpose. Except autopoiesis, all
other purposes are transient.

For a business to be autopoietic, the first condition to
be fulfilled is the ability to reflect on itself and act based
on that reflection. Who are we? Why do we exist as
an organization? What is our purpose in society? Do
we want to change society? Do we want to change who we
are? What do we want to become? What purposes do we
want to give to ourselves? What should be our mission
and vision? What businesses are we in?

In my view, all Level 8 businesses are not autopoietic
even though all of them have the *potential* to be
autopoietic systems. There are very many businesses
which are just money-making machines which have
never gone through a process of reflection. In fact, the
question 'What business are we in' was raised only in
1960 by pioneer marketing academic Theodore Levitt.
Surely individual businesses may have asked this

question earlier, but management, as a discipline, asked this question in 1960. These are thus early days in the journey of autopoietic businesses.

Do not judge a business to be allopoietic just because it works as a money-making machine. If the business reflected on what it is, what it wants to be and decided that it wants to be a money-making business, then it is autopoietic because it decided its own fate. Such an autopoietic money-making machine cannot, however, pass on the rationale for money-making onto shareholders. Also note that since purpose belongs to the domain of the observer, it can change if the senior leadership is changed. An allopoietic system thus has the potential to become autopoietic and vice versa.

A purposive business organization defines its responsibilities to its stakeholders. For example, in 1943, Johnson & Johnson (J&J) formulated its credo which clearly articulates its responsibilities towards various stakeholders like doctors, patients, parents, other users, customers, suppliers, distributors, employees, local communities, the world community and finally the stockholder. The credo prioritizes its responsibilities, keeping the stockholder last and the doctors first. This credo was not imposed by anyone on J&J; J&J adopted it on its own volition. The credo helps it navigate through the ups and downs of business and acts like a moral compass.

Every business with a well-crafted mission or vision statement is not autopoietic. A statement framed on the wall of a conference room serves no purpose. It must be questioned at regular intervals to check whether it needs reformulation or reaffirmation. The purpose of the firm must be visible in the actions of the employees in daily activities. The purpose must be apparent to its customers and society, for they are the final judges of the efficacy of the firm.

To find meaning in existence is perhaps the purpose of life. Managing an organization allows you not one but two avenues for finding meaning. The first is through your personal quest for meaning as an individual. The second is the collective quest for meaning as part of the senior management of the firm. Leaders provide meaning to the collective, and thereby infuse their own life with meaning and a sense of purpose. May this book achieve its purpose by instilling in you the process of reflection indispensable for making a leader.

PART II: THE DOORS

CHAPTER 6

Closed Doors

'Gentlemen, I have arrived. There will be no withdrawal
without written orders and these orders shall never be
issued.'

—Lieutenant General Sam Manekshaw (later Field
Marshall) on assuming command as General Officer
Commanding of the retreating IV Corps during the
Sino-Indian War, November 1962

THE PURPOSE OF an autopoietic system is self-given and
hence difficult to ascertain from the outside. The sense of
purpose ingrained in mission and vision statements may
be too broad and at best provide just an over-arching
sense of direction. The actual roadmap connecting
purpose with the ground reality is the strategy of the
firm. It is an encoding of the purpose, taking into account
the changing customer and competitive landscape in the
context of technological, economic, social, political and
regulatory contexts. This encoding can happen through a
formal strategy formulation process resulting in an annual
plan of action. The encoding can also happen through

an emergent process. In whatever way it happens, there may be parts of these plans which are hidden so that the competitors may not take advantage. Thus, the verbalized strategy incorporated in the annual plan is only a portion of the game plan that the top management has in mind.

It is thus difficult to completely grasp the strategy of the firm unless you are part of the top management. Middle management may be part of the strategy formulation process by providing inputs for the decisions as well as executing the decisions, but they may get only a fleeting glimpse of the big picture and the game plan. Junior management may be mostly dealing with tactical decisions while workers are told what to do. Thus, even if you are working inside an organization, you may be clueless about the strategy by design or default. The situation gets worse when there are frequent changes in strategy or if there are multiple factions in top management, resulting in confusion about the strategy to follow.

If understanding strategy is difficult for an employee, it is much more difficult for an outsider who has to rely on hearsay or news reports. Yet, evaluation of strategy from the outside is needed if you are an analyst tracking the firm or industry, or if you are a competitor. News reports may be part of company propaganda and public relations exercises. Inputs from the marketplace may be noisy, inputs from supply chain partners like suppliers or distributors may provide some direction, but would also have a competitive dimension. Inputs from employees leaving the firm may be biased. All these inputs together provide a picture of the firm, and an analyst or competitor has only this hazy picture to discern the strategy.

A consultant may get a slightly clearer picture since she has access to the firm and its management. However, access is for certain activities only and for a short duration. A consultant thus has to discern the strategy through verbal and non-verbal cues within a short period of time. Think of the challenge of being a management consultant. You are asked to study a managerial problem, which is so severe that internal management felt the need for external advice, and come up with concrete actionable recommendations in a short period of time. And these recommendations would need to be so rigorous that they can pass the test of relevance before a set of diverse employees, many of whom are functional and technological experts with advanced degrees and years of work experience in the firm and industry. This is by no means an easy task. An outside-in solution to this problem is for the consultant to develop and master tools, methodologies and frameworks and adapt them to the specific client context. An inside-out solution is to understand the client's existing strategy and provide guidance based on the experience of working with similar problems in other client contexts. Both these approaches require a rapid sizing-up of the client's strategy.

How do we quickly understand a firm's strategy? We cannot just rely on mission and vision statements as they are too broad, cannot just rely on inputs from customers and supply chain partners as these are too noisy and possibly biased, cannot just rely on scrutinizing the annual plan as it does not provide the big picture, cannot just rely on top management interviews as what is verbalized as strategy may just be a small part of the overall game plan. We have to rely on all these to build a representation of the firm strategy. We need to cross-check with management whether our representation is justified. Most importantly, we have to cross-check the representation with respect to the doors that are closed.

Managers make decisions and decisions involve making choices among alternatives. Many people think of strategy as a plan of action. This definition of strategy focuses on the choice that is made from among the alternatives. My view of strategy is the complement. For every plan of action, there are multiple plans which were not adopted. For every path that is chosen, there are multiple alternate universes that we say 'no' to. For every door we walk through, there are many more doors that we close.

Strategy Is the Art of Closing Doors

It is not easy to say 'no'. Closing doors implies saying no to alternate courses of action. Thus, for each door that the strategist walks through, there are many more doors that the strategist says 'no' to. The strategist must understand the implications of the closed doors and take the responsibility involved in closing them.

To evaluate strategy in terms of plan of action focuses our attention on the chosen path. In contrast, to evaluate strategy in terms of closed doors, we need to evaluate why other paths were not chosen. To evaluate strategy in terms of a plan of action as well as closed doors involves understanding both the path taken as well as the paths that were not taken.

Every closed door is a constraint. A strategy is the set of self-imposed constraints which we choose to abide by. There is a direct connection between strategy formulation and the process of reflection on choices. Just like a Level 7 human being can go through life without ever asking existential questions, a Level 8 business organization can go through plans of action without reflecting on the paths that were avoided by design or were not considered due to lack of awareness. It is this process of reflection of the top management of the organization on the organization itself which creates the consciousness of who we are, why we exist, which customers we choose to service, what value we provide to them, which partners we choose to serve value to customers, how do we choose to create value, how we differentiate our offering from competition and how we create value for our shareholders. Inherent in these reflections are the alternate personas of who we could have been, the customers we chose not to serve, the customer value propositions we chose not to offer, the partners we decided not to have, the value creation processes we chose not to adopt, the competitive positions we chose to ignore, and the shareholder value increment options we chose to forego. These choices were made by us and not forced by anyone else. We created who we are through the process of making these choices. And it is we who will review who we have become by a periodic process of reflection. We may choose to continue being who we have become. We can also choose to change ourselves. This is the existential view of the business. This is also the autopoietic view of the business.

An organization at a specific point of time is thus a collection of closed doors across marketing, finance, HR, operations, supply chain, etc. Not all doors are the same. Some of the doors are tightly shut based on high-level principles. Some of the doors are tactical in nature and are opened or closed based on market conditions. Some of the doors have been closed on the basis of long discussions. Some have been closed for such a long time that no one really remembers why they were closed. Some doors have been opened and closed so frequently that they have become a joke. Some are so trivial that no one cares whether they are open or closed.

Functional managers are concerned with the doors under their watch. A marketing manager decides a target segment and offers them a value proposition. An operations manager chooses the appropriate technology, determines the capacity and the production strategies to align with the choices done in marketing. Once the capacities have been created, the marketing manager in turn has to take production strategies into account for launching new products or addressing new customer segments. Thus, the doors closed in marketing need to be in sync with the doors closed in operations. This synchronization is not automatic, nor is it unidirectional or one-time. Certain door choices in one function may not be interoperable with certain door choices in another functional area. Therein lies the value of the general manager who can periodically align the door choices across functional boundaries to reduce friction and gain synergy. Strategy is not just the art of closing doors; it is the art of *integrated* closing of doors across functional boundaries.

Closing one set of doors results in patterns of interaction among components which would have differed if another set of doors had been closed. Thus, strategy starts shaping the autopoiesis of the organization by impacting the nature of interactions and transformations. A set of doors closed for a long period of time generates stable patterns of interactions and transformations and thereby shapes the culture of the organization. A strong culture may deter the opening of a closed door. Peter Drucker supposedly stated that culture eats strategy for breakfast. Strategy may have given birth to that culture in the first place!

Do not think about door closings with a negative orientation. A set of closed doors allows the will of the organization to flow in certain channels. German philosopher Arthur Schopenhauer perceived, '. . . this world is, on the one side, entirely *representation*, just as, on the other, it is entirely *will*.' I want you to view business strategy as, on one side, purpose, and on the other side, closed doors. Closed doors are like sluice gates which regulate the flow of the organizational will striving for a purpose. Closing a door is not easy, but once it is closed, it focuses and directs the organizational will. In contrast, a business which can open and close any door at any time would not be able to focus and direct its meagre resources. Businesses which aim to provide all kinds of value to all kinds of customers may think that they have not closed doors. Yet, they do not realize that they have closed doors to the option of closing doors! You cannot escape from strategy.

Strategy is an art since it involves philosophical viewpoints which cannot be evaluated in strictly quantitative terms. A set of closed doors which results in synergy of one kind cannot be compared with the synergy achieved by another set of closed doors. Strategy has a beauty associated with it. While the implementation of two strategies could be compared based on performance metrics, the beauty of the strategy cannot be compared. It is difficult to appreciate the beauty of strategy unless you have experienced the friction generated by a jarring set of closed doors. All cars have four wheels and an engine, but only the driver understands the joy of driving a fine-tuned car.

There are so many doors across different functional domains, and each one may be opened or closed. This results in a staggering number of possible combinations. Thankfully, the set of feasible combinations is smaller, since many of the jarring combinations are impractical. A study of the strategies adopted by different kinds of successful firms throws up different patterns of closed doors. While combinations are many, patterns are relatively few. The study of these patterns is thus very helpful if you want to quickly evaluate the strategy of a firm.

As a consultant, look out for closed doors to quickly gather an understanding of firm strategy. Start with the most important choice that a firm ever makes: the choice of customer. Meet the marketing team to understand the paths chosen as well as the doors closed in marketing. Then transition to the operations and supply chain domain and understand the paths chosen and the doors closed. Similarly, gather an understanding of the HR and finance functions. Then ask whether the paths chosen and door closings are synergistic. How is this pattern of door closings similar or different from known patterns? The more patterns you see as a consultant, the quicker you can put a finger on the pulse of the organization. Whenever a firm has a pattern different from known patterns, question why this different pattern exists. It may be due to a unique operating environment or cultural context or organizational history, or simply due to confusion and mismanagement. Occasionally, you may discover patterns which others have not studied before. Fill your professional life with the beauty of the patterns.

If you are a manager, look at the doors you have closed in your workplace. Experience the pain of friction and joy of synergy caused by the interaction effect of doors closed in different departments. Identify patterns of door closings that work together and patterns that don't. Study your competitors and understand their choice of path and doors closed. Ask yourself what changes in door opening or closings are needed in your department and in other departments so as to better serve customers and compete in the marketplace.

Look intently at your own life and review the paths you have chosen and the bridges that you burnt. See the doors that have been closed by religion, society, circumstances or fate, and those that are self-imposed. Understand who you are not, who you do not want to become. Each set of doors that you close defines a different you. What then is your original you, unfettered by closed doors? As Zen Buddhism asks, have you seen your original face? Is it like what Buddha described as transient clouds floating in a limitless sky? When I look at my beloved's face, I see the same transient patterns with a backdrop of limitless possibilities. I recognize the beautiful patterns and claim I have seen her beauty while the limitless possibilities silently mock me.

CHAPTER 7

Decision Areas in
Operations Strategy

'The possibilities are numerous once we decide to act
and not react.'

—George Bernard Shaw

IF YOU GO to a firm as a consultant and ask them which
doors they have closed, you will most likely be shown the
door. So, keep these things to yourself. Instead, observe the
systems and processes and *infer* the doors that are closed. A
framework of decision areas in Operations Strategy allows us
to develop a thorough understanding of the existing choices.
There are eight main decision areas in Operations Strategy.
These are Capacity, Facility, Scope, Technology, Quality,
Planning, Workforce and Organization, as propounded by
Steven C. Wheelwright and Robert H. Hayes.

Capacity comes in large, distinct chunks with
considerable lead time between the time the capacity
expansion decision is taken and the time the capacity
become available for commercial production. Operations

managers need to decide the size of these capacity additions and deletions as well as the timing of the decisions. Lead capacity strategy aims to add capacity ahead of the curve so that an excess capacity cushion is available at any time. In contrast, Lag capacity strategy is conservative and adds capacity when enough demand exists to fully utilize the added capacity.

Figure 2: Lead Capacity Strategy

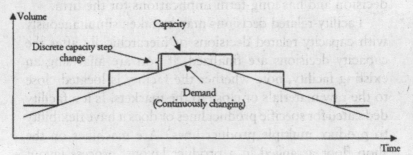

Source: Olhager, J., Rudberg, M., and Wikner, J. (2001). *Long-term Capacity Management: Linking the Perspectives from Manufacturing Strategy and Sales and Operations Planning.*

Figure 3: Lag Capacity Strategy

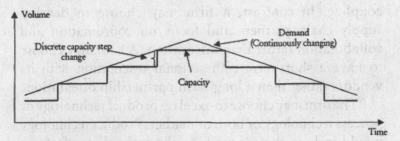

Source: Olhager, J., Rudberg, M., and Wikner, J. (2001). *Long-term Capacity Management: Linking the Perspectives from Manufacturing Strategy and Sales and Operations Planning.*

Capacity sizing decisions are frequently interconnected with the choice of technology involved. For example, the Minimum Efficient Scale (MES) of steel production through blast furnace technology is significantly higher than the MES through electric arc furnace technology. The capital requirements for a technology with a higher MES may be higher, resulting in interconnectedness of capacity strategy with the options available in financing domain. Capacity strategy is thus a top-level strategy decision and has long-term implications for the firm.

Facility-related decisions may be taken simultaneously with capacity-related decisions or hierarchically after the capacity decisions are finalized. If you are analysing an existing facility, note whether the facility is located close to the raw materials or close to the markets. Is it a facility dedicated for specific product lines or does it have flexibility to produce multiple product lines? Are machines on the shop floor arranged in a product layout, process layout or cellular layout? Is the facility fully developed or does it have scope for expansion, horizontally or vertically?

Scope refers to the extent of vertical integration. Is the firm vertically integrated with upstream or downstream players? If so, evaluate the direction and extent of the coupling. In contrast, a firm may choose to develop supply chain partners and focus on coordination and collaboration rather than integration. A firm may choose to have a short-term transactional orientation with its vendors rather than a long-term partnership orientation.

The firm may choose to excel on product technology or process technology or both or neither. Product technology would include choices made in the technology platform that the firm chooses to offer value to customers. Process technology could include the use of general-purpose machines or special-purpose machines custom-designed by external machine tool manufacturers or internally adapted by in-house engineers. A firm may decide to have a high level of automation or more labour intensity. Technology choice also includes the choice of supporting technology like information technology and networking infrastructure. A firm may choose a standard off-the-shelf Enterprise Resource Planning (ERP) software instead of custom-designed information systems. The choice of ERP technology or customer relationship management (CRM) systems could affect the way the firm interacts internally among employees and externally with partners and customers. It could also affect the flexibility of the firm to adapt to a changing business environment.

A firm may choose to have inspection-based quality control rather than quality assurance. The former focuses on product quality while the later focuses on process quality. Firms can choose to compete on different dimensions of quality. Strategic quality management recognizes eight different quality dimensions. These are Performance, Features, Reliability, Durability, Conformance, Serviceability, Aesthetics and Perceived Quality, as per David A. Garvin.

Planning includes various sub-dimensions like production planning, distribution planning, inventory control strategies, scheduling, warehousing and delivery planning. A firm may choose to follow Level or Chase production strategies, adopt continuous or periodic reviews of inventory, assign different scheduling priorities to jobs waiting in queue, design a centralized or decentralized distribution structure, deliver to stockists on

Ready-Stock or Deliver-to-Order basis, choose different transport modes, and for a particular mode decide to send goods on a Full Truck Load (FTL) or Less Than Truck Load (LTL) basis.

Workforce-related decisions relate to the number, type and skill level of employees, whether they are permanent employees or contractual. It includes decisions taken in the sub-domains of recruitment, performance measurement, promotion, incentives and motivation. Workers could be paid on a piece rate or hourly basis or given a fixed salary. Different cadres may have different rules regarding overtime, benefits and perks. Performance can be measured at an individual level and/or at a team level. Firms may choose to provide avenues for self-development and learning or refuse to invest in employee development, fearing attrition. Some firms may choose to rely on an internal pipeline of leaders while others may choose to hire the best talent laterally.

Organization structure can be of various forms like entrepreneurial, machine bureaucracy, diversified, etc., as per Henry Mintzberg. The roles, responsibilities and reporting structure of managers may vary considerably based on the structure. Some firms may have centralized control while others may choose to have a decentralized structure. Span of control can vary based on a flat or hierarchical organization structure and reporting relations can be rigid or in a matrix form.

The above description of choices in the eight decision areas is by no means exhaustive. A full treatment of each of these decision areas is beyond the scope of this book. Many of these are well covered in various textbooks on Operations Management. Here, I would like you to recognize two insights. First, Operations Strategy includes very well-defined discrete choices. You cannot simultaneously adopt a centralized and also a decentralized distribution structure for a specific product in a specific territory, nor can you simultaneously send cargo on FTL and LTL bases for a specific cargo vehicle at a specific time. Choosing one option is akin to closing the door on the other options. Second, given the large number of decision areas and multiple choices for each decision area, the number of combinations of door closings is significantly high, if—and it is a big if—the decision areas are independent. If the decision areas are related, then certain choices in one area may favour the choice in the other. This implies that certain patterns of door closings may be synergistic while other patterns may be unstable given the tension between the two related door choices. The focus of this book is the description of stable patterns of door closings.

The existence of patterns in door closings is dependent on the existence of some kind of coordination mechanism whereby two different decision-makers working in two different departments of the same firm make related choices. What could be an example of such a coordination mechanism? Interestingly, the coordination mechanism is an encoding of the will of the organization. This will is not an abstraction, it is so real that anyone working in a managerial capacity would have faced it but may not have recognized it. Businesses are performance-driven and managers are evaluated on meeting their targets. A target cannot exist without a performance metric. The targets and underlying performance metrics are thus the encoding of the will of the organization. Top-level targets

are broken down into departmental targets and further
into decision areas. Thus, patterns of door closings are
possible if the targets for decision areas are aligned.
Such alignment is not automatic, and the purpose of
general managers is to achieve this alignment not just
across decision-makers in the operations domain but also
across marketing, sales, HR and finance. In achieving
this alignment, general managers are also instrumental
in realizing synergies across departmental and functional
boundaries.

Stable patterns across departmental and functional
boundaries also hold out promise for a quick evaluation
of the strategy of the firm. Remember, stable patterns
are few while combinations are many. If these few stable
patterns are studied in depth then a consultant can
quickly evaluate a firm by comparing to what extent the
doors closed by the firm are similar to the doors closed
in the sample pattern. The door closings which match
the typical pattern are taken as confirmations while those
that do not match are starting points for probing deeper.

CHAPTER 8

Performance Metrics and Dimensions

'What gets measured gets done.'

—Unknown provenance

THE ABOVE QUOTE is not really accurate. However, measurement of performance is key to knowing whether we are achieving progress. It's a different matter that 'not everything that counts can be counted'. What counts in one situation may not count in another. To determine what to measure, we need to start with the most important stakeholder for whom we are performing.

The starting point for analysing the operations strategy of a firm is understanding customer segments and consumer behaviour. According to Peter Drucker, 'Marketing is the distinguishing, the unique function of the business.' Who is our customer? What does the customer value? How would we serve the customer? Operations strategy is intricately linked to the segmentation, targeting and positioning decisions taken in marketing.

Marketing strategy includes making choices regarding Product, Price, Promotion, Place—the four Ps—along with a host of other decisions. The extent to which doors closed in marketing would affect the operations strategy depends on the degree of interconnectedness between the two. A loose coupling between marketing strategy and operations strategy is possible if the customer-facing side can be buffered from the operations side by the use of inventory. Services demonstrate a much higher level of coupling, and it is frequently difficult to determine where marketing ends and operations begins. Even if the existing situation demonstrates loose coupling between marketing and operations, it is worthwhile to note that the extent of coupling is also a strategic decision. A firm can choose to differentiate itself from competitors by eliminating buffers and tightly coupling the operations and marketing functions.

While you are understanding the existing choices in marketing, be sensitive to picking up signals which have a strong impact on the operations design. Two of the most important signals are volume and variety. What kind of overall volumes are we talking of in terms of units to be produced or serviced? Is this firm choosing to serve a small set of customers, or is it a mass marketer catering to everyone with a standardized product, or a mass marketer serving different segments with differentiated offerings? At a firm level, there exists a fundamental trade-off between volume and variety. Think of a firm which sells a hundred cars annually. The sales can range between a single variety of hundred cars sold to a single unit of hundred varieties sold.

The absolute numbers of volume and variety are important, but more important is the sense of how these numbers compare with other firms in the market. The overall market share of the firm needs to be broken down as per customer segments. Is our firm one of the biggest in its chosen segments in terms of sales units? Does it have the largest range of product offerings? Or does it offer the best (or worst) of both worlds? Note that low variety with low volume is possible in crafts-based industries. Such craftsmanship is rare in the industrialized society and can exist if the consumer values the quality of craftsmanship and is willing to pay a premium. In contrast, high volume along with high variety is more of an aspiration. Much more abundant are examples of high volume–low variety and high variety–low volume situations.

Along with volume and variety, we need to understand product characteristics like shelf life and obsolescence rates. Shelf life has high relevance for agricultural products and food items while electronic goods may have high obsolescence rates. Demand characteristics of high importance to operations involve seasonality and extent of demand uncertainty. Seasonality is an example of predictable variability since it can be predicted that demand for fans and air conditioners would peak in summer, but the extent of peaking is unknown. In contrast, there is inherent uncertainty in the demand for fashion products while the demand for staple products and commodities may show low demand uncertainty.

The marketing channel structure needs understanding too. The firm may be selling directly to the end customer or through channel intermediaries like distributors, wholesalers and retailers of various kinds. Each of these channel intermediaries have their own requirements like minimum order quantities, credit and payment terms, etc. The firm may be using different kinds of promotional policies for different kinds of channel partners at different times of the year. The channel could operate on a demand-pull or a sales-push basis. There could be delivery-related expectations related to shorter delivery lead times or delivery reliability.

The quality of products or services on offer need to be benchmarked with the quality available from competitors. More importantly, how do the channel partners and customers view the quality offered by the firm? Quality is one dimension where you need to take management's version with a pinch of salt. No sane management would concede that they are selling low-quality products; instead, they may claim that their product provides value for money.

After you have understood the marketing side, it is time to start evaluating the operating performance of the firm to check if the firm is delivering value to its customers. Evaluation is on the performance on selected metrics. Interestingly, the knowledge of metrics on which the manager would be evaluated may have negative consequences for system performance, as suggested by academic V.F. Ridgway. Metrics could be general or specialized. There are metrics like capacity utilization which are used across industries, and there are metrics like average cost per seat-mile which are used in specific industries. There are literally thousands of metrics and you can find joy in creating a few more. You can combine metrics to create more metrics. You can drown in the sea of metrics. While each of these metrics has its own merits and demerits, too much focus on metrics results in a situation where you miss the forest for the trees. The key is to realize that while metrics are many, operations performance dimensions are few.

There are four main performance dimensions in operations. These are Cost, Quality, Delivery and Flexibility, in no particular order. Just as a point in a three-dimensional space has projections on each of the three dimensions, the operations performance of a firm is evaluated based on the performance in these four dimensions. The metrics that we discussed earlier can be mapped on to these dimensions. To understand the performance of the firm, we need a few metrics covering each of the dimensions rather than a lot of metrics related to one or two dimensions and the rest of the dimensions untracked.

A set of metrics covering all four Operations performance dimensions gives a complete picture for the purpose of evaluation. It also gives a false impression that all selected metrics are equally important. A firm may prioritize one performance dimension over others, resulting in a relatively stronger focus on the related metrics. A fundamental question in this regard is 'Should firms prioritize one operations dimension over others?' Stated in a negative sense, 'Are certain dimensions less important than others?'

Is the dimension of Cost unimportant? All hell will break loose if you ask such questions to the chartered accountant or cost accountant working in the firm. The dimension of cost has grim implications for the profitability of a firm. An operations manager who delivers superlative quality at superlative cost may soon need to update his résumé. Is the dimension of Quality unimportant? Try telling that to an irate customer, and you may face a consumer backlash on social media, resulting in a sales dip and a very angry marketing manager. Is the dimension of Delivery unimportant? Try telling that to the patient being rushed to hospital in an ambulance that it might take a few additional minutes because fuel consumption is not optimal at high speeds. Is the dimension of Flexibility unimportant? Try telling that to your shareholders when your perfectly designed system sputters as customer preferences shift. If all dimensions are equally important, then no doors are closed. Or, maybe the firm has chosen to close the door on strategy itself.

The million-dollar question is: what does the customer want? An easy and oft repeated answer is that the customer wants the best quality at the lowest cost and wants to be served as soon as possible. We do not need the marketing department to tell us this gem of an understanding of the consumer. Which customer would not want the best of all worlds? As a consumer, I would also want to have the cake and eat it too. What stops me from doing so is constraints.

There is no need for strategy in an unconstrained world. It is due to constraints that a consumer may value one dimension of performance more than others. A consumer may have a money constraint and be constrained to choose the best quality product that fits the budget. If this budget constraint is too tight then the consumer may forego the purchase since the products are not affordable. Another consumer may look for the cheapest option among products, meeting a given quality standard. If the quality standard is too exacting then the consumer may be forced to pay a higher amount for the few options available. Different segments of consumers look for different bundles of value. Their sensitivity to price is not the same. The bundle of value chosen by the target segment dictates the relative importance of the operations dimensions. We are thus able to interlink marketing and operations strategy.

From the above logic, it follows that the customer purchasing high-end equipment like a car is more sensitive to quality rather than cost, and hence operations strategy might prioritize quality over cost. Unfortunately, it is not so straightforward. The firm may choose to evaluate the marketing and sales departments on revenue while operations may be seen as the cost centre. After all, profit is maximized when revenue is maximized and cost is minimized. Thus, operations managers may have to deal with an overriding cost focus even when the target customer segment has low sensitivity to price.

A fundamental insight in Operations Strategy is that the choices which minimize cost are not the same as those that maximize quality or those that minimize delivery time. There are inherent trade-offs, and excelling in one dimension may come at the expense of another. The set of doors that needs to be closed for cost leadership is not the same as those for quality excellence. Closed doors lead to patterns of interaction and transformations which are different, finally generating cultural differences across firms excelling in different dimensions.

Can a firm excel in more than one operational performance dimension? Yes, it is possible but difficult to achieve. Before we discuss how it is possible, we need to understand the simpler situations first. We first focus our attention on situations where there is a primary operations performance dimension. We translate the overall performance dimension into functional and departmental performance dimensions, metrics and target. Based on these performance objectives, choices are made in the eight major decision areas of Operations Strategy. The resulting pattern of door closings is a sample pattern for that overall performance objective. In the next section of this book, the sample patterns for various operational objectives will be discussed in detail.

PART III: THE PATHS

CHAPTER 9

Cost Leadership

'And there went out a champion out of the camp of the Philistines, named Goliath, of Gath, whose height was six cubits and a span.'

—1 Samuel 17, *The Bible*

'Yes, at home or on the job, Dad was always the efficiency expert. He buttoned his vest from the bottom up; instead of from the top down, because the bottom-to-top process took him only three seconds, while the top to bottom took seven. He even used two shaving brushes to lather his face, because he found that by so doing he could cut seventeen seconds off his shaving time. For a while he tried shaving with two razors, but he finally gave that up. "I can save forty-four seconds," he grumbled, "but I wasted two minutes this morning putting this bandage on my throat." It wasn't the slashed throat that really bothered him. It was the two minutes.'

—Frank B. Gilbreth Jr and Ernestine Gilbreth Carey, writing about their parents, the renowned efficiency experts Frank and Lillian Gilbreth, in the bestselling book *Cheaper by the Dozen*

COST LEADERSHIP IS a generic strategy, as per economist and strategy scholar Michael Porter. It is also the default strategy against whose background the other two generic strategies of differentiation and focus are contrasted. It does not take long to figure out that gross profit can be maximized when revenue is maximized and cost is minimized. To continue to deliver growth in gross margins, firms can focus on marketing and sales activities to increase price realization, or focus on internal operations to reduce Cost of Goods Sold (COGS) or both. For a large number of firms, the prospect of price increases are difficult to achieve as they may be selling in commodity markets with a large number of competitors. Prices could also be regulated by governments. For these firms, cost leadership is not just an attractive strategy but sometimes the only viable one. The main debate inside these firms is not *whether* to follow a cost leadership strategy but *how* to become a cost leader. The answer lies in first asking *what* kind of cost leader you want to become.

The sources of cost leadership are many. A firm may exploit more than one source of cost leadership. However, there is a pattern in the way cost leadership is attained by firms. The pattern involves the relation between fixed and variable costs of production. Nothing in the world is fixed, so when we say fixed costs, we are identifying those costs which do not vary with quantity produced. Set-up costs may be incurred before a batch begins production. Once the production line is set up, each additional unit produced incurs a run cost. The total cost of production is thus the sum of the fixed set-up cost and the variable cost (which is the product of production cost per item and the number of items produced). The key to cost leadership lies in understanding how total cost changes with production quantity for different fixed and variable cost parameters.

The term cost leadership has a relative dimension built in. You cannot have a leader without a follower. So cost leadership has to be understood in terms of the choices that the firm makes which provide it a lower total cost per unit compared to competitors. One of the crucial choices is the quantity to be produced as the cost per unit varies with the quantity produced. So a firm may choose a technology which necessitates a larger fixed cost if the variable cost is low enough such that at the intended production quantity, the total cost is lower than that of the competitors choosing an alternate technology. This is the essence of the cost leadership strategy.

Figure 4: Cost Leadership

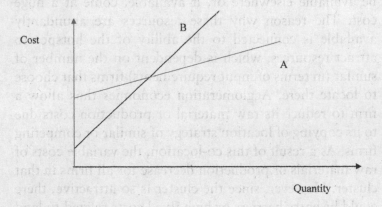

Firm A is a cost leader at higher production quantities

There are several sources of cost leadership. We now enumerate some of these and describe the choices involved in achieving cost leadership using that source. The various sources of cost leadership include economies of agglomeration, economies of scale, economies of scope, efficiency, network effects, coordination and collaboration, and market share. After discussing each source in detail, we will attempt to identify the underlying theme which runs across all these diverse sources of cost leadership.

Economies of Agglomeration: There is a romantic view of start-ups starting off from the garage. While it is true that many successful firms have indeed been launched from the backyard of the entrepreneur, such accounts gloss over the fact that not all backyards are the same. A garage located in Silicon Valley has advantages for a tech entrepreneur that accrue simply due to its location in a technology and venture capital hotspot. It allows access to inputs, resources, expertise and skill sets that may not be available elsewhere or, if available, come at a huge cost. The reason why these resources are abundantly available is connected to the ability of the hotspot to attract resources, which is dependent on the number of similar (in terms of input requirements) firms that choose to locate there. Agglomeration economies thus allow a firm to reduce its raw material or production costs due to its copying of location strategy of similar or competing firms. As a result of this co-location, the variable costs of raw materials or production decrease for all firms in that cluster. However, since the cluster is so attractive, there could be entry barriers or high fixed costs related to land prices, office rentals, etc. In contrast, the rental costs of the entrepreneur's own garage located in a small town could be negligible. The entrepreneur has to thus consider carefully the location strategy offering the choice between a low fixed cost but high variable cost option and a high fixed cost but low variable cost option.

While agglomeration cost benefits are due to location choice, not all sources of location-based cost advantage are due to agglomeration. For example, a firm may benefit from tax holidays or subsidies due to its location in a special economic zone (SEZ) but not benefit from agglomeration if there are a few firms in that location. Commercial firms benefit from being located in big cities, and industrial firms benefit from being located in an industrial belt due to the location of other firms, not necessarily competitors. However, agglomeration benefits are more pronounced for specialized skills or input raw materials which are central to product quality, innovation and profitability. It is here that the firm has to make a conscious choice of co-locating with competitors and sharing input cost advantages versus differentiating from competitors.

All firms in the cluster share similar input cost advantage over firms not located in the cluster. It is thus the cluster which bestows cost leadership on its constituent firms. On the flip side, being located in a cluster may increase distribution costs if the cluster is located away from customers. If the product characteristics are such that distribution costs dwarf the input or production costs then it may not make economic sense to be located in a cluster.

A firm choosing to derive cost leadership using agglomeration economies as a source is thus choosing a me-too strategy and casting its lot with competitors. More potent are firms that not just choose to be located in clusters but also pursue other sources of cost leadership.

Economies of Scale: In simple terms, economies of scale exist if the total cost is less than doubled if the quantity doubles. Note that $T = F + VQ$ where T = total cost, F = fixed cost, V = variable cost per unit and Q = production quantity. As quantity Q is increased, F remains unchanged while VQ increases linearly. So, in this simplest model, the total cost at $2Q$ production quantity is $F + 2VQ$ which is lower than $2T$ by value of F. Hence, as the quantity doubles, the total cost does not double. The average cost, represented by the gradient of the line segments OA and OB, reduces as production doubles. Note the crucial role played by fixed costs in achieving economies of scale. Economies of scale exist *because* of fixed investments. If $F = 0$, there is no possibility of economies of scale and the average cost remains unchanged as quantity increases.

Figure 5: Economies of Scale

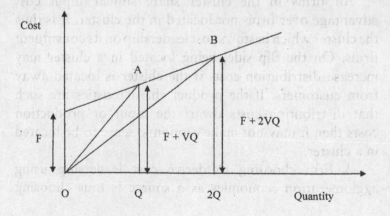

The situation would be different when V itself is a function of Q, that is, the variable cost increases or decreases as production quantity increases. For example, diseconomies of scale may occur at large production volumes due to various causes like organizational inefficiencies, overcrowding, congestion, increase in prices of inputs due to supply constraints, etc. Similarly, F could also change with Q as capacity increase becomes imperative once Q increases substantially. However, the insight offered by the simplest model is profound. To achieve economies of scale, the main focus is on the cost of fixed investments. Consider the situation where $F \gg VQ$. A ten per cent increase in Q would result in a ten per cent increase in VQ but a substantially lower percentage increase in $T = F + VQ$. More importantly, higher the value of F, lower the percentage increase in T. Thus, while any production situation which has a fixed-cost component would show economies of scale, the effect is accentuated for those situations where the fixed-cost component dwarfs the effect of the variable component. Thus, our hunt for cost leadership through economies of scale should focus on production technologies which have high fixed costs but very low marginal costs of production of an additional unit.

Capacity and technology choices become intertwined in the quest for cost leadership through economies of scale. Steel can be produced through blast furnace or electric arc furnace technology but the MES of a blast furnace is much higher than that of an electric arc furnace. The capacity and technology choices are not independent, a low-capacity blast furnace or a super-sized electric arc furnace may not bestow cost leadership.

Economies of scale exist in process industries where production capacity is linked to the size of spherical vessel. This is because the costs may be proportional to the surface area of the vessel while the output is related to the volume of the vessel. Note that for a sphere of radius r, the surface area is given by $4\pi r^2$ while its volume is given by $\frac{4}{3}\pi r^3$.

So, if the volume doubles, $\frac{V_2}{V_1} = \left(\frac{r_2}{r_1}\right)^3 = 2$ and hence the ratio of surface area is given by $\frac{S_2}{S_1} = \left(\frac{r_2}{r_1}\right)^2 = 2^{\frac{2}{3}} \sim 1.6$

This relationship is simplified as the six-tenths rule which states that costs would increase by 0.6 times when the capacity doubles. A bigger boiler or a blast furnace is thus more economical to operate than a smaller one in terms of average costs.

Economies of scale exist in procurement when the seller offers quantity discounts. Even if there are no quantity discounts, economies of scale exist in procurement due to the existence of fixed ordering costs. The Economic Order Quantity (EOQ) model, one of the earliest models in inventory theory dating back to 1913—developed by Ford Whitman Harris and popularized by R.H. Wilson— trades off the cost of holding inventory with the fixed cost incurred every time an item is ordered. Similarly, the Economic Production Quantity (EPQ) optimizes the fixed set-up costs in production. Economies of scale in distribution may emanate from bigger centralized warehouses while economies of scale in transport emanate from the use of larger trucks and palletization.

Economies of Scope: While economies of scale arise due to spreading fixed costs over quantity of production, economies of scope arise from spreading fixed costs over the variety produced. Consider a restaurant which needs to hire chefs for offering two distinct cuisines, continental and Chinese. The restaurant hires a chef specializing in continental cuisine for $X per month and another chef for Chinese cuisine at $Y per month. Subsequently, a chef who is an expert in both cuisines expresses interest and expects a fixed salary of $Z per month. Economies of scope would exist if the salary costs are subadditive, that is, if $Z < X + Y$. Note that while Z could be higher than X or Y, it should be lower than the sum of X and Y for economies of scope to exist. Thus, the restaurant could offer a higher salary to any chef who specializes in both cuisines and still reap the cost advantage through economies of scope.

An important assumption in economies of scope is that the quality of output is not affected by switching from a specialized resource to a multi-specialized resource. A chef who excels in a large number of cuisines would provide huge economies of scope and command a high salary. Not all chefs can attain that distinction. The restaurant may thus have a choice between adopting a string of pearls strategy of assembling a team of chefs each excelling in a chosen cuisine or a jack-of-all-trades low-cost strategy of relying on generalists to offer dishes which do not quite meet high expectations or an economies of scope strategy of hiring chefs who excel in multiple cuisines *without* compromising on quality.

Economies of scope exist when a firm invests in an umbrella brand or company brand whose brand-building costs can be shared across multiple product categories. It exists when a firm invests in market research to understand the different needs of a customer segment which could be satisfied by different products or services. A firm with a single product or brand may find it costly to create an in-house market research team, while a firm with multiple product lines can absorb this fixed cost by apportioning costs over a variety of product lines. Similarly, economies of scope may help in media buying as the aggregated requirement over a large number of products or brands could allow better price negotiations or qualify for quantity discounts. Economies of scope exist in transportation when a shipping container is loaded with a variety of products or a truck is jointly optimized for volume and weight by combining different SKUs with different unit volume and weight.

Efficiency: Efficiency is concerned with obtaining the maximum from existing resources. Once a technology choice is made and the production capacity is made operational, the firm would incur costs related to depreciation and interest burdens. The bigger the capacity put in place, the bigger the depreciation and interest burden and the higher the urgency in recouping investments. The firm would look at an idle resource as a missed opportunity. If sufficient demand exists, the firm could move from single-shift to double-shift to round-the-clock operations. Weekly offs could be staggered so that the plant operates seven days a week. Capacity utilization would increase due to these measures and could soon reach full utilization of the time available for operating the plant. Can there be further improvement of capacity utilization from here on? Yes, it is possible, but requires a scientific analysis of the productive activities.

Frederick Taylor gave birth to scientific management and triggered a fanatical focus on efficiency. Time and motion study of production activities can identify the productive use of time and suggest ways to streamline the sequence of activities or eliminate unnecessary steps. *Introduction to Work Study*, published by the International Labour Office, divides the total time of operation under existing conditions to be made up of four parts: basic work content, work content added by poor product design or materials utilization, work content added by inefficient methods of manufacture or operation and ineffective time resulting from Human Resources contribution.

While the basic work content is the 'irreducible minimum time', the actual work content is bloated by the addition of the other three parts. The search for efficiency thus translates to systematic identification and reduction of excess work content. The reduction of total time of operation allows production rates to be speeded up, thereby increasing output from the same set of resources available in a given time period. An analysis of working conditions, tools and equipment can identify ways to reduce the effort involved, thereby reducing worker fatigue. Jigs and fixtures can be designed to reduce the time and cost of set-up. Preventive maintenance can be scheduled to avoid unanticipated machine downtime. Scientific analysis can be performed to reduce the consumption of raw materials and quality control can focus on improving yields. Inventory can be optimized to balance inventory holding costs with the cost of stock-outs. Standard operating procedures can be put in place to automate decision-making. A culture of identification and elimination of waste (*muda* in Japanese) of different kinds—waste of motion, waste of over production, etc., could permeate the organization. Every facet of the organization, including man, machine, material, money and management, can be reviewed with the objective of making activities more efficient. Efficiency gains arise from insights and learnings related to how work could be done better, and hence is a kind of dynamic economies of scale as opposed to static economies of scale, discussed earlier.

While the quest for efficiency reached its pinnacle under scientific management, its roots can be traced back to much earlier. Division of labour in human societies is a form of efficiency as productivity is gained by repetition of activities. The celebrated pin factory example cited by Adam Smith in *The Wealth of Nations* shows how striking productivity gains are possible by breaking down a manufacturing activity into a series of repetitive steps. Each step is assigned to a specific worker who specializes in that activity. As a result, set-up times and set-up costs are minimized and, in addition, run times may decrease due to the learning curve effect. However, there is more than what meets the eye here. Charles Babbage was the first to allude to the fact that division of labour allows different wage rates to be paid based on the skill requirement of each activity, while lumping of all activities together means that the worker needs to be paid as per the highest wage rate corresponding to the activity requiring most skill. According to Babbage, 'The higher the skill required of the workman in any one process of a manufacture, and the smaller the time during which it is employed, so much the greater will be the advantage of separating that process from the rest, and devoting one person's attention entirely to it.'

Frederick Taylor was the first to recognize and implement this scientifically, thereby not only gaining productivity improvements but also reducing the size of the workforce and paying differential wage rates based on skill involved. In the book *Shop Management*, he stated the main challenge as 'What the workmen want from their employers beyond anything else is high wages, and what employers want from their workmen most of all is a low labor cost of manufacture. These two conditions are not diametrically opposed to one another as would appear at first glance. On the contrary, they can be made to go together in all classes of work, without exception, and in the writer's judgment the existence or absence of these two elements forms the best index to either good or bad management.'

His solution lay in segmenting workers based on productivity. According to him, 'The possibility of coupling high wages with a low labor cost rests mainly upon the enormous difference between the amount of work which a first-class man can do under favorable circumstances and the work which is actually done by the average man.'

However, increase of labour productivity was also contingent on a much greater role for management. In order to solve the problem of soldiering, a practice where workers deliberately or out of laziness adopted a slow pace of work, Taylor not just identified an above-average man and offered him a higher wage rate, but also took control of work away from the worker. 'Well, if you are a high-priced man, you will do exactly as this man tells you tomorrow, from morning till night. When he tells you to pick up a pig and walk, you pick it up and you walk, and when he tells you to sit down and rest, you sit down. You do that right straight through the day. And what's more, no back talk. Now a high-priced man does just what he's told to do, and no back talk. Do you understand that? When this man tells you to walk, you walk; when he tells you to sit down, you sit down, and you don't talk back at him. Now you come on to work here tomorrow morning and I'll know before night whether you are really a high-priced man or not.'

This example, cited by Taylor in the book *Scientific Management*, is for a gang of originally seventy-five men manually loading pig iron weighing 97 pounds into railroad wagons at the Bethlehem Steel Plant. Productivity increased 3.8 times, from a man handling an average of 12.5 tons of pig iron per day to 47.5 tons per day; while the wage rate of the selected workers increased only 60 per cent from $1.15 to $1.85 per day. The increase in labour productivity and the resultant decrease in workforce size and total labour cost incurred is the root of the success of the cost leadership strategy achieved by early adopters of scientific management. The efficiency gains from division of labour are more pronounced for labour-intensive operations.

Not surprisingly, Marxist historians and economists like David Harvey have pointed out the way the quest for efficiency in the form of division of labour has deskilled the worker and made him a commodity while ultimately reducing his wage rate and bargaining power. At the same time, the reduction of direct labour is accompanied by an increase in indirect and supervisory manpower. 'Routinization of tasks at one level often requires the creation of more sophisticated skills at another level. The job structure becomes more hierarchical, and those at the top of this hierarchy—the engineers, computer scientists, planners and designers, etc.—begin to accumulate certain monopolizable skills.' In the example cited by Taylor, the increase in labour productivity was preceded by a time and motion study to specify the target productivity of 47.5 tons per day as well as analysis and segmentation of the workers to identify capable workers who would be interested in monetary incentives, and day-to-day planners who would instruct workers on when to work and when to rest. These are *investments* that are necessary for increasing efficiency and productivity.

Frederick Taylor has also contributed immensely to our understanding of the role of variability in manufacturing systems. If all the sub-activities constituting a bigger activity are homogenous in requirement of a high level of skill then division of labour is not likely to reduce the wage bill. Higher the existing variability, higher the potential for cost savings. Scientific management embarked on a quest to identify variability and introduce standardization. In pre-industrialized society, the artisan and his tool were inseparable. The artisan crafted his own tool, maintained it and passed it on to the next generation. In India, craftsmen still perform puja of the tools and venerate Vishwakarma, the God who crafted this entire world. An apprentice learning the trade would consider it an honour if the craftsman bestowed his tools to the apprentice.

Today, computer programmers and managers may think it is a sign of progressiveness if a firm has a policy of 'Bring Your Own Device' (BYOD), but even in the early years of the Industrial Revolution, craftsmen would bring their tools to the factory. Taylor considered this practice unscientific as it did not allow standardization of work practices and made determination of work content difficult. He argued that if workers bring their own shovels then the amount of material shovelled would differ based on the variation of size of the shovel, making it difficult to set the expected amount of material shovelled that constitutes a fair day's worth of work. Consider the shock then when the craftsman is told that he need not bring his tools to the factory. The factory would have a standardized set of tools which would be allocated to the worker on a daily basis, to be deposited back at the end of the day. Perhaps there is no better milestone of the journey from skilled craftsman to factory worker than this severance of bond between the craftsman and the tool. The tool becomes profane, anyone can touch it just like the transformation of the ustad (master artisan) into a daily labourer. Scientific management decrees that standardized tools would be used by workers wearing uniforms and paid standardized wages to work on standardized activities using standardized raw materials as per standardized work practices and evaluated as per standardized quality standards.

The journey of standardization had begun a century earlier when Eli Whitney introduced the concept of interchangeability of parts to the production of muskets for the US Army in 1798. The possibility that any random lock could be paired with any random stock or barrel to produce a complete firearm was revolutionary as it meant not just ease of manufacturing and assembly but also repair. The focus of scientific management on standardization brought about a similar revolution by introducing a different kind of interchangeability. While Henry Ford may be infamous for saying, 'Any customer can have a car painted any colour that he wants so long as it is black', the scope of standardization is not limited to components (for example, the components of a musket) or characteristics of the product (the black paint of the car), but also something much more radical. In the insightful book, *The Machine That Changed the World*, James P. Womack, Daniel T. Jones and Daniel Roos state that 'Ford not only perfected the interchangeable part. He perfected the interchangeable worker.' Just as interchangeability of parts is contingent on the standardization of the interface between parts; interchangeability of workers is contingent on the standardization of (i) individual activities and processes and (ii) interactions between individual activities and processes.

Division of labour and standardization of activities and processes together can lead to cost efficiencies. In craft production, a highly skilled fitter would have '. . . gathered all the necessary parts, obtained tools from the tool room, repaired them if necessary, performed the complex fitting and assembly job for the entire vehicle. Then checked over his work before sending the completed vehicle to the shipping department.' The source of cost reduction comes from two different sources. First, there is a difference in skill level between the different activities undertaken by the fitter, but he is likely to be paid a high wage rate based on the most complex skill involved in the composite activity. Division of labour allows the highly skilled worker to concentrate only on the activity requiring a high skill level and get a high wage rate while the other activities with lower skill requirements can be allocated to workers with lower skill levels who get paid lower wage rates. This unbundling of work content in terms of skill requirements and segmentation of wage rates as per skill requirements results in cost reductions. Second, the dedication of a specific worker to a specific task results in learning effects and the reduction of task duration and improvement of accuracy emanating from repetition of the task.

The quest for standardization transcends the physical processes in a factory and applies equally to information systems. Off-the-shelf ERP software represents standardized software which has modules which can be customized to customer requirements. This customization is not in terms of understanding the specific and perhaps unique requirements of the client and designing a software to serve the need. The customization offered by most ERP packages is the choice of parameter settings pre-designed in the off-the-shelf modules. If the parameter settings fit the client requirements, then all is well. If they do not, the ERP vendor is likely to press client management to change policies or processes or systems of the client to match ERP functionalities. Scarier is the use of the loaded term 'best practices' to sell default patterns of parameter settings in off-the-shelf modules. If all competitors adopt the so-called 'best practices' peddled by ERP vendors, the world would be made up of copycat systems. Standardized software thus represents both an opportunity and a threat. Due to standardization, a firm can buy a world class ERP system at a lower cost than if that same quality of IT systems had to be developed from scratch. At the same time, the firm chooses to commodify its information processes and sacrifice uniqueness and differentiation at the altar of the lower-cost promise of standardization.

Standardization allows cost savings as duplication of resources can be minimized due to an increase in interchangeability. This is an internal-focused understanding of why standardization reduces cost. The external-focused explanation connects the quest for standardization to a quest for increasing the predictability of the work environment. If the variations in the work environment in terms of machines, workers, tools, raw materials, ambient conditions (weather fluctuations, noise levels, etc.) can be minimized then work can get better designed. The factory thus operates in an island of predictability buffered from the variations in demand through finished goods inventory and variations of supply though raw material inventory. The work-in-process (WIP) inventory buffers internal processes with different production rates from one another. The adoption of standardized work processes and worker training decreases the individual worker's discretion and hence increases predictability. The adoption of a Level production plan maintains a constant, and hence a predictable production rate. The need to have predictable output quality requires a focus on the sourcing of predictable quality of raw material, thus necessitating investments in vendor development so that not just product quality but also service quality in terms of On-Time In-Full (OTIF) deliveries can be predicted. The quest for efficiency thus not just permeates the firm but also transcends the firm boundary.

At its fanatical extreme, the cult of efficiency sacrifices the human and the humane in the quest for a little more of the same. Man is turned into a robot, with each action of the left hand and the right hand defined, timed and accounted for (do not mention to the industrial engineer the fact that the left leg and right leg are idle, someone may devise a way to extract a little more efficiency from there too). The regimentation of work robs the workplace of the space for reflection and innovation, the relentless pace of work makes the worker weary and increases absenteeism and attrition and encourages militant trade unionism. The relentless focus on changing the environment to increase predictability and thereby increase standardization and efficiency leads to an eventual 'McDonaldization' of society. In an interesting chapter in his book, sociologist George Ritzer details how McDonaldization has virtually converted the summiting of Mount Everest into an assembly line of climbers. The fact that this system can put a climber of modest physical fitness on the top of the world is simultaneously an occasion to rejoice and a cause for concern. While the paying customer may demand to summit the mountain, the variability of environmental conditions may occasionally turn too severe, thereby risking a catastrophic failure.

Network Effects: Network effects are exemplified by Metcalfe's Law—named after Ethernet inventor Robert Metcalfe—in telecommunication networks, which estimates that in a network of n nodes, value is a function of n^2 while cost is a function of n. So, as n increases linearly, cost increases linearly while value increases exponentially. This value increase is made up of two parts—increase in the number of transactions and increase in the willingness to pay. In a telephone network, if there are n subscribers, each subscriber can potentially call $(n-1)$ other subscribers and hence the total number of potential telephone calls is $n(n-1)$. As n increases, the number of possible transactions increases as a function of n^2. In addition, a customer may be willing to pay a higher fee per transaction as n increases. For example, in telecom, a person who calls only a few numbers may be enticed by a scheme where low rates apply for these specific numbers, thereby price discriminating with respect to those customers who call a large variety of numbers. For the telecom network, the first sale is incredibly difficult to make since the first customer has no one to call. The second customer can only call the first customer. So, telecom revenue increases exponentially as n increases due to not just the increase in the potential number of other customers that each customer may call, but also in the customer valuing this ability to connect to a wider group. Stated in a different way, the cost of convincing an additional customer to join the network decreases as n increases.

Different kinds of networks exhibit different extents of network effects. In broadcast networks, like cable TV, value increases linearly with the size of the network. Peer-to-peer transactional networks like telecommunications exhibit value growing at n^2. Group-forming networks (GFNs), as per computer scientist David P. Reed, are networks where individuals can create groups or communities, like Facebook groups or WhatsApp groups. Since the total number of possible groups is 2^n, GFNs have the potential to scale even faster than that predicted by Metcalfe's Law.

Network effect is thus an example of demand-side economies of scale in contrast to supply-side economies of scale, discussed earlier. Note that in the telecom example, nothing prevents the firm from reaping supply-side economies of scale in addition to demand-side economies of scale. Thus, the firm may invest in switching technology with a higher fixed cost but lower marginal costs, and thus reap the benefit of lower total costs as n increases compared to competitors. The marginal cost per transaction could also decrease as n increases. For example, the telecom firm may have to pay an inter-connect charge if a call originating from its network needs to be connected to a node in the network of a competitor. If both the originating and destination nodes are internal to the telecom firm's own network, then this inter-connect charge does not apply. The bigger telecom network thus has a cost advantage over the smaller network. As network size increases, the increase in profits can come from the revenue side (network effect) or cost side (scale effect) or a combination of both.

The existence of network effect frequently propels a firm to adopt the Grow Big Fast strategy. While supply-side scale economies imply the need to Grow Big, the addition of 'Fast' is necessitated due to the winner-takes-all nature of network effects. Quickly capturing market share is thus as much an imperative as building scale. The firm thus needs to not just have deep pockets but it also needs to make upfront investments rather than stagger them conservatively over the time horizon. The financial risks involved in such ventures are considerably high, and mistakes in understanding the customer or overestimating technology capability are fatal. The competitive intensity is fierce as other firms strive to gain market share from each other.

In telecom networks, the customer initiating a call in one instance can be the one receiving the call in another. In other words, customers are of one type only. In contrast, platforms connect different types of user groups. Multi-sided platforms (MSPs) like Uber and Airbnb need to serve the different needs of different types of users. The network effect for MSPs is dependent on not just the total number of users of different types, but the composition of different user groups too. The MSP has to Grow Big Fast on as many fronts as there are user groups but also maintain a balance in the relative proportion of each type. A marketplace with all sellers is as meaningless as a marketplace with all buyers, even though the absolute number on the platform may be high. The addition of each buyer thus has a same-side effect on the other existing buyers, and a cross-side effect on the existing sellers. The challenge in growing MSPs emanates from the fact that while cross-side effects can be positive, same-side effects can be negative.

Coordination and Collaboration: Traditional cost leadership took a firm-specific view and focused on cost reduction opportunities internal to the firm. The flowering of the domain of supply chain management has urged us to look at the total delivered cost to the customer and analyse how that cost can be minimized due to the activities of various firms involved in the supply chain. The Bullwhip Effect, a concept introduced by Jay Forrester, explains how order variability can be amplified upstream even when downstream demand is relatively flat. The culprit is information distortion in supply chains arising from various causes like (i) demand forecast updating (ii) order batching (iii) price fluctuations and (iv) shortage gaming, explain Hau L. Lee, V. Padmanabhan and Seungjin Whang. Instead of each stage of the supply chain taking an independent decision, the total cost can be reduced if decisions are coordinated across the supply chain. The implementation of Just in Time (JIT) pull systems can reduce inventory holding costs. By reducing supply lead times, Quick Response (QR), as studied by Ananth Iyer and Mark E. Bergen, can increase forecast accuracy and reduce demand–supply mismatch costs in situations of high demand volatility and short selling seasons. While the value of coordination is easy to see, taking the coordinator's role requires long-term commitment, effort and investments. The coordinator needs to not just understand how cost reductions are possible but also negotiate, incentivize and share gains with other firms to change decisions and practices in firms over which the coordinating firm has no financial control or authority.

The act of coordination between multiple firms, each having its own set of managerial objectives and shareholder expectations, requires the cultivation of an atmosphere of trust and collaboration. This is in striking contrast to the adversarial relationship that permeates the transaction orientation of price negotiations with suppliers. Low price is not the same as low cost, and the arm-twisting of suppliers in terms of lower prices or longer payment terms may only result in the supplier eventually passing on the cost to the firm in the form of lower quality or unreliable supply. Cost leadership through coordination is thus an enlightened view of how costs are accumulated in the supply chain, and an effort towards achievement of a global optima rather than a sum of local optima for each firm.

Market Share: The quest for higher market share is a quest towards market dominance with promises of a higher price realization. A dominant firm in a market can be a price-setter, either as a monopolist or in collusion with competitors in an oligopolistic situation, thereby attracting adverse scrutiny and regulations. Dominant market share also has the ability to provide opportunities for cost reduction. For example, a retailer has little option but to carry the category leader, and hence lesser bargaining power against a firm with dominant share than a firm with low market share. This low bargaining power of the retailer results in a lower slotting fee and hence a lower cost of sales for the FMCG market leader. Dominant market share also helps a firm in implementing product, technology or process standards that are helpful in reducing costs. A firm with a higher market share has the option to invest in advertising campaigns as it could spread this fixed cost over a larger quantity of sales compared to a competitor with a lower market share who may be constrained to only play around with promotional discounts.

A firm may wish to gain market share through a merger with or acquisition of a competitor. The combined entity may lower competition intensity in the industry, thereby reducing costs of sales for both firms. In situations where start-ups are burning investor cash to gain market share by providing consumer discounts, such mergers can reduce the overall cash burn and lengthen the runway, and are hence preferred by the private equity or venture capital firms which hold a stake in both start-ups.

Unless the total market size is diminishing, increasing market share also implies a larger-sized firm in terms of revenue. A larger-sized firm has more ability to afford indirect fixed costs like corporate staff functions. It is thus much more economical for a larger market share firm to hire management or technical consultants, specialized services like trademark protection, public relations experts or crack legal teams. At its extreme, dominant firms may become so big that they represent systemic risks for the economy. By becoming too big to fail, the dominant firm cushions its downside risk since the government may be forced to bail it out in an adverse situation. At the same time, becoming too big may attract unwanted scrutiny and threat of a government takeover, anti-trust proceedings or NGO activism.

Fundamental Principle of Cost Leadership: The previous discussion on the sources of cost leadership has identified several different kinds of sources. There seems to be a large number of ways in which a firm can gain cost leadership. But a deeper review of the different sources reveals a very fundamental pattern which characterizes all the different sources of cost leadership. To achieve cost leadership, firms have to employ a two-stage process involving investing and utilization of invested resources to the fullest.

Mantra of Cost Leadership:
Invest and Utilize to the Fullest

In the first step, the firm invests in creating capacity of different kinds. This capacity could be manufacturing capacity located in a specific location to get agglomeration benefits. It could be investments in a production technology with a large minimum efficient scale to get economies of scale. It could be investments in a resource or technology which provides economies of scope. It could be investments in Total Quality Management (TQM) to reduce costs of quality and thereby gain efficiency. It could be investments in product promotions to increase adoption and gain loyalty in networks and platforms. It could be investments in information networks to enable flow of information between firms collaborating in a supply chain. It could be investments in trade promotions to steal market share from competitors. It could be investments in building trust in supply chains to reduce demand–supply mismatch costs. It could be investments in any source of cost leadership. The fundamental insight is understanding that the key is *investments*. You cannot gain cost leadership without investments. The type of investment may vary but the need for investments is paramount if cost leadership is to be achieved.

We need to distinguish between costs and investments. Investments buy us something in the future. The money invested in buying a house gives us benefits over years while the rent paid for a specific month is a cost that provides benefits for that month only. Investments in plant and machinery can be recouped over the productive life of the assets. Once the investment is made, the firm has to earmark depreciation on the assets and pay interest on the borrowings that funded the assets. The depreciation and interest charge are thus annual fixed costs which do not vary with the quantity of production. They may change from year to year based on the depreciation method adopted or the structuring of the loan, but the amount charged in a particular year does not vary with production quantity. Higher the investment, higher the fixed cost on a yearly basis and hence higher the urgency in recouping the money invested.

Once, an investment is made in an asset, the focus then shifts to 'sweating out the asset' by increasing the amount that can be produced using it. Merely investing in capacity produces no financial benefit unless the capacity is utilized. The extent of utilization is captured in the metric of capacity utilization. For a cost leader, the ideal capacity utilization is 100 per cent. At this level, the maximum rated output is being produced and the fixed costs are being spread over the maximum number of units possible. While the target capacity utilization may be 100 per cent, the actual capacity utilization could be lower due to unforeseen production stoppages resulting from various causes like employee absenteeism, machine breakdown, quality issues, raw material unavailability, etc. Note that capacity utilizations higher than 100 per cent are possible only if the plant is operated beyond its stipulated working conditions (for instance, by reduction of planned maintenance hours or by instituting a third shift when originally a two-shift operation had been envisaged, etc.) or if there is a change in production technology.

Becoming a cost leader thus entails investing in the right type and quantum of capacity and utilizing the capacity to the fullest. Large capacity with low capacity utilization is high on potential and low on delivery. Small capacity with high capacity utilization is low on potential and high on delivery of the installed potential. Both these situations are suboptimal. The ideal situation is when the firm has invested in a capacity that dwarfs competitors and operates that capacity at near full capacity utilization. We call such a firm an Elephant.

An Elephant is a firm which invests to gain cost leadership. A manufacturing Elephant invests in technologies which provide scale or scope economies. A brand Elephant invests in brand-building and leverages brand equity to sell a diverse product line. An R&D Elephant in the pharma domain may be investing decades worth of research in the quest for the next blockbuster molecule.

The first thing that you notice about the Elephant is the size. The scale is gigantic. It needs marshalling of resources on a scale which ordinary entrepreneurs can only dream of. Bigger the Elephant, better the potential cost savings if it is driven at full capacity. The competition between Elephants is thus based on who has the bigger capacity and whether the capacity is being utilized to the maximum. An Elephant may not shy away from dropping prices to shore up capacity utilization. It may not shy away from dropping prices below cost to crush a new entrant by not allowing it to gain volumes and reach break-even point. The older entrenched Elephants may have depreciated their assets and have relatively lower interest burdens than the new entrant who is saddled with depreciation and interest burdens. The brutal Elephant battle philosophy calls for crushing the new entrant when it is still weak by aggressive price wars; as it would be costlier, if not impossible, to dislodge the new entrant once it establishes itself.

The fact that Elephants may not shy away from a price war does not mean that they would engage in one. Low competitive intensity would allow Elephants to maintain relatively high prices while reducing costs and minting money for shareholders. Low costs need not translate into low prices, and brand Elephants and R&D Elephants may simultaneously enjoy high prices and low costs.

There are several ways in which you can identify an Elephant from an outside observer's perspective. An analysis of the cost structure of the Elephant should reveal large fixed costs and low fixed costs per unit output. An analysis of market share could reveal the dominant market position of the firm. An analysis of pricing moves could reveal the Elephant as the price leader. An analysis of capacity additions in the sector could reveal the Elephant as the firm with the largest capacity increments. An analysis of industry benchmarks may reveal the Elephant as having the highest capacity utilization or efficiency parameters.

If you have access to the internal working of the firm, either as a consultant or as an employee, look for the performance metrics that permeate the entire firm from shop floor to the board room. If the firm is an Elephant, you cannot miss the overriding focus on capacity utilization as the primary performance metric to assess the health of the business. The specific version of the capacity utilization metric would vary from one industry to another. Power plants would be evaluated on Plant Load Factors (PLFs), paper manufacturers on tons of output, airlines on cost per seat mile. In certain industries, the cost focus is so overwhelming that metrics based on capacity utilization become default benchmarking metrics. In such industries, the Elephants stand out as the firms with industry-best capacity utilization metrics. These industry leaders are very difficult to dethrone unless there are technology advances which disrupt the way value is delivered to customers.

Doors closed by Elephants: Elephants have a distinctive pattern of closed doors. The focus on maximization of capacity utilization means that many strategic decisions are swayed by the option which results in better utilization of assets. Thus, an Elephant is likely to choose a Lag capacity strategy where capacity is added conservatively once enough demand is assured. While the Lag capacity strategy may give up on some unfulfilled demand, the cost of lost sales is deemed by the Elephant as less costly than the cost of any idle capacity. Elephants are more likely to adopt a Level production plan since such a plan minimizes hiring and firing costs and allows the plant to have a stable production rate. In the process, the Elephant values full capacity utilization of production assets as more beneficial than the cost of holding inventory or the cost of stock-outs. You are more likely to find the Elephant located near raw material sources than close to markets. Sometimes, you will find the Elephant co-located with its suppliers. The demand from a big Elephant could be large enough for suppliers to dedicate production units near or even inside the premises of the Elephant mother factory. The proximity of the Elephant with its suppliers may not be just physical. Progressive Elephants may invest in vendor development by deputing their own engineers to develop systems and competencies of the supplier or invest in inter-firm coordination mechanisms to enable JIT supply. In the process, the Elephant closes the door on transactional orientation in supplier relationships.

In economies with high wage rates, Elephants may invest in automation and robotics to reduce the headcount. Automation may also change the workforce composition from higher-skilled craftsmen to lower-skilled machine tenders, thereby reducing costs. The plant layout of Elephants is likely to be product layouts in the form of assembly lines or continuous flow lines. The Elephant thus closes its door to process layouts. The high-volume manufacturing environment allows the Elephant to institute tools like Statistical Quality Control (SQC), thereby moving from product inspection to quality assurance of the process.

The Elephant is likely to have a well-defined and detailed planning process with periodic review of long-term and medium-term forecasts. The annual plan may take several months to finalize and could then be converted into three-month rolling forecasts and monthly sourcing, production and distribution plans. The monthly plan could have a frozen window during which no changes can be made to the production plan. In the process, the Elephant closes doors to instant reactions to volatile demand situations. While the Elephant can choose to be reactive, it can only respond to fluctuations within a band and require long lead times for changing plans. The finished goods are likely to be transported using transport modes which are low-cost like shipping of full containers over ship or rail or full truckloads for road movements using bigger trucks. In the process, the Elephant closes doors on partial or LTL movements or responding to last-minute orders by using air freight.

The internal culture of Elephants is distinctive. A work ethic which prizes discipline and hard work.

Work routines characterized by standard operating procedures. A command and control regime supported by strict hierarchy. Near cult-like adherence to process improvement tools like TQM, Total Productive Maintenance (TPM) or Lean principles. The culture is best exemplified by the joke that Ford engineers in the heyday of the 'cult of efficiency' would have decreed that typists write efficiency with one 'f' since that would mean less effort and time to type. Those halcyon days of cost leadership have thankfully passed. Still, it is difficult to imagine an Elephant without a preponderance of deviation-counteracting feedback loops which aim to stipulate and maintain all aspects of Elephant existence.

While focus on efficiency improvement may exist in any part of business, the impact of efficiency improvement initiatives depends on the cost structure. A firm which has a relentless focus on improving labour efficiency may not gain much if labour costs are a miniscule proportion of total costs. Instead of an overarching philosophy of achieving cost leadership on all fronts, a firm can identify the biggest cost sources and strategically focus efficiency improvement initiatives on those fronts where there is maximum potential.

Look around you and see the Elephants roaming around. They are easy to spot in stable industries or commodity markets. In these situations, the whole industrial sector seems to be made up of Elephants of varying degrees, established Elephants along with wannabes and strugglers. They are easy to identify in monopoly situations or platform businesses where there are only a few potential winners. Whenever you see an Elephant, check out the source of cost leadership and you would start seeing the way the culture of the Brand Elephant is different from the culture of the Manufacturing Elephant or the Supply Chain Elephant.

The established Elephant is a veritable money-making machine with its low-cost structure, stable pricing and enormous war chest. It is extremely difficult to dislodge an Elephant and gain market leadership by anyone other than another Elephant. The Goliath towers over ordinary firms and beats them every time till one day David appears with a new technology and disrupts the entire industry. The victory of David is so celebrated because it is so rare. It is the exception to the norm of the Goliaths reigning over the business landscape.

CHAPTER 10

Time Responsiveness

'A stitch in time saves nine.'

—English proverb

ELEPHANTS COMPETE ON the dimension of cost, and there are a variety of different cost heads that make their presence felt in an analysis of the cost structure of a firm. However, there is one particular cost head that is conspicuous by its absence in the profit-and-loss statement of any firm. And this cost head is so important that it can literally mark the difference between life and death.

The Cost of Time

What exactly is the cost of time? Nothing, if you ask the hermit meditating under a tree. Boredom, if you ask the station master of a remote train station with only a couple of trains in a day. A lot, if you ask the top-notch professional charging by the hour. Life, if you ask the doctor treating patients in the emergency ward of a hospital. The cost of time would vary depending on who you ask and when you ask. And that makes the accountant highly sceptical, and rightly so, of the valuation of this cost head. The solution? Follow conservative accounting principles and just disregard this cost in the books of accounts. The accountant is happy, but it is a sad day for the sales and operations managers. Forever they will have to answer audit queries on why their effective systems are so cost inefficient. The high cost of the stitch made in time is real, the cost of the additional nine stitches avoided is notional savings and hence disregarded by the wise auditor.

Whose cost of time are we dealing with? The cost of time for a firm originates from the cost of time of the set of customers it serves. If there are distinct customer segments with different costs of time, the firm has to select which segments to serve and design the operating strategy accordingly. The design for the low cost of time system could be quite different from the high cost of time system.

If a patient walks into a big hospital for a consultation, she may be first asked to register in the outpatient department (OPD) and then asked to wait outside the consultation room. There might be several patients waiting in the queue and the waiting area may be a common one for a group of consultation rooms. The scene can be quite chaotic with staff members directing people to different doctors and medical testing departments. In some of the well-regarded hospitals, the number of patients could be significantly large and even overwhelm the number of doctors and medical personnel available. There could be too many patients waiting for the doctor's attention.

In this world, someone waits for someone. The clue in designing operating systems is finding out who waits for whom. The fundamental insight is that the resource with a lower cost of time waits for the resource with a higher cost of time.

In the OPD, people wait patiently for the doctor since their cost of time is lower than the doctor's given the demand–supply imbalance. In the same hospital, there would be an emergency department where doctors are assigned duties without knowing how many patients needing what kind of emergency treatment would turn up. The doctors wait here patiently for the patient to turn up (hopefully, there will be none). The design of the emergency department is quite different from the OPD. The access to the emergency ward is straight from the road, with the facility for an ambulance to drive close to the door of the emergency department. There is no registration or paperwork and the patient is provided immediate attention. In fact, the emergency service starts even earlier when the ambulance, fitted with life-saving equipment, picks up the patient. Here, doctors, medical personnel and the ambulance wait for the patient since the patient's cost of time is life.

We are thus not stating that the doctor always has a cost of time which is higher. Different segments of patients may have quite different costs of time, varying from low cost of time for elective consultations to high cost of time for emergency procedures. Additionally, a patient who came in for a regular consultation can suffer a heart attack while waiting in queue. The patient's cost of time could thus change over time, necessitating a change in the operating system. The basis of segmentation is thus not type of individual (doctor vs patient) or type of service (OPD vs emergency) but the relative cost of time of the customer and the service provider.

An OPD can be designed to be cost efficient, but an emergency service needs to be effective in terms of providing the right treatment as soon as possible. This effectiveness comes at a cost. The uneven workload in emergency departments means that dedicated doctors, medical personnel and ambulances would be idle for a significant portion of time, and this is surely an inefficient use of a resource. Ambulances could be stationed in different areas of the city to minimize the time to pick up patients. It might have been much more cost-efficient to house all ambulances in a centralized location. For the same service level, a centralized emergency facility would have reduced stocking of costly drugs and low shelf-life consumables due to statistical pooling than if these were stocked at decentralized locations. And relaxing the inventory-fill-rate-related stocking norms of life-saving items like blood supplements or anti-venoms would surely reduce costs. Let me not provide any more of these gems lest some efficiency experts actually get motivated to implement them. A manager who questions the cost of effectiveness should just pray that he/she does not have to visit a cost-efficient emergency facility as a patient.

The focus on effectiveness is not limited to emergency medical services. Sliding down a fireman's pole is not particularly elegant but helps in a faster response. Fire service departments may use smokejumpers who parachute close to forest fires in a bid to contain the fire before it is too late. In countries where the use of wood for housing is prevalent, it is not uncommon to have a community firefighting system at the village level so that any incidence of fire can be quickly handled. These village-level voluntary firefighters may not be paid by the state but train and maintain a high level of preparedness. Thus, the cost of effectiveness is borne not by the state but by community members. Cities maintain emergency hotlines and 24x7 call centres for different kinds of support like calling the police, reporting an accident or suicide crisis lines. There must be adequate staffing in these call centres so that every call can be speedily responded to. Countries may invest in quick response teams for disaster relief, flying them in dedicated planes fitted with specialized equipment. Commando teams are expected to use unconventional methods and surprise the enemy with the speed of the operation. Sending in the army may be relatively cost efficient but there are certain operations where the high-cost, high-responsive commando is indispensable.

Business is far removed from the world of smokejumpers and commandos, but the need for speed of response is not alien to management. Cities hosting mega sporting events like the Olympics may need to build and develop a host of sporting as well as transport facilities under strict timelines. The core set of projects funded by the state would give rise to spin-off projects in the commercial sector like construction of hotels, restaurants and entertainment facilities. Every mega project can be subdivided into smaller projects with interlinked deadlines, and a delay in one project may have a cascading effect on other projects. Projects are ubiquitous. They range from small improvement projects on a factory shop floor to building factories, dams, bridges and cities to large multilocation teams working round the clock on software projects, to projects captivating a nation's imagination like sending a man to the moon. The tremendous variety of project environments have one thing in common: a fanatical focus on completing the project before the due date. A project manager has to worry about both cost and time overruns, but finishing on time is more important. The cost focus is limited to choosing the least cost alternative such that the time deadline is achieved. The primacy of the time dimension in projects is apparent with textbooks featuring chapters on project crashing to achieve a deadline, by trading off increased cost for a faster completion. While project 'decrashing' (involving reducing project costs by settling for a relaxed deadline) is theoretically possible, it merits no more than a cursory mention in a footnote.

In nature, a faster response may mean food for the predator and life for the prey. Different predators have different response speeds based on the differences of anatomy which are uniquely suited for their choice of prey. Lions, tigers, cheetahs, leopards, jaguars all belong to the *Felidae* biological family, but differ in terms of weight, speed, stalking behaviour, killing method, time of hunting or whether they hunt alone or in packs. There is no ideal predator. The characteristic of the terrain in terms of open savannah or dense tropical forest, and the characteristic of the prey in terms of weight and speed, etc., favour one predator over another. The peak speed of the tiger at 49–65 km per hour is about half that of the cheetah at 110–120 km per hour, but that does not make the tiger any less lethal in the dense forests of the night.

The cheetah in comparison has much poorer night vision and prefers to hunt only during the cooler morning and evenings rather than the heat of the day. It has much lesser weight than a tiger, and it does not even have the tiger's phenomenal power-to-weight ratio that can kill a lion with a single paw strike. It cannot climb trees like a tiger nor is it as adept at swimming. Poor cheetahs, they cannot even roar! They purr like household cats. Before you start thinking of having one as a pet, consider the one dimension where the cheetah stands out.

The cheetah is the fastest land animal. It holds the record not just for the top speed but also for the fastest acceleration. It is this acceleration which is the cheetah's key to a successful hunt. It first narrows the distance between the prey and itself by creeping up to the prey using the cover of the tall savannah grass and its camouflage. Once the prey starts running, the cheetah quickly accelerates. Most hunts are over quickly—either the cheetah catches the prey or gives up. It cannot continue running at that high speed for a long period of time. This is because of the enormous amount of energy required for the sprint. The cheetah can produce 120 watts per kg of body weight, in comparison, researchers estimated in an article published in *Nature* that Usain Bolt used 25 watts per kg in his record-breaking run in 2019. This enormous burst of energy would increase the core body temperature, and the cheetah must stop running to cool down. The cheetah is thus the fastest only in small bursts. As an athlete, the cheetah should never ever compete in a marathon, it is built for the 100 metre dash.

Start looking around you to identify business contexts which are time-sensitive. The cheetah has a small window of opportunity in which to make the kill. There are businesses too which operate with a small window of opportunity in which to convert a customer into a revenue stream. The time window may originate from several different sources. It may originate from the time window of the customer or a patient, like when the time window of a souvenir seller is based on the time window the tourist has for some souvenir shopping at a tourist attraction before boarding the tour bus, or the time window available to a farmer to spray pesticide before a pest attack destroys the standing crop, or the time available to administer life-saving drugs to a critical patient. A customer may display differential willingness to wait for a product—at certain times agreeing to wait for an out-of-stock branded product and at certain times refusing to wait and instead willing to try an alternate brand or settling for a substitute. The more loyal the customer to a brand, lesser the need for time responsiveness; the more fickle the customer, the greater the need to seal the transaction before the customer has a change of heart. The time window may originate from competitor presence, like the need to steal market share from a competitor by converting a sale before the customer is aware of a favourable competing offer. The souvenir seller has to worry not just about the time left before the bus departs but also the time left before other souvenir sellers start offering discounts to lure away the tourist. The third source of the time window is any time-window-related promise made by the business itself. Such time window promises may be explicit, as when a business promises a turnaround time for a particular service, or implicit, when a business promises to deliver hot food to a customer. A fourth source of a time window may be the existence of a high-season spread over a few months, like the sales of cold drinks, ice-cream, fans and air-conditioners during summer; or a fashion season, like spring–summer or fall–winter; or a festival season like Christmas or Diwali. A fifth source of a time window may be retailer-specific sales promotion dates offering large discounts on all or a subset of products in all or a subset of stores (offline or online or both). A sixth source of a time window could be related to product characteristics—supply-side considerations like low shelf life of perishable products or technology-related considerations like the rapid pace of technological advancement in the product category, resulting in high obsolescence rates of hi-tech gadgets.

Cheetah businesses compete by promising ever shorter delivery lead times or promising ever increasing delivery reliability within an ever shorter time window. In the first situation, the customer derives value if the service is provided as early as possible. Such a situation may exist, for example, if there is a contingency or breakdown and the needed service or part is holding up a bigger operation or project. In the second situation, the customer is indifferent as long as it is within the defined time window. JIT deliveries from suppliers to an assembly line are scheduled within a time window, and an early delivery is problematic as there is little storage space, and a late delivery would result in stopping the assembly line. A Cheetah competing on shorter lead times has to go all out on the accelerator pedal. In a Formula 1 race, there is no prize for just completing the race, and cars try to squeeze out the last ounce of speed even if that risks a breakdown. They are Cheetahs that run like there is no tomorrow. In contrast, Cheetahs competing on delivery reliability have to balance speed and reliability by offering a high enough reliability at high enough speed. They can steal market share from another Cheetah by offering an earlier start of the time window or offering precision in terms of a shorter time window or offering increased reliability while keeping the time window unchanged.

Frequently, a business may promise not just to serve a customer within a time window but offer to compensate if the promise is not met. Such offers are great marketing tools as they convey to the customer the confidence that the Cheetah has in its own competence to catch the deer within the promised time window. 'Trust me, I am not just fast but reliable too, and I put my money where my mouth is,' says such a Cheetah. A consumer who trusts a Cheetah's competence in delivering on time may be willing to pay a premium for the service. Other predators may be forced to try to match the Cheetah. However, there is a thin line between machismo and foolishness. That is the moment when the men are separated from the boys.

If the marketing or sales department of a firm wishes to match the promise of timely delivery made by a competing Cheetah, it must do so only after appraising whether the firm has the capacity and capability to run like a Cheetah. The promises made by marketing are thus tightly coupled to the operations. In such a situation, the primacy is to operations rather than marketing. Promises are to be made based on operations capabilities already in place rather than first making the promise and then worrying about capacity-building later. The competing

Cheetah would eat your lunch every time if you make promises without a basis. It is much better to ask yourself whether your firm has the capacity to run like a Cheetah before you make a service delivery promise based on a time window. And you must be suicidal to promise compensation if the reliability of the run has not been established.

The first thing that a firm wishing to compete in the time dimension needs to put in place is a measurement system to accurately capture the timelines of events related to the service, and derive performance metrics related to the responsiveness of the service rendered. While this seems elementary, I am aware of a firm which established a strict service delivery deadline for a service which was known to take a lot of time and was habitually late. The firm subsequently reported a stellar performance as not a single customer request was late as per the stricter time window, as reported by the in-house ERP system. This remarkable improvement was not due to an actual reduction of service lead times but due to the fact that the personnel recorded the arrival of the service request in the ERP system only when the service was almost complete! Instead of a Cheetah, the firm had become a paper tiger or, shall I say, an ERP Cheetah. A real Cheetah is built on a much stronger base.

A cheetah is built for the kill. The tremendous power to accelerate comes from a drastic increase in metabolism supported by an oversized heart, lungs, liver and adrenaline glands. To enable flow of air to the lungs, the nasal passages are wider. The spine is long and flexible; it allows the back feet to be positioned before the front feet during the course of the run. The legs are long, allowing the cheetah to cover a larger distance in a single stride. The cheetah body is aerodynamic to reduce friction, and the cheetah stays more in the air than on the ground during a run. The feet have hard pads, like tyres, and semi-retractable claws which increase traction while taking turns. The muscular tail acts like a counterbalance to its body weight while taking sharp turns. The cheetah weighs much lesser than other predators as its bones are lightweight. Each of these individual design elements support the ability of the cheetah to run fast. More important is that each of these design elements operate synergistically. From the bones to the muscles to the internal organs to the claws to even the tip of the tail, every single feature is fine-tuned for just one thing: speed. What a beauty of a system design.

A cheetah hunt takes less than a minute. For the rest of the twenty-four hours, the cheetah just walks around with its oversized heart, lungs, liver and adrenaline glands. You do not need a huge capacity of heart or lungs just for walking around. What a colossal waste of resources. Thank God there are no auditors that nature has to face. Otherwise surely they would have highlighted the significant over-capacity in the system. As a consequence of this over-capacitated system, the cheetah has very low capacity utilization during rest periods, with spikes in the capacity utilization metric reaching close to full utilization only during the run. In other words, it works at peak efficiency only for a small fraction of time and is highly inefficient otherwise. While the cheetah is indeed 'built for the kill', it is not optimized for the rest of the time when it is not running. Nature has poured all its efforts in designing the cheetah to optimize it for a few minutes of running in a day. What a beauty of a system design.

Nature has closed the door to full capacity utilization as an ideal while designing the cheetah. Over-capacity surely has a cost but also has a benefit. It allows a firm to react to customer demand as and when it originates. An Elephant operating close to full capacity utilization does not have the spare bandwidth it needs to react to unplanned requests. The structured monthly planning process, the production freeze windows, the long set-up times needed to changeover from one product to another, the huge backlog of existing orders, the long pipeline of raw materials, WIP and finished goods inventory, the Level production plan—all favour a steady work plan rather than erratic running around after ephemeral customer opportunities. The Elephant chooses a Make-to-Stock production system by buffering itself from peak and non-peak demand conditions through the existence of an adequate finished goods inventory. The Cheetah chooses a Make-to-Order production system by eliminating the finished goods inventory and reacting to customer demand. Since the Cheetah has little control over quantity, timing or type of customer order, it necessarily has to keep its idle resources in readiness for a quick response. The idle capacity allows the Cheetah to ramp up production on demand and ramp down as demand drops. An Elephant operating at full capacity has no headroom to ramp up production. In contrast to the Level production strategy of the Elephant, the Cheetah adopts the Chase production strategy.

It is very intuitive to understand that a Cheetah needs to chase demand. The fundamental insight about *how* to chase demand is not that intuitive. A Cheetah must have the capacity and preparedness to chase demand. The interaction between the act of chasing and the capacity to chase is the primary determinant of the success of the chase. The capacity utilization metric is a succinct way to express the extent to which the act of chasing has used the available capacity. A firm having low capacity utilization has better *potential* to run as a Cheetah. Mere potential is not enough; the Cheetah must also be prepared for the chase.

Mantra of Time Responsiveness: Keep spare capacity and be prepared

---

To ensure spare capacity, the Cheetah adopts the Lead capacity strategy and adds capacity ahead of demand. The Lead capacity strategy and the resultant spare capacity enables the Chase production strategy by providing a capacity cushion. Thus, the act of chasing is fundamentally connected to a Lead capacity strategy. The characteristics of the chase depend on where, when and how much spare capacity is provided.

The location of the spare capacity in the supply chain defines the point from where the Cheetah can start the run. A firm choosing a Lag capacity strategy in manufacturing and a Lead capacity strategy in distribution intends to run like a Cheetah only in distribution while another Cheetah may choose a Lead capacity strategy for both manufacturing and distribution, thereby building a capability to run from an earlier point in the supply chain. The extent of Cheetah operations would thus vary across Deliver-to-Order, Assemble-to-Order, Make-to-Order, Engineer-to-Order and Design-to-Order situations. The Cheetah operations of an engineering procurement construction (EPC) firm which designs, engineers, procures, produces, transports, erects and commissions an industrial project under strict timelines are thus substantially more challenging than the Cheetah operations of an online retailer which stocks inventory and delivers on customer demand. The EPC contractor needs to adopt a Lead capacity strategy for a larger set of resources than the online retailer.

The location of spare capacity is also dictated by the type of supply chain. A firm may have a diverse range of products and employ a cost-effective supply chain for products with low demand–supply mismatch risk, and a time-responsive supply chain for high-risk products. The mismatch risk would be higher for products with high demand uncertainty (measured by the coefficient of variance of demand) or high financial implication of a mismatch (measured by product price). Thus, the Cheetah strategy is likely to be adopted for high price or high demand uncertainty products while the Elephant strategy is adopted for others. The location of spare capacity in such a supply chain would correspond to the resources which serve the Cheetah supply chain.

The timing dimension in spare capacity can arise from seasonality. A firm selling a product with a highly seasonal demand needs spare capacity during the peak season. The sales loss for ice-cream or cold drinks during summer, due to lack of availability in a retail outlet, cannot be replaced by any amount of supply during winter months. Minimization of sales loss during peak season requires access to spare production and distribution capacity during peak season. During off-peak season it would not matter if this spare capacity is employed elsewhere as there is little need to be time responsive. A customer buying an air conditioner in winter may be willing to wait much longer than the same customer during summer. The customer's sensitivity to cost of time thus varies over time for seasonal products, and the need for spare capacity varies accordingly.

The question of how much spare capacity is needed depends on the speed of responsiveness desired. It might not be intuitive that as capacity utilization increases, the lead time for supply increases. In my experience of teaching queueing fundamentals, I have always noticed that a section of executives think high capacity utilization is a good thing as it implies the server is working harder, and hence the queue should be quickly dealt with. This argument is correct in deterministic situations but breaks down in real life where customer arrivals and service times are stochastic. What is even more non-intuitive is that the rise in lead time is not linear. The exact relationship between capacity utilization and lead time can be determined using queueing theory. For an $M/M/1$ (single server, Poisson arrival, exponential service times) queueing system with capacity utilization ρ, the average queue length $L = \rho/(1- \rho)$, $\rho < 1$. At $\rho = 0$, $L = 0$ and as ρ tends to 1 (that is, full capacity utilization), the queue length tends to infinity (Figure 6). The rise in average queue length L results in rise in mean lead time W, as per Little's Law ($L = \lambda W$, λ being the arrival rate). At high values of ρ, the system exhibits a large backlog of orders and hence any new order takes much more time to be served than at lower ρ values. For example,

L increases from 1.5 at $\rho = 0.6$ to 4 at $\rho = 0.8$ and 9 at $\rho = 0.9$. Keeping higher spare capacity implies lower ρ values and hence faster response times. The lead time promised to customers could be used to determine L using Little's Law and the necessary capacity utilization ρ. For example, for an $M/M/1$ system, the mean lead time could be reduced by two-thirds by reducing capacity utilization from $\rho = 0.9$ to $\rho = 0.75$. Similar results hold for more complex queueing models. A more detailed analysis may involve the use of simulation models to quantify the percentage of customers served within the promised due window. The other option is to use thumb rules to specify target capacity utilizations. Prior experience in an industry may specify a range of 60–75 per cent, beyond which the Cheetah loses the ability to outrun the prey or other predators.

Figure 6: Queue Length for M/M/1

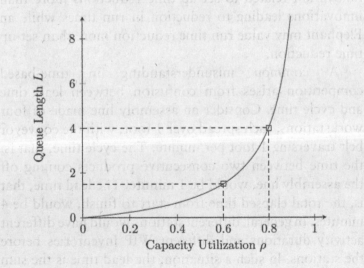

The need to keep spare capacity and respond quickly to customer orders dictates the choice of technology. In production, this is seen in the use of machines with small batch size requirements and lower set-up times. Production lot sizes are smaller, and frequency of changeovers is higher. The production schedule is frequently interrupted as the Cheetah changes order quantities and priorities based on a fast-changing demand landscape. The implication for running after small customer orders also means that the Cheetah would have a large variety of products to make and deliver, giving rise to a high-variety low-volume quick-turnaround production context. The low volumes imply the infeasibility of a learning curve for decreasing run times, but the high variety also presents an opportunity for set-up time and cost reduction. A decrease in set-up time frees up capacity and hence improves both efficiency and effectiveness. A Cheetah values process innovation related to set-up time reductions more than innovations leading to reduction in run times while an Elephant may value run time reduction more than set-up time reduction.

A common misunderstanding in time-based competition arises from confusion between lead time and cycle time. Consider an assembly line made of four workstations, each spread over 1 foot, with the conveyor belt traversing 1 foot per minute. The cycle time, that is, the time between two consecutive products coming off the assembly line, would be 1 minute. The lead time, that is, the total elapsed time from start to finish, would be 4 minutes. In general, different stations would have different activity durations and different WIP inventories before the stations. In such a situation, the lead time is the sum

of processing times and the wait times for all activities
that a job/customer undergoes. Rearranging Little's Law,
we get $W = (1/\lambda)L$ or Mean Lead Time = (Average Cycle
Time) x (Average WIP) (expressed as $MLT = CT \times WIP$).
While we reserve the use of $L = \lambda W$ for service situations
and $MLT = CT \times WIP$ for manufacturing situations, we
note that lead times and cycles times are characteristic
of all operations situations, whether manufacturing
or service. Any operational intervention (for instance,
increase/decrease in batch sizes, set-up times, run times,
inventories, etc.) may have implications for one or both of
lead time and cycle time. The strategic difference between
Elephants and Cheetahs emanates from the purpose of
the intervention. A Cheetah is likely to pursue all possible
tactics which increase responsiveness through reduction
of lead time, any concomitant reduction of cycle time,
if at all, being a bonus. An Elephant is likely to pursue
all possible tactics which increase productivity through
reduction in cycle time, any concomitant reduction of
lead time, if at all, being a bonus. A Cheetah focuses on
lead times, an Elephant on cycle times.

The Cheetah may prefer technology choices in logistics
that offer faster modes of transport even at a higher cost.
The delivery fleet could use smaller-sized vans to offer
more weekly or daily deliveries rather than bigger capacity
trucks delivering the monthly requirement. In peak season,
the frequency of delivery could be increased to several times
a day, incurring high transport costs but minimizing sales
loss. To achieve this level of responsiveness, the Cheetah
needs not just spare capacity but also an ability to identify
stock-outs or predict potential stock-outs emanating from
demand and supply volatility.

All predators need good eyesight or other sense organs to locate and track the prey. A Cheetah organization aiming for quick responsiveness thus needs to invest substantially in information technology (IT) in tracking its own activities (through ERP systems) as well as those in the supply chain (through EDI). A firm which sells to distributors needs real-time demand information of not just the immediate customer but also the downstream wholesalers, retailers and consumers. It also needs visibility of stocks at different stages of the supply chain along with item-level detailed information like expiry dates to reduce the demand–supply mismatch.

The extent of visibility could vary from little visibility of downstream operations to visibility of stocks at different stages of supply chain to visibility of stock and sales on a monthly basis to visibility of stock-outs on a real-time basis to visibility of end customer requests for own products which could not be serviced (own sales loss visibility) to visibility of end customer requests for competitor products (competitor visibility) to visibility of end customer unmet demand for products that neither the firm nor its competitors produce (unmet demand at category level) to insights about unarticulated needs of the end customer (unmet needs). The extent of investments in IT mirrors the extent of visibility deemed necessary for the Cheetah. Extended visibility into the supply chain needs a partnership approach in linking the IT systems of different entities. A firm taking a transactional approach in its distribution system is unlikely to gain the visibility needed to respond to a quick-changing demand landscape. Such a firm should understand that a blind elephant can survive because grass does not run away. A blind cheetah would starve to death.

The need for investing in partners is also important in upstream supply. A Cheetah needs responsive suppliers if it has to be responsive to its customers. This implies that purchase managers should not award supply contracts based on lowest cost only. The contract needs to specify the delivery window and provide incentives for adhering to the same and penalties for non-compliance of quality and delivery parameters. Going beyond the contract, purchase managers also need to keep a tab on the spare capacity with the supplier and control the flow of orders so that target capacity utilization at the vendor end is maintained, leading to a reliable lead time of supply. Vendor development activities could focus on making the supplier more efficient in set-up time and set-up cost reduction so that capacity is freed up. The Cheetah thus needs to educate its vendor regarding the Cheetah mantra of keeping spare capacity and being prepared.

Spare capacity is something that can be bought, preparedness is something that needs an attitude, culture and practice. A firm which has a sacrosanct policy of always sending FTLs may have spare capacities but does not have the ability to respond to a part-load demand. A Cheetah needs an entrepreneurial spirit in the sales organization, a hunting orientation rather than a farming one. The customer-facing sales and logistics personnel need to take quick decisions and implement them. A culture where the manager needs to fill up forms in triplicate and obtain permission from headquarters for the most mundane decisions is least likely to foster a Cheetah. A Cheetah needs decentralized decision-making and empowerment of front-line personnel to take quick decisions in a fast-moving environment. Some of those decisions could turn out to be wrong, some may result in rework due to the hurry. An organization culture which provides little room for error and takes the success of the deer hunt as a given is unlikely to breed Cheetahs. A Cheetah that is severely reprimanded for losing a deer would take the easier route the next time and promise a less strict delivery window.

In my experience of teaching the Cheetah orientation to sales managers, I invariably notice a devious kind of excitement when the topic of empowerment of customer-facing personnel is raised. Empowerment does not mean the ability to do anything, it is surely not a passport to indiscipline. It's a freedom within a boundary. In fact, a Cheetah firm needs to be far more disciplined than the slow and steady Elephant. An airline pilot is empowered to take split-second decisions that may put the lives of all passengers and crew at stake. But the same airline pilot also goes through hours and hours of practice in a simulator and smaller planes before this huge responsibility is assigned. The simulator trains the pilot for different types of emergencies and about standard operating procedures for every conceivable situation. Cheetah organizations cannot predict the fast-moving demand landscape but can perform scenario planning and train frontline customer-facing personnel on the best course of action in a particular scenario.

The role of coordination is much more acute in a Cheetah, since delivering value to the customer may imply team effort under time pressure. The team must understand each other, be aware of the intricacies of the roles performed by all members, and believe that serving the customer needs a coordinated effort. A quick response to a customer may need the procurement, production, logistics and sales functions to coordinate their activities. This is easier said than done in a bureaucratic, departmental silo-based organization structure; unless top management prepares for the Cheetah run by designing appropriate reporting mechanisms or creating interdepartmental teams. The team also needs to be staffed with personnel having an entrepreneurial and a problem-solving mindset rather than people who are just content to carry out orders. The inherent variability in the environment also dictates that the staff in a Cheetah firm should be of a higher skill level than those at the Elephant where variability is lower and surprises are comparatively fewer. As a result, the Cheetah is likely to incur a higher wage rate too.

A Cheetah is costly. The increased cost comes from a host of sources like spare capacity, preparedness, lack of scale economies, etc. The auditor is right in pointing out this inefficient use of resources, but the audit function must also be cognizant of the strategic benefits of time responsiveness. There is perhaps a need to formulate specific audit standards for Cheetah organizations. There is little justification in running such high-cost operations unless cost inefficiencies are more than compensated by increased revenues. This increase in revenue can come from two major sources: price premiums and decrease in lost sales. A customer who values the time responsiveness offered by the Cheetah should be willing to pay a premium for this added benefit. The marketing department of the Cheetah should thus understand the benefit the customer gets from the time responsiveness and accordingly set the price premium. Different customer segments may have different costs of time, and hence price discrimination could be achieved through a differentiated service offering different levels of responsiveness. The second avenue for increasing revenue comes from minimizing lost sales through quick response to stock-outs or potential stock-outs. If the revenue increase from time responsiveness is higher than the additional costs, the Cheetah strategy is justified economically.

A stitch in time may hypothetically save costs of nine but is unlikely to impress the auditor if the costs of the additional nine stitches are claimed as a benefit of time responsiveness. In contrast, the added revenue from time responsiveness is not hypothetical. Instead of bemoaning the auditor's focus on costs that are real, there is a need for the Cheetah to determine the added revenue and show that the inefficiencies of the Cheetah are more than compensated for by the added effectiveness. A Cheetah which cannot show this analysis may be blind to the extent of value it is creating. Such a Cheetah deserves to be shut down or converted to an Elephant unless it improves its eyesight. A blind Elephant can survive, a blind Cheetah cannot since it was built for the kill. Oh, what a beauty!

CHAPTER 11

Cost-Cutting

'As Gregor Samsa awoke one morning from uneasy
dreams he found himself transformed in his bed into a
gigantic insect.'

—Franz Kafka, *Metamorphosis*

THE CHOICES MADE in terms of doors closed by
Elephants and Cheetahs are fundamentally opposed
to each other. This leads many students to the wrong
conclusion that the opposite of the Elephant is the
Cheetah. The Elephant is focused on the dimension of
cost, Cheetah on the dimension of time. These are two
different dimensions, not necessarily opposites. If there
exists anything which can be considered the opposite of
an Elephant, it is an Insect.

Insects are made up of diverse species and constitute
among the largest number of life forms on the face of
the earth. While there is tremendous diversity in the way
insects look, there is one thing that is common to all
insects. They cannot grow big. J.B.S. Haldane explored
the question of why an insect can be tall and flat and

long but not big in his article 'On Being the Right Size'.
Insects lack lungs and blood. Hemolymph, the equivalent
of insect blood, is used to carry nutrients and metabolic
waste to and from their cells, and it has no function
in the transport of oxygen and carbon dioxide. Insects
breathe from minute air pipes called trachea, through
which oxygen reaches each and every cell via the process
of diffusion. The process of diffusion works over short
distances. So, while the insect can breathe even without
investing in lungs or blood, it can grow only as thick as
the distance oxygen and carbon dioxide molecules can
reach through the process of diffusion. This distance
is quite small, and hence an insect cannot grow to the
size of an elephant given its lack of investment in a
circulatory system.

Remember, the mantra of the Elephant is 'Invest
and Utilize to the Fullest'. To attain cost leadership, the
Elephant has to invest and gain scale economies from
that investment. As a result, the Elephant has to carry
a lot of fixed costs, the saving grace being that high
volumes imply a low fixed cost per unit output. The
fixed cost is essential to this business model, since high
volumes are made possible by the investments in fixed
assets. However, this is not the only business model
which can allow the firm to offer a low price in the
market.

The Insect firm takes a very different approach. It
aims to offer low prices to the customer, not necessarily
at a low cost. To achieve a low price, it takes the very
opposite strategy to the Elephant. It closes the door
on investments. By not investing, the Insect avoids the
substantial fixed costs that weigh down an Elephant.

As a natural corollary of not investing, the Insect sacrifices scalability.

> **Mantra of Cost-Cutting: Incur Bare Minimum Cost Required for Survival**

The Insect firm is likely to invest in the lowest possible production capacity which allows it to pursue the business. The technology choice is likely to be the cheapest, most easily available, off-the-shelf option. Why invest in the latest technology and big capacities when the business challenges are so demanding? It makes sense to minimize the capacity risk by investing in machines which have a better salvage value. Anyway, everyone else is buying these standard machines, so why should I bother? Be with the masses, copy what everyone else is doing. If there is a new product in the market, shamelessly copy it. Not for me the challenge of investing in product development. Research and development—you must be joking, right? Who has money for burning in R&D? If I had that kind of money, I could have invested in building a brand. At least the product packaging could be a little different than the well-known brand I ripped it off from. But the fact is, I don't have that kind of fancy money to burn. I am living a hand-to-mouth existence; watching over cash flow is more crucial to my existence than fancy investments. The supplier has threatened to stop deliveries if I do not pay my dues soon. Perhaps I can cut some costs by moving to the other supplier with dodgy quality. There must be some way to replace some ingredients to cut costs. My competitor down the street just slashed his price again.

How do I match his price? Which costs can I cut this time?
Perhaps replace the skilled workers with trainees and
interns? Oh well, trainees and interns are young, and they
cost less and can work twice the time of the old hands and
they learn quickly. Wait, what good is training anyway?
Training would only strengthen their resume in the job
market. Better look for loyalty rather than competence.
Why would a competent guy work with an Insect like me?
He would just get the training and run to my competitor.
Let me stop training, it would cut some more fixed costs.

   With a keen eye, the Insect entrepreneur hunts
down any fixed cost and mercilessly removes it. No
investments in R&D, product development, brand-
building, quality processes, vendor development
or learning and development (L&D) activities.
Rudimentary investments in production capacity of the
most basic variety, rudimentary and obsolete IT tools,
minimal investments in employee engagement, career
planning, succession planning, minimal marketing
activities, with low price being the biggest bait. The
Insect has closed doors to investments of all kinds,
except the absolutely essential.

   The Insect firm is a minimalist. You can be sure that if
you remove any item from the Insect business, the whole
thing could come crashing down. There is frequently
no back-up plan or asset, since buying an asset and
keeping it idle is anathema for the Insect. The absence of
redundancy implies that Insects can get wiped out with
just one unfavourable turn in the business environment.
A business continuity plan is a luxury an Insect engaged
in a daily battle for survival can only dream of. If only I
had a little more money . . .

Insect firms are caught in a vicious cycle. They have little investible surplus and hence lesser ability to differentiate themselves through investments in product, process, technology, manpower or brand. Since they use standardized machinery to produce me-too products using raw materials sourced from common suppliers, there is little to differentiate themselves in the marketplace from competitors. The lack of differentiation may extend to similar choices in locating factories or stores, resulting in clustering. The only way to attract more business is to cut prices and offer discounts. The Insect would rationalize the low price by resorting to marginal costing. Since lowering prices is not due to lowering of costs, the margin is depleted, resulting in lowering of investible surplus, thereby completing the vicious cycle. If margin is maintained, then the lower price has to be compensated through some form of cost-cutting, and it is most easily achieved by further eroding the fixed investments made in the firm.

With low investments, Insects do not face the same pressure as an Elephant to maximize capacity utilization. To gain efficiency, the Elephant invests in not just high-throughput machinery and robotics but also work study and quality improvement processes, including a variety of shop-floor practices like TQM, TPM, Lean, etc. These investments include a sufficient number of qualified engineers and staff functions tasked with improvement projects. The Insect has little money to invest in or attract high-quality engineers to improvement projects. Thus, though Insects would have benefitted the most from putting the house in order, their operations are far from efficient. As a result,

Insects exhibit low machine and labour productivity and consequently incur high costs.

Figure 7: Vicious Cycles in Cost-Cutting

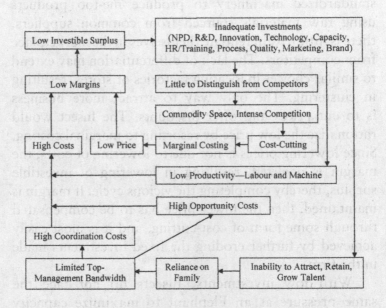

The lack of an employer brand also implies that Insects face difficulty in attracting and retaining talent. Who among you want to work for an Insect? There is little to no investment that the Insect would make in your career growth and learning. From the Insect viewpoint, it is foolish to invest in the development of employees. The Insect knows that if it invests in improving the skill levels of its workers then they would run away to greener pastures. So, the intuitive choice for an Insect is not to train its workers and make them employable elsewhere.

Instead, if it keeps the workers from upgrading their skills, they will be unemployable elsewhere and hence would have no option but to be loyal to the Insect. The Insect would any day prefer an incompetent loyalist than a competent professional who is valued by competitors. The lack of a career growth trajectory for a competent employee in an Insect firm also emanates from the fact that everyone in the firm knows that the senior and top management positions are to be held by family members by default. For Insects, trust is easily placed on blood relations rather than professionals. A competent professional is likely to leave the Insect, leaving senior managers surrounded by hand-picked yes men. The senior managers, instead of performing their horizon-scanning function of understanding how the technology and customers and competitors are evolving, feel important as they busy themselves with micromanaging the day-to-day operations and tactical decisions that should have been taken care of by the non-existent middle management layer. The Insect may even be happy with the cost reduction achieved through the elimination of middle management, oblivious to the increase in coordination inefficiencies and opportunity costs. Or they may complain that they are all for delegating middle management jobs but, you see, it is so very difficult to find a loyal employee these days! The vicious cycle is complete, there is no escape for the Insect.

And who among you would wish to lend money to an Insect? What are your chances of getting your principal back? The lack of investments results in poor quality of the balance sheet. The significant default risk is accentuated by the lack of hygiene factors like following proper accounting standards. There could be multiple books of accounts—one for the family, one for indirect tax calculations, and one for income tax reporting. While the Insect may take joy in the underreporting of income and the consequent reduction in direct and indirect tax incidence, it pays dearly through lack of access to capital through formal banking channels. It pays usurious rates for money it can raise from moneylenders. The Insect, very predictably, complains that it would have definitely invested in the business, if only capital was available at lower interest rates. *If only*! If only Insect firms could do soul-searching and realize that they are Insects!

Instead of focusing on engineering an improvement, Insect firms excel in bricolage, the process of making do with whatever is at hand. The Insect environment is characterized by extreme resource shortage, and bricolage is essential to survival. Instead of dedicated tools for each activity, Insects are experts in repurposing resources. Thus, a tool originally meant for one particular purpose could be used in a context that its designers had never dreamt of. The innovation of the Insect is best described by the Hindi word *jugaad*. The focus of the Insect is not on the engineering orientation of optimization, but on the practical orientation of sufficiency. The objective of repurposing is to just get a quick fix on the problem at hand using available resources, not to get high efficiency or effectiveness. To the Insect, it is important that the solution works *now*, it is not important that it creaks and seem to be coming off at the seams. We will worry about it the next time.

The Insect way of cost-cutting involves cross-subsidization. The personal and professional worlds collide, and it becomes difficult to separate the accounting. Family members work in the business and help out as much as they can. The payments made to family members may be much lower than the market wage rate. The use of family members is an effective way to reduce labour cost, especially the fixed overheads related to managerial fees. Cross-subsidization could also involve sharing of real estate or rental costs. The front side of the house could serve as a retail outlet with the back side being used as a small warehouse, with the family living upstairs.

No modern trade retailer can match the labour and rental cost structure of the mom-and-pop retail shop. Retail Elephants like supermarkets have to invest in costly IT systems just to know how much stock of which items are located where inside a large supermarket. The Insect retailer knows the exact amounts in her small shop and does not require a sophisticated IT system or analytics support. Retail Elephants also have to worry about pilferage by employees, a cost head alien to owner-managed mom-and-pop retail stores. The small store may sit in prime real estate and yet not pay astronomical rentals since the property would have been bought generations ago. The small scale of the Insect may thus be beneficial in certain ways. While managers in Elephant retailers must bother with raising and servicing huge debts needed to fuel national and international expansion, the Insect retailer has neither competence nor interest in taking in debt to expand to a second location. Neither depreciation nor interest cost would weigh down the Insect which does not want to grow. Don't look down on the Insect entrepreneur. He may have a much more content life than you can ever dream of. He may be in charge of his work–life balance, choosing to speed up or speed down his professional or personal life based on what is important at that moment. He is the master of his own destiny while you, working in an Elephant, cower before your boss.

I want you to ponder about this point. Does the word 'Insect' have a negative connotation in your mind? Especially when you contrast Insects with majestic creatures like Elephants and Cheetahs? I want you to start seeing the beauty of Insects. Nature is beautiful. Insects, like say, cockroaches, may not look beautiful to you but you may not be seeing them from cockroach eyes. The fact that Insects still exist in a world full of Elephants is a testament to their extreme survivability.

There is an urban legend regarding cockroaches which says that in the event of a nuclear war the only species that would survive is the cockroach. This may or may not be scientifically true, and surely, I would not propose an experimentation to find out the truth. But this urban legend does highlight that cockroaches are difficult to kill. The extreme survivability of Cockroach entrepreneurs stems from their very low fixed-cost structure and the ability to cross-subsidize professional and personal costs. In the event of a severe downturn in demand, given the low break-even point, the Cockroach may be the only business still operating long after the Elephants have downed their shutters. They may be the first set of businesses to spring back to life after a natural calamity or economic downturn. Given the small-scale, decentralized and highly distributed nature of business, Cockroaches are the life blood of an economy. Thank God for the Cockroaches.

The Cockroach as a species seems indestructible. Cockroaches are numerous, they sniff out opportunities and establish businesses wherever they can find a customer need to fulfil. They have little fixed assets on the ground and hence can move quickly to a new place or to a new line of business in case the consumer needs a change. They sniff out opportunities using their long antennae. They have an amazing social network from where they get inputs on the latest trends in technology, raw material costs and changing customer needs. They are quick to copy and latch on to the latest bandwagon. If a Cockroach sees two other Cockroaches in a crevice, he expects some food to be there and joins them. Seeing the three Cockroaches huddled together, the fourth Cockroach rushes in to join the party. Seeing the four of them, the fifth Cockroach is absolutely certain that there must be food there. Soon the whole place would be teeming with Cockroaches, each trying to take its bite from a rapidly deteriorating commodity marketplace. There is little to differentiate one Cockroach from another except that the early Cockroach got its belly full. If there ever was a situation of perfect competition, the competition between Cockroaches would fit it perfectly.

While I have asked you to see the beauty of Insects, let me also caution against any undue romanticism. The cost-cutting mantra of Insects can soon degenerate into cutting corners. Cockroaches have a fondness for darkness. The cockroaches in your kitchen may be having a nice party at midnight but the moment you switch on the light they vanish into the darkness. Cockroach firms too love markets with regulatory darkness. You would find these small firms in the dark underbelly of large cities or in economies with a large informal sector. The Cockroach can slowly start descending into darkness by progressively cutting corners, employing tactics which an established firm in the formal sector cannot and should never adopt.

Cockroaches can cut corners by employing illegal immigrants at wage rates substantially lower than legal norms. They can employ child labour when the practice is illegal. Their employees may have working hours much longer than the legal norms and they may be denied weekly offs or vacations. The employees may be working in hazardous conditions without sufficient safety equipment or training and may not have access to proper medical facilities. The Insect may delay payment of pension, provident fund or gratuity and may even not offer such facilities in the form of consolidated pay. Women employees may be discriminated against in terms of pay and are unlikely to be offered support like a crèche or maternity benefits.

The downward spiral may continue with Insects cutting customer support in a bid to reduce costs. An Insect may sell goods on a caveat emptor basis, and deal with fake and counterfeit products. There may not be any warranty on its products, and goods once sold cannot be exchanged or returned even if there is a quality problem. The transactions could be in cash and without receipts and hence the customer may not be able to prove a deficiency of service. The Insect may choose to shortchange the customer if the consumer protection rules or enforcements are lax in the region. Such shortchanging can occur by packing less weight than the amount specified or by varying ingredient composition in a bid to reduce costs.

The Cockroach may cut corners by not depositing tax collected with the government or delaying the process as far as possible. It can evade taxes by underreporting revenues and by cooking up books of accounts. It can be complicit with the customer by offering differential prices based on whether the customer insists on a receipt, thereby sharing the amount evaded in tax. The evasion of taxes provides the Cockroach a substantial cushion in their price war with Elephants and other Insects.

At the extreme, the Insect may degenerate into a business focused not on being a sustainable business but the very opposite—a vanishing business. The entire business model of this Insect is to suck money from unsuspecting customers and suppliers and one day just vanish into thin air. I find it apt to compare them to leeches. A prominent feature of a leech is its mouth with its jaws and teeth, and it attaches itself to a host and sucks the host's blood till it is full. The leech even injects the bite area with an anticoagulant to keep the blood from clotting. Leech firms are similarly highly sophisticated when it comes to projecting a sense of business as usual, only for the purpose of deception. A lot of these Leeches may raise funds from stock markets during bull runs by showcasing capacity addition plans. Investors who think they are investing in future Elephants are deceived when the Leeches vanish after having their fill.

Compared to these devious Leeches, the humble Insects which just focus on investment avoidance seem almost angelic. At least they do not wish to harm employees, customers, investors and defraud governments. Their business model simply wants to keep things small-scale and they are content to trade off growth in business with cost control. Since their cost reduction is not based on scale economies, they have no option but to be extremely wary of fixed costs and always on the lookout to reduce variable costs. These ethical Insects are the bedrock of the economy.

How does an Insect escape the vicious cycle of the lack of an investible surplus? There is little chance of breaking the cycle unless the Insect starts investing. Perhaps luck will smile on it, and the Insect may get a windfall. A more practical opportunity beckons when an established business lends Insects good engineers and managers as a part of vendor development. In itself, the Insect may never be able to afford the high-quality advice. However, these engineers and managers on deputation should also try to refine their advice to the absorption capacity of the Insect rather than simply advocating the copying of Elephant practices. Vendor development initiatives also need to be systematic rather than sporadic so the Insect can slowly learn and adopt. Vendor development is thus a win-win for both the Elephant and the Insect supplier. The Insect can access expertise without investments in building and retaining the expertise, while the Elephant can reduce costs in the supply chain by bringing in efficient work practices.

When you look at a market and see different firms competing on price, you need to distinguish the Elephants from the Insects, and among Insects distinguish between the law-abiding Insects, the Cockroaches and the Leeches. All of them would compete by lowering prices, but the similarity ends there. While Elephants reduce prices as they benefit from cost reductions due to scale economies, Insects reduce prices as they reduce fixed costs, and Cockroaches and Leeches reduce prices by cost-cutting and cutting corners. The doors closed by each one are different. A manager working in an Elephant firm may get exasperated with Cockroaches undercutting him by resorting to tax avoidance. There is little that this Elephant manager can do. Trying to stomp out Insects is a futile act as newer Insects take the place of old ones. My advice to the manager in the established Elephant is to stop focusing attention on the Insects. Don't waste your time trying to eliminate the Cockroaches; the Cockroaches are invincible as a species though not as an individual. Instead, try to be a bigger Elephant by developing the market so that the share of the informal sector is reduced.

To understand price-based competition, it is thus important to change perspective from the lofty Elephant to the humble Insect. Our view of the Cockroach may be biased, and worse still, we may take a condescending view of the Insect. But have we ever considered asking the Cockroach how it sees itself, let alone how it sees Elephants? There is a serious deficiency in our communication with Cockroaches. Management science owes its origin to the scientific management of Frederick Taylor, who used science to make Elephants more efficient, thereby attempting to stomp the Cockroaches to extinction. There is very little work which has looked at the Operations Management challenges of the Insect entrepreneur, partly because perhaps the Insect anyway has no money to invest in paying consulting fees to management scientists. The Insect may never be able to afford hiring the managers produced by business schools and may never read the magazines and journals where management research is published. Management books too may take the investment orientation as granted. We are thus compartmentalized in our different worlds, unable to communicate. Like Gregor Samsa in *Metamorphosis* by Franz Kafka, the Cockroach entrepreneur is the vermin we instinctively loathe but never really try to understand, till one day, in a cost-cutting frenzy we start cutting corners and find ourselves trapped in a Cockroach shell.

The saddest sight in a business landscape is to come across former Elephants that, having fallen on hard times, are unable to turnaround and instead metamorphose into Insects. First, they start underinvesting in the business, then stop investing altogether and then start cutting costs and finally end up cutting corners. The slide of the Elephant into the Cockroach is gradual, but the metamorphosis is alienating. There is a sense of apathy around the place. Expectations about annual salary increments get replaced by monthly worry about the employer's ability to pay wages, the perks vanish, the support staff become skeletal, the working hours lengthen and the work itself turns into drudgery. Then the asset sales start as lenders take control and try to salvage what is left. The firm may survive, but only by retreating into the shell of the Cockroach, unable to come to terms with the loss of the earlier self, nor able to accept its new reality. The bigger the former Elephant, the more widespread the alienation. Entire neighbourhoods or even factory townships and regions inhabited by these Elephants may show signs of decay. Layoffs trigger population degrowth and result in declining tax revenues for municipalities. Broken windows are not fixed due to lack of investments, resulting in more broken windows and a degeneration of civic sense and increased criminal activities. No one sheds a tear when Gregor Samsa finally dies.

CHAPTER 12

Superior Quality

'Quality is free.'

—Philip Crosby, quality guru

THE WORD 'FREE' is magical. People might even take poison if it is free. And it is irresistible if the item being peddled as 'free' is quality itself! Who on earth can say 'no' to free quality? But caveat emptor, how come quality is free when there is no such thing as a free lunch?

Who on earth can show us the truth? The use of the word 'guru' while describing thought leaders in the quality domain is equally interesting. Seldom is this word used for describing thought leaders in other branches of management. Neither did we encounter the word while navigating cost leadership or time responsiveness strategies, though there are plenty of thought leaders out there. The reason for the preponderance of gurus in the quality domain stems from the vexing nature of quality itself. Before we ascertain for ourselves if quality is indeed free, we need to first address what the hell is quality.

Quality is conformance to requirements/specifications (and not some vague ideas about 'goodness' or 'elegance') as per Philip Crosby, while Joseph M. Juran defined it as fitness for use. Surely these are two different views, the first internally driven and the other externally. A firm may claim to produce quality goods using Crosby's definition without asking whether the specifications make any sense. That seems awful, but Crosby also stipulated that we need to not just conform to specifications but also periodically review if they are in accordance with customer requirements. The specifications could be based on a translation of customer voice through a rigorous Quality Function Deployment (QFD) exercise. And fitness for use takes the customer orientation but seems to be a warm, mushy concept. Whose use is it anyway? Internal customers? External customers in the supply chain? End consumers? All of them? And if so, whose fit gets more importance? Would a product be better quality if it fits the needs of the retailer to a smaller extent and the need of the distributor to a larger extent than if it was the other way around? How do we quantify the fitness? Compared to this confusion, conformance to specification seems an easy way out. Or could it be that neither of these definitions capture the elusive truth about quality?

Is quality better described as an absence, like the implied presence of quality in the utopia of Zero Defect and Doing It Right First Time (DIRFT)? Or instead of absolute standards, do we need a relativist standpoint; would a firm be called high-quality if it is continuously and forever improving, as commanded by quality guru W. Edward Deming? But wait again, Zero Defect and Continuous Improvement both assume an observer. Does a system produce superior quality if the products have a defect that the observer is unable to detect or if the system improves but the observer is unable to perceive it? As George Berkeley asked, 'If a tree falls in a forest and no one is around to hear it, does it make a sound?'

Notice how easily we have transitioned from the mundane world of defects to the abstract world of philosophy. Philosophy allows debate and divergence of opinion. Multiplicity of views enriches the intellectual inquiry but may mystify and confuse the manager handling day-to-day quality challenges on the factory shop floor. But curiously, sales and marketing managers are never confused about quality. Every firm on the face of the earth promises quality to the customer. Period.

It is this hypocrisy which marks out quality as a competitive dimension apart from cost leadership or time responsiveness. A firm which decides not to be a Cheetah would not promise a quick response time to its customers. But no firm can afford to tell the customer that at the price you are paying you better expect lousy quality. Instead, they proclaim through advertisements that only the finest ingredients have been used by the most skilled workers using state-of-the-art technology to produce the flawless piece of beauty that the consumer can buy at the best value for money. No top management can admit in an annual general body meeting with the shareholders that the firm has compromised quality to achieve volumes. So, every firm mouths the same platitudes about quality, decorates their boardrooms with nicely framed copies of their quality policy, which none of their employees can remember, and goes about their business of extracting value. The casualty of this mass delusion is the firm which really competes on the dimension of quality. Its voice is swamped in the cacophony of the market.

To identify the firm which competes on quality, we must first identify those firms that do not. We cannot base this identification on any promises made to customers due to the limited ability to distinguish between genuine, overambitious and outright fake promises. Ranking of firms based on customer complaints could benchmark the quality offered but does not provide insight into whether the top-ranked firm is striving wholeheartedly to give its best or just keeping abreast of competition. The key to the identification of the firm striving for superior quality lies paradoxically in an analysis of costs.

In my career I have met many managers who are aware of the contributions of Deming. In contrast, very few managers are aware of Juran and his pioneering work. Yet, it is Juran who laid the foundation of our understanding of what it really means to compete on quality. He introduced us to a fundamental concept.

The *Cost* of Quality

Everyone understands that costs and quality are different. They may intuitively understand a trade-off involving the two. But Juran connected cost and quality by asking what is the cost *of* quality. Bow down to our guru, Juran. Juran systematically identified a large number of cost heads based on whether the cost is incurred when the product is inside the boundary of the firm (internal failure costs) or outside (external failure costs). Internal failure costs include costs related to rework, retesting, etc. necessitated due to a quality failure identified inside the firm. External failure costs include costs related to product recall, warranty, etc., which arise if a quality failure happens in the hands of customers. To minimize the internal and external failure costs, a firm invests in quality appraisal like inspection and quality control activities (appraisal costs) as well as invests in preventive activities like designing and implementing quality frameworks like ISO 9000, Good Manufacturing Practices (GMP), Six Sigma, etc. (preventive costs). Note that preventive- and appraisal-related expenses are really of the nature of investments rather than costs. A firm invests in preventive and appraisal activities to decrease internal and external failure costs.

None of these cost heads (rework costs, retesting costs, etc.) are unknown to a firm. The genius of Juran lies in systematically identifying any expense related to quality and classifying it either as a cost or an investment. For example, the fee paid to a lawyer to fight a case in a consumer court due to an alleged quality problem would have earlier been classified as an administrative cost of business at the headquarters rather than a cost traced back to a quality issue at a factory. This lawyer fee would not have existed if the firm was producing high-quality products. The analysis of costs using the lens provided by Juran allows a firm to create a dashboard of costs related to quality. This exercise can be very revealing to a firm as it stacks up the costs and investments and determines the implication of quality in monetary terms. A firm may be confused regarding the definition of quality, but there is no ambiguity regarding the monetary value of costs and investments made related to quality. By connecting quality to costs of quality, Juran starts to make sense to a businessman focused on making money. He does not

lecture the businessman on quality, he shows them the
gold in the mine. Money makes the world go around, not
quality. Bow down to our guru, Juran.

Is it starting to make sense to you? Not yet? By putting
a dollar value on quality, Juran allows one firm to be
compared to another. A dollar value of costs of quality
allows the same firm to be compared over time, revealing
if the firm is making progress on costs of quality. A firm
can be accused, rightly or wrongly, of being a hypocrite
in claiming quality before an outsider but there is no
hypocrisy in claiming quality has improved because the
cost of poor quality has decreased. A claim of quality
improvement due to better fitness for use is difficult to
verify. In contrast, a claim of quality improvement based
on costs of quality is internal rather than external in
orientation, and verifiable. More importantly, a dollar
value on quality changes incentives for the firm. Quality
improvement is no more flowery talk, it is an opportunity
to reduce costs and improve profitability. Which selfish
business can say no to making money? Juran thus finesses
the selfish business to improve quality. Bow down to our
guru, Juran.

Every firm carries costs of quality, some are aware
of the dollar value, some are not. Can a firm claim to
compete on quality if it is not even aware of the costs of
quality it is incurring? If you are an executive working in
a firm, let me ask you a simple question. Do you know
the cost of quality your firm is incurring? If you are not
aware, if this concept is alien to your firm, if this amount
is not a focus of action, on what basis do you claim
your firm competes on quality? You want to end this
hypocrisy? Bow down to the lotus feet of our guru, Juran.

Figure 8: Costs of Quality

Internal Failure Costs	External Failure Costs
Appraisal Costs	Preventive Costs

Juran goes further than just putting a dollar value on quality. His work allows us to understand how each firm carries a *portfolio* of costs related to quality. Estimation of the different elements of costs of quality allows us to determine the percentage of money that is spent in each of the four heads. Two firms having the same costs of quality may be quite different in terms of the percentages of cost. A firm having a hundred percentage of costs in external failure costs is surely different in its quality orientation from a firm having a hundred percentage of costs in preventive costs. The worst type of costs is the external failure costs, followed by internal failure costs, appraisal costs and preventive costs. The proportion of costs across these four heads is thus like a distinct signature of the nature of the portfolio of costs of quality. Different firms with the same absolute dollar value of costs of quality could be quite different in terms of the quality signature. A firm with a higher proportion in failure costs shows less maturity in the quality journey than a firm with a higher proportion in appraisal and prevention. Do you know your firm's quality signature? If not, bow down to the lotus feet of our guru, Juran.

Is it now starting to make sense to you? Not yet? Just putting a dollar value and introducing an ability to gauge the quality maturity does not enable us to improve quality. Juran unequivocally shows us that to improve quality we need to invest in appraisal and preventive activities. The path to higher quality is through investments. As a result of these investments, the internal and external failure costs would decrease. As we proceed on this quality journey, the costs related to investments in quality keep increasing while the costs related to failure keep decreasing. What is the net effect of these two cost curves? This is the masterstroke by Juran. He postulates that the total cost curve, being the sum of all costs related to quality, would be a U-shaped curve. Initially, investments in quality would provide the firm a much higher return in decreasing failure costs, thereby producing a downward sloping total cost curve. However, the law of diminishing returns would eventually result in a situation where more and more investments would be needed for lesser and lesser decrease in failure costs, resulting in an upward sloping total cost curve. The total cost would be lowest at the optimal conformance level.

Figure 9: Minimizing Costs of Quality

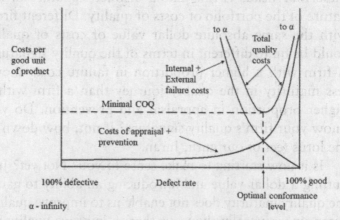

Source: Juran J.M., and Gryna, F.M. (1993). *Quality Planning and Analysis.*

Where is your firm located on this U-shaped curve? Is it to the left or the right of the optimal conformance level? If you are to the left, you can decrease your costs by investing in quality. If you are to the right, you can decrease your costs by scaling back investments in quality. A firm on the left side can simultaneously improve costs and quality by investing in quality. A firm on the right has to make a choice. Does it want to keep investing in quality even when its total costs would increase? Or does it want to scale back on investments in quality to achieve a lower cost? The firm on the left has no dilemma, quality is truly free for this firm. Have the cake and eat it too. The firm on the right faces a real dilemma, should it decrease cost or improve quality? Quality is not free for this firm, it comes at an ever-increasing cost. Where is your firm located? Not sure? Yet you claim to compete on quality? Bow down to the lotus feet of our guru, Juran.

A firm which weighs the pros and cons of investing in quality and decides to scale back to the optimal conformance level may masquerade to customers as a high-quality firm, but in its heart it knows that it is just an Elephant. It is an Elephant which invests in quality and reaps cost leadership. There is absolutely nothing wrong in being an Elephant investing in quality and operating at optimal conformance level. Such a firm has much higher quality than the other Elephants which have under-invested in quality or the Insects which are far away to the left of the optimal conformance level. However, this higher quality has not been achieved through closing the door on costs. On the contrary, this higher quality is the by-product of a cost leadership strategy. The objective of such firms is to provide the customer optimal quality at optimal costs.

Firms truly competing on quality are the firms which deliberately choose to provide high quality at high costs. These firms operate on the right side of the optimal conformance level. They do not trade quality for lower costs, resisting the temptation to lower costs by scaling back on investments in quality. Instead, they recover the higher costs by charging customers a premium for higher quality. Would the customer pay this premium when there are 'good enough' products available from Elephants at lower costs? The existence of the Artist solely depends on the answer to this question.

Who is an Artist? A true Artist is driven by passion, not rationality. The Artist keeps on investing in their art since the goal is perfection, not 'good enough'. Good enough quality is for the rational Elephants to achieve, perfection is for the passionate Artist to aim for. Good enough quality is attainable, perfection is a never-ending journey. To attain good enough quality, you have to trade-off costs and quality. Trade-off is the language of the engineer. Trade-off is a dirty word for an Artist. The biggest insult for an Artist is when it is accused of having compromised its art for the sake of commercial considerations. An Artist would rather face extinction than compromise and sell its soul for money.

Mantra of Superior Quality: No Compromise

'No compromise' is the mantra of the Artist. 'Trade-off' is the mantra of the Elephant.

Do Artists actually exist? You bet. In many industries, you will find firms which are much smaller in size than reigning Elephants and which do not compete on cost. Their prices could be high, even outrageous, but there is a niche customer segment of connoisseurs which patronizes and keeps alive the tradition or the craft. The Artist focuses complete attention on perfecting the craft without bothering about marketing or sales. True genius is hard to keep secret. Word travels and connoisseurs seek out and scale mountains to reach the Artist. They do not buy the product or service, they experience perfection.

Perfection is multidimensional. Perfection on all dimensions is perhaps the realm of the Divine. Mortals have to be content with glimpses of perfection in one or a few dimensions of quality. David A. Garvin has presented before us not one but eight dimensions of quality: Performance, Features, Reliability, Durability, Aesthetics, Conformance, Serviceability and Perceived Quality. Some of these dimensions also have sub-dimensions. For example, an Artist may focus on excelling in designing and building the fastest cars while another may focus on building cars with the highest fuel efficiency. Both acceleration and fuel efficiency are dimensions of a car's performance. In addition, excelling in fuel efficiency may necessitate choices in product design which compromise acceleration, and vice versa. The Artist perfecting fuel efficiency is thus distinct from the Artist perfecting acceleration as they eschew compromise on different performance dimensions. Similarly, a firm choosing to excel in the dimension of reliability may close doors, distinct from the firm choosing to excel in serviceability. One firm says their product would break down very rarely, but if it does, you would need to buy very costly replacement parts, available, if at all, in only some repair outlets. The other firm makes no guarantee that their products would not break down, but if they do, you would be serviced quickly anywhere in the country using parts that are easily available and not costly. Both firms produce quality products, but on different dimensions. Both firms produce lousy products, but on different dimensions. Both are Artists.

Competing on quality is thus going all out on one or a few dimensions and hoping that the customers value those dimensions so much that they would pay a premium to cover the added costs. Instead of the comfort zone provided by optimality, competing on quality pushes a firm into making strategic choices of dimensions to excel in and hence choose dimensions *not* to excel in. The firm thus closes doors on not just certain quality dimensions but also, more importantly, on optimality itself. Its choices are suboptimal in terms of costs but strategic in terms of quality.

So, what is the mantra you would give to a firm to compete on quality? Use loudspeakers to repeatedly remind the mass of Insects and Elephants that 'quality is free', and appeal to their selfish interest in cost reduction through investments in quality. Only very rarely would you encounter a true Artist. When you meet the Artist, take him aside and whisper, 'No compromise.'

If the Insects and Elephants bother to listen to you, start with assessing how far away they are from the optimal conformance level by evaluating the extent of investments in prevention and appraisal. For the weakest of the Insects, you may start with first instilling a sense of discipline by goading the firm to practice the 5Ss. You may find that 5S practices may need to be extended to the home of the worker. If the worker does not practise cleanliness and hygiene at home, how can we expect the same worker to metamorphose into a quality conscious worker the moment he or she steps inside the firm?

For firms further into the quality journey, you may adopt the set of practices which are most suitable. There is a plethora of quality improvement tools, techniques and systems to choose from. Firms struggling with specific challenges may benefit from the top-down, centralized, time-bound, target-oriented approach of Six Sigma. Firms wishing for a more bottom-up, decentralized, continuing, real-time, problem-solving approach may benefit from the Lean philosophy. Firms with very strong departmental silos may benefit from adopting a TQM framework. Firms with capital-intensive mass production may benefit more from a TPM focus. Firms may benefit from adhering to applicable ISO standards and the periodic third-party review. Firms in specific industries may need to follow established quality frameworks like GMP and Good Distribution Practices (GDP) in pharmaceuticals or Capability Maturity Models (CMM) in IT. Instead of hair-splitting and nit-picking to determine which is the best practice, remember that the fundamental requirement of improved quality is investments. Let the firm choose the path that appeals to it. As long as it is investing in reducing failure costs, the specific path does not matter. All that matters is the *faith* that adopting the path would result in improving costs as well as quality. Have faith in our guru, Juran.

If you encounter an Artist, you may discover that in many respects the Artist may be worse than an Insect in terms of investments in quality. This is shocking since you may expect that a firm to the right of the optimal conformance level would have higher investments than one to the left. This apparent contradiction may exist because the Artist chooses a few dimensions to excel in. It is in these chosen dimensions that you will find the investments made by the Artist to far exceed anything that the Insects or Elephants can dream of. The Artist may be obsessed with these chosen dimensions and neglect others. It is in these chosen dimensions that he proclaims 'No compromise', in others the extent of compromise may put an Insect to shame. So, your analysis of the kind of investments necessary for the Artist requires an understanding of the strategic choices made by the Artist. Would such an uneven pattern of investment pay off for the Artist? The true Artist could not care less. His *faith* is in his art form. He bows down to perfection in his art form. We bow down to our guru, Juran.

Did I just use the word 'faith'? Science has no faith in faith. Yet, so much quality literature is devoted to gurus and rituals that it is impossible to avoid it. Quality orientation is like a religion. It has rituals, cults, converts, believers and non-believers. It has gurus and fake gurus. It has long-held traditions and new-age fads. Having faith in the cost–quality trade-off curve presented by Juran is also like believing in a cult. The curve presented by Juran can be questioned. It does not incorporate opportunity costs of poor quality, like lost sales. Has any firm actually reported paying infinite costs to achieve zero defects? Why should the U-shaped curve be symmetric? I am yet to see a firm which has traced out the exact nature of the investment and failure cost curves applicable to itself.

This is because the curve states *if* you invest, your failure costs will come down. There is no way to scientifically prove the veracity of this statement unless you have faith and invest first. You may say that you would first have faith and then look at the result after a year. But the failure costs are period costs while investments in quality culture have benefits that accrue over a much longer time horizon. Accurate estimation of return on quality investments is difficult. In addition, the relentless pace of change means that products are changed, product characteristics and features change, machines are upgraded, production technologies are improved, employee training and motivations evolve, and supplier capabilities change over time. All these may mean that the old cost–quality trade-off characteristics may not be relevant any more, and there is a need to evaluate a new cost–quality trade-off curve every time you want proof before you take the leap of faith. So, the trade-off curve presented by Juran is best seen as a conceptual tool rather than a proven fact. Faith in the cost of quality concept may be more helpful in improving quality than waiting indefinitely for proof.

Science and faith can continue their deliberations. Meanwhile, in the cacophony of the market, the Insects are busy undermining quality to cut costs, the Elephants are busy investing in quality to achieve optimal quality at optimal costs, and both are busy beating their own drums about delivering quality while the Artist silently strives after perfection. Oh, what a beauty.

CHAPTER 13

Superior Design

'During all those years of experimentation and research, I never once made a discovery. All my work was deductive, and the results I achieved were those of invention, pure and simple. I would construct a theory and work on its lines until I found it was untenable. Then it would be discarded at once and another theory evolved. This was the only possible way for me to work out the problem. . . . I speak without exaggeration when I say that I have constructed 3000 different theories in connection with the electric light, each one of them reasonable and apparently likely to be true. Yet only in two cases did my experiments prove the truth of my theory.'

—Thomas Alva Edison

'Genius is one per cent inspiration, ninety-nine per cent perspiration.'

—Thomas Alva Edison

160

'If Edison had a needle to find in a haystack, he would
not stop to reason where it was most likely to be, but
would proceed at once with the feverish diligence of
the bee to examine straw after straw until he found the
object of his search. . . . His method was inefficient in
the extreme, for an immense ground had to be covered
to get anything at all unless blind chance intervened
and, at first, I was almost a sorry witness of his doings,
knowing that just a little theory and calculation
would have saved him ninety percent of the labor. But
he had a veritable contempt for book learning and
mathematical knowledge, trusting himself entirely to
his inventor's instinct and practical American sense.'

—Nicola Tesla

'When Jobs was still in his twenties, he once explained
his vision of design to me, using as a symbol the object
whose name he appropriated to name his computer
company. "Fruit—an apple," he said. "That simplicity
is the ultimate sophistication. What we meant by that
was when you start looking at a problem and it seems
really simple with all these simple solutions, you don't
really understand the complexity of the problem. And
your solutions are way too oversimplified, and they
don't work. Then you get into the problem, and you
see it's really complicated. And you come up with all
these convoluted solutions. That's sort of the middle,
and that's where most people stop, and the solutions
tend to work for a while. But the really great person
would keep on going and find, sort of, the key,

underlying principle of the problem. And come up
with a beautiful elegant solution that works."'

—Steven Levy writing about Steve Jobs,
The Perfect Thing.

A BEAUTIFUL, ELEGANT solution is the fruit of a superior
design process. Anyone can see the beauty embodied
in an elegant solution; it is the rare few who have the
privilege to witness the beauty of the organizational
systems and processes that give birth to the elegant
solution. It is rarer still to witness the choices inherent
in the design of the design process itself. I want you to
see this meta-beauty inherent in this meta-design process,
if I may call it that. The beauty of the different ways
in which operating systems can be beautifully designed
to ultimately innovate beautiful products and services.
Instead of arguing whether Edison was a bigger genius
than Tesla or Jobs, let us see the beauty in each approach.
Maybe, tomorrow, my friend, *you* would make your
own design choices and set up and manage departments
or organizations producing breakthrough innovations.
What a beauty that would be.

I can almost hear you say, 'I am not a genius, I am just
a manager. I don't have delusions of grandeur.' That may
or may not be true, but it is a fact that geniuses are, perhaps
by definition, rare. The extraordinary competencies of a
genius are surely a beauty to behold. What is even more
beautiful is to behold the system which employs ordinary
mortals and produces extraordinary results. A genius
may gift the world a breakthrough innovative product or
service, but the system which produced this breakthrough

is fundamentally dependent on the competencies of the genius and hence is not autopoietic. The system cannot continue producing breakthrough innovations after the genius leaves. The fact that you are not a genius makes you eminently suited to recognize your limitations and thereby focus on bringing together a network of other mortals with complementary skills who could work as a team and deliver results. Oh, what a beauty to witness an autopoietic New Product Development (NPD) system made of ordinary mortals which consistently and sustainably produces innovative products and services.

Note the tension between the words 'consistent' and 'innovative'. Consistency may be boring, but it is extremely challenging to achieve. There is a beauty in systems that can produce the same end state, whatever the variations and variabilities involved in incoming raw materials, manpower, machines, work practices or environment. Innovation is the opposite of consistency; it involves producing something entirely new. There is a beauty in systems that can employ ordinary mortals, machines and raw materials to produce a product which did not exist earlier. To design a system to deliver consistency, we require deviation-*counteracting* mutual causal processes. To design a system to deliver innovation, we require deviation-*amplifying* mutual causal processes. Oh, what a beauty to witness a system designed to deliver innovation consistently, requiring both deviation-counteracting as well as deviation-amplifying mutual causal processes.

We are thus concerned with the challenge of designing a system to *consistently* deliver innovations. We are less concerned either with innovations produced by a genius or one-off innovations produced by a firm merely by accident, fluke or chance. The main question before us is not whether we want to design a system to consistently deliver innovation but *how* we achieve this. And before we talk of strategies for consistently delivering innovation, we need to understand the essence of the work involved in design and innovation and how it differs from other work in the factory.

Think of the challenge in measuring productivity and the effectiveness of an R&D department or NPD process. The output of the design and development activities could be measured in the number of new products which have been commercialized by the firm or licenced out to other firms. It could also be measured in terms of the number of patents filed or the number of research articles published in peer-reviewed journals. Thus, the output of the design and innovation process may not be only the fully functional commercial product but also abstract ideas which may have an intrinsic value of their own. Thus, in contrast to the factory, the WIP inventory of the design process may have an intrinsic value apart from the role it plays in the value of the finished goods (FG). The intrinsic value of patents is difficult to ascertain as the willingness to pay (WTP) would be different for different potential buyers and the various uses that the buying firm may have for these patents. The intrinsic value of basic research published in peer-reviewed journals are public goods whose worth may be even more difficult to ascertain or appropriate. Merely counting the number of patents may not provide an idea about the quality of the patents measured in terms of their usefulness. A firm may be productive in terms of generating patents as well as commercializing products but then these patents or products may not be effective in generating revenues. Similarly, the number of citations received by journal articles may be low even though the productivity of researchers could be high.

The quest to understand what constitutes a superior design performance is further complicated when we look at intermediate activities prior to patent filing and commercialization. How do we, for example, evaluate the productivity or effectiveness of a product visualizer who generates sketches or a laboratory assistant who performs experiments? Merely counting these intermediate artefacts like sketches, prototypes, sub-assemblies, code fragments or experiment reports do not allow us to evaluate progress. We may be progressing quite a lot very quickly with excellent quality towards an ultimate dead end. And finally, much of the design work may be happening inside the head of the designer, without any external artefact as output. We may have no means to quantitatively or qualitatively evaluate progress in such situations.

We need a framework to understand what constitutes progress in the design and development environment. This framework should be sufficiently broad so as to be applicable across diverse industry sectors as well as technology environments. What could be common to design work done across diverse sectors like the design of consumer goods, consumer durables, engineering solutions, drug discovery, fashion design, interior design, construction, architecture or software development?

We turn to the work of Edison to understand the essence of a design and development factory which churns out innovations. Think of this factory as a machine which does experiments. As Stefan Thomke argues, experimentation is the heart of innovation. At the core of a system for innovation is the repeated testing of ideas. A design concept is nothing but a hypothesis that this concept or idea can be realized and holds promise in meeting certain needs. The movement from this ideation stage to final product commercialization proceeds through a long series of experiments to check if the product would not just meet customer and societal expectations but can also be produced by existing or new technologies at a cost that makes it commercially viable. We may hypothesize that a specific set of raw materials may be used or combined in specific ways by using specific tools, equipment or technologies to produce an end product which serves the specific needs of a target segment of customers. Our initial hypothesis, in part or in whole, most likely would not be valid. It is through experimentation that we find out which parts of our overall working hypothesis do not hold. We then use our creativity to overcome the specific hurdles, thereby refining our working hypothesis, and then proceed to retest the idea.

The genius of Edison is in realizing that the systematic experimentation requires an enabling environment which includes access to knowledge bases, a network of highly skilled machinists, tool-makers, equipment designers and laboratory workers, apart from access to funding. The nature of the interactions between these highly skilled personnel with complementary skill sets is perhaps the most important decider of whether a creative spark in one person's mind would ignite sparks in other minds and lead to changes made in raw materials, tools, equipment, work practices, techniques, technologies, etc., to finally produce a completely new product or solution.

The system for innovation should not just create the ambience for the initial spark but also have an interconnectedness so that a spark in one domain can start new experimentations with altered ideas, raw materials, processes or technologies in another domain. The genius of Edison lies not just in creating the light bulb but in creating the interconnected system of innovation which feeds off and feeds into experiments in diverse domains. Instead of a component-focused view, his approach was essentially taking a systems-focused view of innovation where *interactions* between the components resulted in transforming the creative ideas into commercial realities.

We thus understand experimentation to be the core activity of the design and development process. But what is the output of an experiment? At a primary level, it is just the acceptance or rejection of the working hypothesis. At a second level, the systemic testing of ideas generates new data and insights. The experiment may generate new data about performance characteristics of the configuration being tested or throw up new insights about how the different sub-assemblies and components of the configuration interact with each other. The insight may also be in the form of an understanding of what would not work and why. A negative result in the form of rejection of the working hypothesis is thus not a setback, it may actually be a blessing in disguise. A negative result earlier in the development cycle may be instrumental in turning the search process towards more promising areas, thereby avoiding unnecessary time and money investments. A negative result may also force designers to confront and reassess their mental models of the product or solution, thereby refining the working hypothesis. By pondering on why the model did not work as expected, the designer can get a deeper understanding of the problem and hence reformulate the original problem statement and devise a better solution. The output of an experiment is thus learning—learning what works, what does not, what works in some contexts but not others and why.

> **Mantra of Superior Design: Experiment and Learn**

We are now able to appreciate what is meant by quality of the experimentation process. A high-quality experimentation process is one which allows us to learn rapidly about the current problem statement and the prototype which represents the proposed solution. Low quality in this context does not imply negative results in hypothesis testing, it implies that the experimental set-up was faulty in design or execution, resulting in no new data or insights or learning. As Stefan Thomke puts it, we should 'fail early and often, but avoid mistakes', that is, avoid experiments that do not provide new data or insights because they were inadequately designed or executed.

The system for innovation is essentially a search process for an elegant solution to a need. We start with a nebulous idea to solve an initial problem statement and develop a prototype to test the idea and learn from it. A prototype is thus the physical or logical embodiment of a conceptual hypothesis. It is tested to check if it meets the needs and requirements of the user as well as the constraints imposed by production technology and target costing. The requirements can be varied, emanating from multiple internal and external customers and stakeholders, and could be contradictory in nature. The designer's job is frequently to balance these contradictory requirements, to find a candidate solution that satisfies all requirements and constraints. Thus, the design search process is more of a feasibility search than a search for an optimal solution. At various nodes of this search process, we may refine existing prototypes, generate new ideas or abandon earlier ideas when the experiments we carry out either support or reject the working hypothesis. The output of the design process is thus not only the final prototype selected for commercialization but also the mass of learning gained through the process of experimentation. The final prototype is just one node of the search tree with various other nodes—nodes that failed to meet some of the requirements and constraints, nodes that were alternate prototypes which were equally promising, nodes which were abandoned for being too costly or difficult to achieve with current technologies but which could become attractive with shifts and advances in technology, nodes which were left unexplored due to paucity of time, nodes which were yet to be fully conceptualized, etc.

With this understanding of innovation as a search process, we can look back at the quotes from Edison, Tesla and Jobs at the start of this chapter. Edison seems to be performing a thorough examination of all possible nodes of the search tree, a process which is not just time-consuming but also inefficient, as Tesla points out. Indeed, if large parts of the search space could be eliminated through scientific analysis (for example, the process of calculating a lower bound in a branch and bound search process in a mathematical programme) then the search process could have been speeded up without compromising solution quality. Tesla seems to make sense. But, hold on. Tesla's observation would be correct if the objective function is well-defined. If you are searching for a needle in a haystack, you have a pretty good idea of what a needle looks like and what a straw looks like. What if we are not aware of what a needle looks like or what if we are not even sure that we are searching for a needle? The process of examining every single blade of straw may actually lead us to start recognizing different kinds of straw, and who knows, we may end up discovering an entire science behind what makes each blade of straw differ from another. Edison was not just inventing the light bulb; he was the pioneer in the then nascent branch of electrical engineering with so many secrets waiting to be uncovered. The process of doing an exhaustive search in the form of the 3000 theories that he built and tested, to the exasperation of Tesla, seems inefficient if we think Edison knew he was searching for a needle. At the same time, all those experiments allowed Edison to know more thoroughly the science of the straw he was sifting through. The needle, when finally found, was just the icing on the cake.

The search process involved in design problem-solving is not one but two different search processes. One viewpoint is the search for the solution to the design problem. The other, in the words of Herbert Simon, is a process '. . . for gathering information about problem structure that will ultimately be valuable in discovering a problem solution. The latter viewpoint is more general than the former in a significant sense, in that it suggests that information obtained along any particular branch of a search tree may be used in many contexts besides the one in which it was generated.' The statement by Steve Jobs at the start of the chapter reflects this second type of search process.

The designer starts with a simple problem statement because he is yet to understand the full complexity of the search process. As he continues to better understand the complexities involved, he may go back and review and refine the objective function. The move from a simplistic solution of a simple problem statement to a convoluted solution of a complex problem statement is easy, but the move from a convoluted solution to an elegant solution is contingent on uncovering the underlying principle of the problem, as Jobs puts it. The search is thus a search for this underlying principle, the nature of which or even the existence of which is not known at the beginning of the search process. We are not searching just for the needle. The needle is incidental, the underlying principle of Steve Jobs, or the problem structure of Herbert Simon, is the holy grail.

The accumulation of learning about problem structure may seem to be a by-product of the main task of finding a solution to the problem statement. Nothing could be further from the truth. A firm which innovates once in a blue moon may be so elated with the new product or solution and the prospect of new customers and markets that it devalues the accumulated learnings gained and fails to capture them. It misses the search tree for the node. A more progressive firm may understand the value of this learning and try to monetize it in terms of spinoffs and follow-up product launches. It is only the rare firm which understands that the learning about what works and what does not and why is the true asset the firm has created through the systematic experimentation of which the product being launched is just one by-product. This is a paradigm change, the paradigm of learning gained as the main output and products commercialized as a by-product vs the paradigm of commercialized products as the main output and learning gained as the by-product. A firm investing in systematic testing to gather learning is more likely to produce a series of breakthrough innovations rather than one-off products. These investments in building a system for experimentation could be costly, but have economies of scope as they can be recouped over a large number of innovative by-products.

One experiment may not result in any significant learning, but as new data and insights are connected with the repository of data and insights gained earlier, the pace and quality of learning improves. Consider the same experiment being done by two firms, one with a substantially higher base of retained learnings due to longer experience in performing related experiments. This more experienced firm may be able to design and perform the experiment or interpret the results or transform the learning into a feasible product better than the less experienced one. However, longer experience does not automatically mean the theoretical model that the designers are grappling with has reached maturity. The quality of an experiment, in terms of its potential for a breakthrough, is contextual. Human beings have for long observed apples, coconuts, comets and a host of other objects (including fish) falling from the sky. One apple ignited a breakthrough thought process in Isaac Newton's mind not because there was anything special about that apple or the physical setting of the event. Newton would have been grappling with certain questions, and the falling apple allowed him the breakthrough insight. The apple is incidental, the build-up of the thought processes about alternative theoretical models is deliberate. The breakthrough requires not just the trigger for the ignition (the falling apple) but also the gathering of the combustible material (the thought processes in the search space).

In a way, the experienced firm has developed an absorptive capacity—explained by W.M. Cohen and D.A. Levinthal—for further learning. It may be able to place the results of the experiment in the context of previous related results and gather insights through association which are not apparent to the less experienced one. Moreover, the absorptive capacity developed by the firm helps it in assimilating knowledge not just from experiments conducted by itself but also new information available from external sources like competitors or other industry partners. Similar to absorptive capacity for knowledge, a firm can also develop absorptive capacity in other related activities like transforming the ideas into commercial products, as suggested by S. Zahra and G. George. Thus, a firm with a superior investment in transformation and exploitation sub-dimensions of absorptive capacity can be more effective in turning a new insight into a commercial product than another firm which lags in investments in absorptive capacity. Development of absorptive capacity is thus path dependent; it depends on not just the length of prior experience but also the kinds of previous design and development challenges that the firm encountered.

When we say that a firm has built absorptive capacity, we are treating the firm as a single unit. In reality, the firm is a collection of individuals working in different departments, divisions or business units. These individuals are in constant state of flux—getting hired and introduced to the learning environment, transitioning from project to project, leaving the firm (perhaps for a competitor) or retiring. While each individual designer has an absorptive capacity which changes with time, that capacity is lost when the individual leaves the system. For the system to have an absorptive capacity, it must invest in knowledge management systems so that previous learning is institutionalized. A repository of knowledge base could be in the digital space in the form of a collection of notes and insights from the different experiments. It could be in the form of patents filed or journal articles or reusable code fragments in software development, or it could be in physical form in the form of a box containing unique models, prototypes or sub-systems developed during earlier successful and failed projects. Designers could rummage through these artefacts in search of creative ideas.

A repository of knowledge may be of little value if designers do not interact with it. A big repository does not imply an effective repository as one could drown in the data. A repository could also become less effective as technologies evolve at a faster pace. A focus on the repository may lead a firm to the component view of innovation—to be innovative, you just need to develop or, if needed, buy a repository. This firm has failed to understand the prime importance of *interactions* between components. An innovative firm needs to develop an ecosystem which allows close and meaningful interactions between the various personnel involved as well as with internal repositories and external libraries, expert communities, user groups, etc.

How do we design a system which allows meaningful interactions? To answer this question, we need to first ask: Who are the people who need to interact with each other and work closely on a design assignment? Where exactly is design work located?

A naive answer is that design work is done by . . . well . . . designers. We could thus co-locate the designers in one office, design the workplace to enable formal and informal small group meetings and interactions, and expect breakthrough innovations to follow. This view of design work entrusts the design function in the hands of design specialists. This disenfranchises the other employees—the customer service representative dreaming about changes to an existing product or service offering which could have solved problems with the current design, the production supervisor thinking about redesigning the product to get productivity enhancements, the safety officer worrying about how injuries could be prevented by product redesign, the logistics manager who could have given inputs about the form factor of the product which could have eased storage and transport, the sustainability officer who could have provided inputs about product recycling, the packaging specialist who could have suggested changes which would have reduced transit losses—the list includes almost everyone who comes in contact with or is affected by the product or service to be designed. Just as TQM espouses that quality is not the baby of the quality department only and requires everyone to be quality conscious, the design work may also not be the baby of the design department only but also be the responsibility of everyone. Design thinking needs to permeate the entire organization.

The interactions thus should not be designed to be just among designers only. The design ecosystem should allow interactions among designers as well as between designers and line and staff functionaries who have ideas about product and service improvements. One way to facilitate such interactions is to create multifunctional teams which include representatives from different internal departments and external stakeholders. A multifunctional team may be better placed to interpret the design requirements from a multiple stakeholder perspective in situations where the problem is not an absence of stimulus but the condition of equivocality with the existence of multiple contradictory stimuli having varied interpretations. While the members of the multifunctional team may bring in complementary skills, for the team to work synergistically there is a need for building understanding and trust among members selected from varied backgrounds. In turn, the multifunctional team approach may result in individual departments getting more familiarity about the design process and new product pipeline, enabling them to voice their concerns and hence have a say in the design process. Building familiarity and allowing a say in the design process allows downstream departments to act as partners in the new product development process rather than as passive observers who may resent the imposition of new products with production processes different or more challenging than existing products.

While multifunctional teams increase the design footprint across departmental boundaries, the next step in that journey is to break the firm boundary and include suppliers and customers. The interactions now need to be designed between supply chain partners either upstream in terms of component or sub-system suppliers or downstream in terms of channel partners like distributors and retailers. From the viewpoint of design work, the list of customers whose needs have to be met is long. There are internal customers like engineering, manufacturing, quality, packaging, logistics, etc., but also external customers like distributors, transporters, wholesalers, retailers, end customers, etc. Of these internal and external customers, a strong focus needs to be on understanding the requirements of the end user.

There are various ways in which the user can be a part of the design process. At one level, user testing of the product and service allows the design team to observe how the user interacts with the prototype. Before user testing, designers have just a hypothesis of how they think the user would navigate the functionalities, what functionalities they are likely to prefer, dislike or seldom use, or even to what use they would apply the product or service. The design team may try to refine their hypothesis by using various employees to test out the prototype, but the real learning comes from putting the prototype in the hands of real users and allowing them to use their own imagination to make sense of it and adopting and adapting the prototype to solve their own problems. By putting the prototype in the hands of different segments of users, learning and insights can be drawn about the different ways in which the prototype could be used, and hence provide valuable insights for market segmentation, targeting and positioning.

In user testing, the user interacts with a pre-existing design prototype. A step ahead is when the user participates in choosing some of the design parameters, perhaps through a computer simulation or a toolkit which allows the user to mix and match modular components to produce the end product. Such customer-led design and innovation, explained by Stefan Thomke and Eric von Hippel, may allow the firm to offer the precise configuration or taste in a high-variety environment, thereby reducing its market risks. However, the firm has to invest in developing the simulation or toolkit which allows the customer to innovate. In contrast, von Hippel had shown that lead users may be tinkering, modifying and adapting an existing product to their specific needs because firms may not be aware of their specific needs or may feel that the segment is too small to merit a product variant. This kind of bricolage by the lead users is an example of a design originating completely outside the firm or supply chain. While innovations by lead users provide the design team with prototypes to further explore and refine, the challenge is to find such lead users and understand their needs. A further step is when a firm crowdsources the innovation, thereby outsourcing a major part of the search process. The firm may not even be aware of which person or set of persons would contribute to its crowdsourcing initiative and where they are located. As the location of design and development activity shifts from within the design office to within a firm to within a supply chain to a random user site to a lead user site to a set of unknown users at unknown sites; the kind of technologies (face-to-face meetings, informal meeting places, digital collaborative tools, open innovation marketplaces, etc.) and the quantum of investments needed for interaction facilitation should also change. What will not change is the need to facilitate interactions.

We can look at design and development activity through the prism of Operations Strategy dimensions. Static capacity deals with the number of experiments, aggregated over all new product development projects, which can simultaneously be performed. The capacity can be enhanced by hiring more designers, increasing the number of multifunctional teams, contracting out to research agencies or specialized agencies (for instance, outsourced clinical trials), crowdsourcing, etc. Dynamic capacity deals with the increases in absorptive capacity with experience.

Facility-related decisions involve choosing layout of offices so that meaningful interactions are facilitated; as well as decisions whether the design activities would be concentrated within one firm or dispersed among supply chain partners, or extend further involving customer locations, lead users in fields, offices of outsourced service providers and homes of workers in gig economy. Technology-related decisions involve investments in specialized equipment for rapid prototyping, computer simulations, IT tools for digital collaboration, etc. Scope-related decisions involve the extent to which upstream and downstream players collaborate on joint design of products and services. Planning-related decisions involve decisions regarding adoption of planning techniques like House of Quality, Design Structure Matrix (DSM), Concurrent Engineering, Agile vs Waterfall Model in software development, etc.

Workforce-related decisions focus on hiring, training and retention strategies for highly skilled designers as well as fitters, craftsmen, tool and equipment designers; creation, nurturing and disbanding of multifunctional teams, etc. Quality-related decisions involve ways to minimize Type I and Type II errors related to evaluation of candidate solutions and decisions to either proceed further, pause, prioritize or abandon the particular line of inquiry. Organization-related decisions involve whether the design function is treated as a sub-department under manufacturing or engineering or accorded a separate departmental status (for instance, R&D department, centres of excellence) or whether the design function is more diffused across the organization with a matrix reporting structure or whether design has high visibility and importance to top management.

If we try to fit the new product development activities into the product–process matrix, we realize that the true nature of design activity is a project. However, NPD projects differ from other kinds of projects (like civil construction projects) in that we really don't know what we will finally build or whether we will be at all successful in achieving a breakthrough. The progress of a construction project (say, construction of a bridge) can be monitored by determining adherence to time and cost overruns compared to the original project plan. The project plan can accommodate uncertainties related to activity durations (known unknowns) by using techniques like Program Evaluation and Review Technique (PERT). However, Critical Path Method (CPM) or PERT assumes that we know the set of activities to be performed and the sequence in which they would be performed. In contrast, designers may only have faint ideas about the different activities they would have to perform in an NPD project, resulting in uncertainties in the work breakdown structure (WBS). In addition, NPD projects may have a significant number of iterations among activities, certain activities may be contingent on the achievement of breakthroughs in other activities, and the activity list may be modified as the project progresses. Modelling this project network may require advanced techniques like Graphical Evaluation and Review Technique (GERT) and the need to estimate probabilities of achieving success in different nodes of the search tree. One option is to build capacities in forecasting these probabilities, the other is to confront the reality that we may be trying to predict the unpredictable. Instead of spending considerable time with questionable accuracy in precisely determining unknown unknowns, we may be much better off in visualizing the design process as a set of iterative steps like Empathize, Define, Ideate, Prototype and Test with simple visual charts showing the status of each NPD project as per these broad buckets. While there are different versions of these iterative steps, essentially they are variants of the Generator-Test Cycles, involving generation of alternatives and testing of alternatives, first discussed by Herbert Simon.

The insight that the design process is iterative is fundamental. It frees us from the sequential, directional logic permeating much of engineering, manufacturing, logistics, operations and traditional project management. The circularity of an iteration is in contrast to the unidirectional arrow. A traditional project network takes unidirectionality for granted, in fact, we explicitly check if the underlying network is acyclic before using CPM or PERT. In such networks, the unit of analysis is the individual activity. In contrast, in iterative processes like design, the unit of analysis could be the iteration itself.

We are now in a position to look at design work done at different firms and observe differences in approach. A firm may like to reduce the time taken for an iteration, thereby moving quickly to the next phase of product development. This firm may be aiming for rapid prototyping where learnings and insights from earlier experiments are quickly incorporated into the next round of experiments. Time is of essence in these firms, perhaps because there is a premium in being the first to launch a product in a market or develop a software solution for a time-sensitive client. The focus here is on getting a working product to market which satisfies most of the customer needs. The focus is not on running a large number of experiments to better understand the problem structure or explore all the search nodes or optimize the offering. A quick and dirty solution emanating from a depth-first search strategy would suffice. Note that this does not automatically mean that the firm does not value quality. The firm may introduce the quick and dirty solution in the marketplace, reap financial gains from being an early innovator, and then go back to the drawing board and start the next round of rapid prototyping. The quality of products coming out from this design philosophy would gradually improve over time. A version of this thinking process is evident in software design based on the Scrum methodology which relies on frequent product launches based on time-bound sprints.

Compared to the Cheetah experimenter described above, the Elephant experimenter is most concerned about research productivity. Such a firm is more concerned with increasing the number of experiments that can be simultaneously performed by existing designers so that fixed costs related to R&D could be apportioned over a larger number of experiments or products developed. The problem is that overloading designers with a large number of projects may imply that the designers need to cycle quickly between a large number of research projects assigned. There could be a considerable set-up time involved in immersing oneself in the search space for each project. And when a designer does get immersed in a specific search space, it might take time to forget the same and move to the next. Indeed, design work may not cease when a designer leaves the office, the mind continues to grapple with the challenges on the way back home, over dinner and even while sleeping. The double helix of the DNA revealed itself to the researcher while in a dream. A designer juggling a large number of projects under the able guidance of an Elephant manager is likely to experience nightmares related to project deadlines and cost overruns rather than breakthrough insights in dreamland.

The logic used by Elephant managers in assigning a large number of new design initiatives to the designers is equivalent to increasing the capacity utilization of a server to gain scale economies. We already know that as capacity utilization increases, the lead time and the WIP also increases. In design work, the impact of increase in capacity utilization on lead times could be even more detrimental than in manufacturing or service situations. In these situations, set-up time of an activity is generally constant and does not vary due to the presence of other jobs done by the same worker. Sometimes the set-up time in manufacturing is sequence-dependent, but this variation in set-up time depends on the previous job rather than the number of competing jobs. In contrast, a designer may take more time to reimmerse in a particular design problem if there are multiple projects vying for attention simultaneously. And while working on this design problem, the attention could be constantly diverted to thinking about or responding to colleagues' or managers' information requests regarding other pending projects. Interactions seem to be a burden to this designer, each interaction with another co-designer working on another project breaks the stream of thought, requiring a further set-up time to return to the current problem context. Yet, it is these interactions which hold the key to a superior design. Increasing the capacity utilization of designers may thus adversely affect not just the design lead times but also the design quality. Conversely, a firm can witness both improvements in quality and reduction in lead times by reducing its capacity utilization.

This is a little counterintuitive—how can compressing a design lead time improve quality? We tend to think that hurrying an activity would negatively affect quality. While it may be true that a person can take shortcuts while hurrying, thereby compromising quality, it can also be possible that the reduction of design lead time can actually improve quality. The key to understanding this phenomenon is interactions between iterations.

Traditionally, the design process used the same sequential logic permeating the rest of the manufacturing organization. System specification must precede sub-system design which must precede component design which must precede support system design. This is intuitive. How can we start designing sub-systems when the basic specifications of the overall system have not yet been finalized? It is true that work on basic specification must start before work on sub-system design can start. It is also true that work on basic specification must end before sub-system design can end. But it is not true that sub-system design cannot start before the end of basic specification activity. These two activities can work concurrently for a period of time when basic specifications have not been finalized, but work on sub-system design is in progress based on the partial set of basic specifications available at that time.

The benefit of this kind of concurrency is two-fold. First, concurrency reduces the total lead time for design activity by running several activities in parallel. Second, concurrency improves quality by jointly optimizing the design through facilitating interactions between experimental iterations of preceding and subsequent activities. In the absence of this joint optimization, a choice made at an earlier stage of the design process becomes a binding constraint for a designer working at a later stage. This designer, working on, say, component design, may unearth a flaw in the overall specifications or realize that a particular component characteristic is unattainable. In a sequential design process, the overall specifications have already been finalized, and hence the information available at a later stage is of little use in coming up with a better overall specification. Going back on the overall specifications may imply huge rework since a change in overall specifications may have a cascading effect on other sub-system and component designs. The firm may decide against the cost and time overruns that this redesign may entail, instead settling for some workaround. Instead of this sequential logic, if the firm employs concurrency then there is a chance that the overall specifications have not yet been finalized when the component level flaw is identified, leading to a better overall specification and hence a superior design.

The interaction between two sequential design activities is thus interactions between the Generator-Test iterations that constitute each activity. Note the way in which interactions between designers affect quality. If the designers are working on different projects or if the set of designers have the same projects but have no mechanism to synchronize their activities then interactions between them may require more set-up times, thereby negatively impacting lead times and quality. On the other hand, if designers are working on different aspects of the same design project then they could jointly optimize the design while reducing the lead time. The key is to have the designers interacting on the same design problem, thereby ensuring that they are working on the same search space concurrently. This would mean that design productivity can improve not by loading designers with more projects but by creating a design team and allocating only one or a few projects to the team at a time. The Cheetah experimenter would value the reduction in lead time the most, the improvement in quality being a welcome addition. The Elephant experimenter would value the reduction in lead time for the increase in the number of new products that can be launched with the same investments in R&D, the improvement in quality being a welcome addition.

In contrast, the Artist experimenter would value the increase in quality of the design process more than the benefit of reduced lead time or the reduction in cost per experimentation. Instead of the quick and dirty approach of the Cheetah, the Artist with a 'no compromise' attitude would focus on high-fidelity experiments which would allow the uncovering of the underlying problem structure. The experimental context would be as close to real life as possible, by getting the real target segment of users to try out the product or service using prototypes which are as close to the final product as possible in terms of look, feel and functionality. The Artist may not be concerned with being among the first to launch the product in the marketplace but have faith that the marketplace would value an elegant solution when it is presented with one. The premium paid by the consumers for this superior design would offset the costs incurred while discovering the elegant solution. Its search is for perfection. Its biggest asset is understanding the search space. Its biggest competitor is not any Elephant or Cheetah. Its biggest headache is the Praying Mantis.

A praying mantis is a master predator which uses not just speed but also deception to hunt for prey much larger than its size. It lies in wait, camouflaging itself and blending into the foliage, waiting motionless as the prey wanders into range. Its eyes are a collection of (i) two large compound eyes composed of thousands of miniature eyes and (ii) three simple eyes. The eyes track the prey unblinkingly, with the head having the ability to rotate 360 degrees while tracking the prey. The praying mantis sways from side to side to get depth perception, the only insect that has 3D vision. And when the praying mantis lashes out, it grips the prey with sharp hooks in its serrated forelimbs and starts munching on it while the prey is still alive. The female praying mantis even has a taste for biting off the head of a male after mating. It is not a pretty sight, but there is beauty in the way nature has designed this killing machine.

Neither is it a pretty sight when an Imitator starts eating up the revenue of an Artist by offering a much cheaper imitation to the marketplace. The Imitator does not need to spend on R&D investments to develop a product, nor in advertising to develop a market. It just needs to track the Artist with unblinking eyes, taking a 360-degree view of the product being designed by them. What raw materials does the Artist use? Where from does the Artist buy these raw materials or components? Can it also approach these raw material or component suppliers to get insights on the product being developed? What are the machine tools used by the Artist? Can it approach the same machine tool manufacturers to buy similar equipment? Can it get current designers of the Artist to spill the beans on the products being developed? Who are the disgruntled current and former employees of the Artist? Can it interview these disgruntled employees for a fictitious job opening to get them to rat on their previous employer? Can it hire consultants engaged by the Artist to glean their thinking process? Can it unearth some information from regulatory or patent filings or advertisements or product demos? Can it hack their computer systems to steal the design documents? The Praying Mantis is obsessed with its target, collecting all possible information about it, through means legal as well as illegal and unethical. The target is not just an Artist, it could be anyone, even other Praying Mantises. Not a pretty sight, I warned you.

Copying a design by stealing design documents or bribing is outright illegal. Reverse engineering, in contrast, has a lot of respectability. An ethical Praying Mantis— yes, those organizations do exist—feels no need to go to extremes like its more desperate cousins. It awaits the new product launch of the Artist, sends its own employees to buy the product from the market legally and then asks its engineers to disassemble the product and study each and every sub-system and component to understand the design and decipher how much it would cost to make and hence how much is the margin the Artist is making. The more revolutionary the product launched by the Artist, the more premium it commands in the marketplace, and hence its margin is likely to be mouth-watering. The prey is now locked-in; the target has been acquired—to flood the market with cheap copies of the original products. Easier said than done.

Contrary to popular belief, copying is not easy at all. It is relatively easy to disassemble a product into its individual components. The physical dimensions of these components are easy to measure, relatively more difficult is specifying the chemical and material characteristics like grade or alloy of steel used and the hardness specifications. But the key to successful copying lies not in the individual components but in the *interactions* between the components. Mechanical interactions are relatively easier to glean, more difficult are electrical, electronic, chemical or software interactions. Even more difficult are interactions between components in the presence of stress or thermal deformation. The way certain components interact at room temperature may be quite different when the same components interact under operating conditions characterized by heat, stress and strain, humidity, atmospheric pressure, etc. Reverse engineering is anything but easy; a one-off attempt at reverse engineering is likely to be unsuccessful. It is a competency which is honed over time through practise. A firm develops absorptive capacity as it repeatedly attempts to reverse engineer new product launches. Reverse engineering is practised not just by Praying Mantises but also by Elephants and Cheetahs and even Artists. The objectives behind reverse engineering could range from making cheap copies to achieving the holy grail in design—insights about the search space.

Design is a search for a solution in a search space. A product is a physical realization of a particular design intent achieved by a collection of choices that the designer made based on the current understanding of the problem structure. By attempting reverse engineering, a competing designer can peek into the minds of original designers, not just for understanding the specific choices made but also to uncover the alternate design choices facing the original designers. Design intent is uncovered by asking why the original designers made a specific choice. What were they trying to achieve? Each reverse engineering attempt brings additional information and insight to the Praying Mantis, not just about the search space but also how the original designers were thinking in that search space.

Copying is not copying the product, which is just one realization among a multitude of other equally possible product offerings emanating from the search space. The holy grail in copying is the copying of the search space and uncovering the design intent of the original designers.

A Praying Mantis which has reached this holy grail need not bother about illegal or unethical means. It peers into a newly launched product of the Artist, just as a connoisseur or art critic appreciates a painting by a master hanging in a museum. The specific painting may be a beauty, but there is a bigger beauty in understanding the mind of the master and putting the painting in perspective of the evolution as a painter that the master went through. The difference is that the connoisseur or art critic is happy with the insight and the beauty, the Praying Mantis hastens to make a cheap copy for commercial gains. If it had tried to do some original experiments and developed an original design intent, the Praying Mantis would have metamorphosed into an Artist in its own right. Alas, the mentality of not investing in R&D would not enable the Praying Mantis to be an Artist. A Praying Mantis is, after all, an Insect. A predatory Insect which invests in little apart from absorptive capacity.

How does an Artist experimenter guard against the innumerable Praying Mantises looking to make a meal out of the Artist? The key to this challenge is again *interactions*. Interactions between a few components and sub-systems are relatively easier to glean than those among a larger number. Thus, a joint optimization of the specifications of a large number of components leads to the generation of tacit knowledge whereby the designer has private knowledge of how these components interact, which is not written down or shared with others. The joint optimization may start with two frequently interacting components and gradually encompass frequently interacting modules, and finally the entire product architecture could be jointly optimized. An integrated product architecture may be so complex in terms of interactions that Imitators are unable to fully realize the design intent. However, it also very challenging for the Artist to handle all this complexity, more so when the different sub-systems or components may involve different kinds of technologies which are developing at a rapid pace. An integrated product architecture for a desktop computer maker would need the firm to be a master of diverse technologies like semiconductor design, operating systems, display technologies, storage technologies, etc., each with its own peculiarities, competencies, investment requirements and technology trajectories. A modular design, in contrast, specifies the interactions between the modules, leaving individual firms expert in each technology to innovate and develop each technology further.

Modularity thus has an interesting impact on innovation and imitation. The standardization of the interface leaves each component maker to focus on adopting the latest technology and jointly optimizing *within* the component boundary. The standardization of the interface does not allow a joint optimization *between* two components, which might require a rewriting of the interface specifications. Rewriting interface specifications requires consensus among a large number of fragmented component makers, many of whom are likely to resist changes as it may mean new investments or expenses. Thus, once an interface specification has been standardized, it may take huge coordination efforts to effect a change. At the same time, the stability of the interface standard gives component-makers confidence in investing in new technologies in that domain. Modularity may thus help incremental innovations involving component-level changes, but hinder breakthrough or radical innovations requiring joint optimization across components. The writing down of the interface specifications is also an invitation for the Imitators because they get the earlier tacit knowledge on a platter. The more modular a product architecture, the easier it would be to copy. The more integrated the product architecture, the more difficult it would be to copy.

The ease of copying is also affected by the clockspeed of innovations—a concept introduced by Charles H. Fine—the frequency with which new innovations are introduced. A high clockspeed implies that the Imitator has little time to understand the search space before the search space itself changes with the advent of newer technology. An Artist can thus aim to be at the forefront of technology innovation, without bothering too much about Praying Mantises which are copying products from the earlier generations. This Artist can design its proprietary integrated product architecture and have a vertical structure with presence in all the components and sub-systems making up the end product. However, clockspeeds may decrease over time as the industry and technology mature, leaving the Artist vulnerable as the Praying Mantises catch up with the latest generation. If innovation clockspeed slows down substantially then consumer preferences could also change towards more budget-friendly alternatives. The industry could then move away from integrated product architecture and vertical industry structure towards modular product architecture and horizontal industry structure with a few Elephants emerging in each component space. The Elephants would focus their R&D investments in the chosen component and recoup the costs by selling innovative components adhering to the set interface norms across all competitors who have chosen to adhere to the modular design standards of the end product. The Artist who stays apart with its proprietary integrated product architecture needs to have a significant volume of sales as well as margins to invest in diverse component technologies and handle their integration challenges. Any slip-up and consumer preferences can drastically change, leaving the Artist as just a footnote in history.

One artificial way in which an Artist in a mature industry can still maintain a higher clockspeed is by maintaining frequent launches where the new products are still architecturally integrated, but with only slight variations in the architecture design and component specifications. These slight variations ensure that repairing a used product is difficult as replacement parts are not available and the currently available parts don't fit the earlier-generation product perfectly. An existing user is forced to buy a new product from the Artist even if only a minor component malfunctions, leading to increased sales of the integrated product when a modular product architecture would have entailed increased sales of a specific component-maker. The periodic refreshing of the product aims to maintain the aura as an innovator, creating an illusion of progress. While this is a sharp commercial practice aimed at defending the high-margin innovator image, its success in commercial terms hides the truth that the Artist is now living on borrowed time. The Artist desperately needs a breakthrough, a completely new design architecture integrating the components into a product which actually has a soul.

How easy is it to design an integrated product architecture which represents a breakthrough? How easy is it to handle a search space which includes diverse technologies with different clockspeeds of innovation? How easy is it to not just choose an integrated joint optimization of product specifications but also develop the right manufacturing technology if such process technology does not exist? How easy is it to not just innovate in terms of products and manufacturing processes but also design the entire business model including sales channels, after-sales service, etc.? How easy is it to create a new soul? An Artist who works over such a large canvas deserves to be called something more.

An Artist is different from a Conductor and a Composer. An Artist could have a 'no compromise' attitude towards the design of a specific component or sub-system. An Artist can be a violin player passionate about bringing perfection to her art form. A Conductor is a different kind of Artist who needs to integrate a diverse set of musicians, each an Artist in his or her own right, to recreate a musical score. A Composer is an altogether different kind of Artist who brings together a diverse ensemble of Artists to create something which did not exist before. A Composer is an Artist who has to make sure that the different musical instruments are coordinated, each supporting and contributing to the bigger picture. A Composer has this vision of the bigger picture where each of the selected musical instruments has its own role to play, none more important than the rest. The musical score is then a complete whole, greater than the sum of its parts. A Composer brings a new soul into existence in terms of a musical score or an integrated product architecture. A Conductor recreates the score, mostly adhering to the original with some artistic freedom for reinterpretation. One involves deviation-amplifying mutual causal processes, the other involves deviation-counteracting mutual causal processes.

Why does the Composer create a new soul? It would denigrate the Composer if we assign a commercial motive to the act of creation. Would it be right to portray the world of the Composer to be a bleak one, always concerned with the hordes of Praying Mantises trying to deprive the Composer of the fruits of its labour, or the Elephants intent on undercutting on price? While the Composer does inhabit a cut-throat world, a world of crass commercial interests, surely this commercial world does not inspire the creativity. It is not the dreary world of commercial profits and competing against Praying Mantises that inspires the Composer.

O Freunde, nicht diese Töne!
Sondern laßt uns angenehmere anstimmen, und
freudenvollere.
Freude! Freude!

[O friends, not these sounds!
Let us sing something more pleasant, more full of
gladness. O Joy, let us praise thee!]

And with these words, Beethoven proceeded to incorporate Friedrich Schiller's 'Ode to Joy' in the final movement of his greatest composition, the Ninth Symphony. It was a breakthrough, the first time that a choral movement was part of a symphony, the symphony was also bigger in terms of the orchestra as well as had a longer duration. More importantly, Beethoven's Ninth has a soul. In the words of commentator Tom Service in the *Guardian*, 'The whole symphony charts a story from the birth of music, out of this prehistoric sonic murk, to the birth and betterment of civilisation, climaxing with the Ode to Joy in the choral finale.' The beauty of the Ninth is the outpouring of joy that it fosters in the listener. It is an affirmation of the source of all creativity—the joy of the creation. It celebrates the moment when a creation starts sensing the Creator and feels the brotherhood of His creations. It is an Ode from a composer to his Composer. Yet, this masterpiece was composed only a few years before his death when he was in ill health and had become deaf.

Ordinary mortals can try making a musical composition by playing different notes and checking how they sound. This trial and error requires the operation of a feedback loop involving the act of hearing. To compose music when you cannot hear it properly means that the composer has a search space where feedback need not only rely on the act of physical hearing. The search space is alive, the notes play in the mind's ear. Behold the Genius Composer, rising above the limitations of mere mortals.

It is a moment of great sadness when a human being loses the ability to hear. It is a catastrophe when a musician becomes deaf. It is an incalculable loss when the musician is one of the greatest composers that mankind has seen. But how does this person react to his deafness and declining health? Beethoven contemplated suicide and rejected it in favour of living through his art. He wrote his will at the age of thirty-one when he realized he had no hope left of recovering from his condition.

. . . —with joy I hasten towards death—if it comes before I shall have had an opportunity to show all my artistic capacities it will still come too early for me despite my hard fate and I shall probably wish that it had come later—but even then I am satisfied, will it not free me from a state of endless suffering? Come when thou wilt I shall meet thee bravely—Farewell and do not wholly forget me when I am dead . . .

Heiglnstadt, October 10th, 1802, thus do I take my farewell of thee—and indeed sadly—yes that beloved hope—which I brought with me when I came here to be cured at least in a degree—I must wholly abandon, as the leaves of autumn fall and are withered so hope has been blighted, almost as I came—I go away—even the high courage—which often inspired me in the beautiful days of summer—has disappeared—O Providence— grant me at last but one day of pure *joy*—it is so long since real joy echoed in my heart—O when—O when, O Divine One—shall I feel it again in the temple of nature and of men—Never? no—O that would be too hard.

—Alexander Wheelock Thayer, *The Life of Ludwig van Beethoven*

Providence did not grant him a cure for even a day, prolonging his suffering till death occurred decades later in 1827. But providence did grant him immortality through the ability to bring the feeling of pure *joy* in the hearts of listeners through a long list of compositions climaxing, very aptly, in his finest masterpiece set on 'Ode to Joy'!

Many years later, another terminally ill Genius Composer would present the world with iconic products of elegant beauty while his health was deteriorating, the iPad being launched a year before his death. Like Beethoven, Steve Jobs worked on a large canvas, integrating design choices over products, processes and business models to give the world a sense of joy.

The search for a superior design is thus not a search for a needle nor for the science of the hay. It is essentially a search for joy.

So, if you are a true designer, aim to bring joy to consumers who would use your product. If you are a manager innovating a business model, aim to bring joy to all stakeholders as the firm brings joy to the world through its products or services. Commercial considerations take care of themselves. And as you make new compositions, empathize with the fellow designers working in Elephants, Cheetahs, Artists and even Praying Mantises. See them as brothers who are all united in a quest, join them in wondering about the Composer of Composers who created this whole world. Ordinary mortals can only reach the level where they sense Him and empathize with His other creations. Only a designer can empathize with Him as a fellow designer! Designer, behold His product—this world. Can you sense His

design intent? It is nothing but pure joy. And it is through
the realization of joy, His Design Intent, we can hope to
reach Him.

> Joy, thou source of light immortal, daughter
> of Elysium
> Touched with fire, to the portal of thy radiant shrine
> we come.
> Thy pure magic frees all others held in custom's
> rigid rings;
> Men throughout the world are brothers in the haven
> of thy wings.[1]

---

[1] Translated by Louis Untermeyer from Friedrich Schiller's 'Ode
to Joy'.

CHAPTER 14

Convenience

'It was one Sunday evening early in September of the year 1903 that I received one of Holmes's laconic messages: *Come at once if convenient—if inconvenient come all the same.*—S.H.

The relations between us in those latter days were peculiar. He was a man of habits, narrow and concentrated habits, and I had become one of them. As an institution I was like the violin, the shag tobacco, the old black pipe, the index books, and others perhaps less excusable. When it was a case of active work and a comrade was needed upon whose nerve he could place some reliance, my role was obvious.'

—*The Adventure of the Creeping Man*,
Sir Arthur Conan Doyle

CONVENIENCE IS ASYMMETRIC in relation. While Sherlock Holmes finds it convenient to fall back on the support of Watson, the convenience of Watson is immaterial to him. Just like the dog that did not bark, the clue to unravelling the asymmetric nature of convenience lies in the word missing in the laconic message: 'Please.' The true nature of this message is that of an order. Holmes neither feels it necessary to extend a courtesy, nor to express regret for any inconvenience caused to Watson. The services of Watson are taken for granted; like the inanimate violin or the pipe, he too has become a familiar fixture in the life of Holmes.

The Holmes–Watson partnership is purpose-driven. Holmes sometimes needs a partner in the detective work and Watson fills the need. What need does Holmes fill in Watson's life? They are comrades but instead of the equality of brothers-in-arms fighting side by side in trenches, theirs is more of a superior–subordinate relationship characterizing a detective and the assistant. The assistant may over time learn the tricks of the trade, yet his primary purpose remains the job of providing assistance to the maestro. Over time, the maestro may delegate certain relatively simpler tasks to the assistant so that he can concentrate his faculties on tasks that he finds more meaningful or challenging. The time and effort put in by the assistant saves the time and effort of the maestro.

There could be several economic justifications for transfer of work content from maestro to assistant. The maestro may be time-constrained with too much work and too little time and sees value in offloading some work to a reliable assistant. Here, the rationale is offloading of less quality sensitive work to increase the maestro's focus on what he deems more important. The important point here is reliability—the maestro expects the assistant to deliver consistently rather than achieve any quality or efficiency gain. At an advanced level, the maestro feels not just satisfied that his assistant is reliable, but also benefits from quality and efficiency gains resulting from the assistant developing competencies to complete the assigned job faster, better and more efficiently than the maestro.

The maestro may also transfer the work content, even when he is not overburdened, to focus on more meaningful (to him) activities like playing the violin. This is an example of a hedonic activity which is pursued for its own sake rather than as a means to another goal. The time required for performing a hedonic activity is perceived as an investment rather than as a cost. A reduction of time and effort in daily chores allows us to free up time for enjoying ourselves through hedonic activities. Holmes enjoys playing the violin, perhaps Watson enjoys being the detective's assistant. We all value the time invested in hedonic activities more than an equal amount of time spent in chores.

Would there be an economic rationale for convenience if everyone was equally overburdened and everyone had the same skills? A world where the maestro and the assistant have the same skills negates the idea of a maestro. In this undifferentiated skill universe, the convenience of one would necessarily come at the cost of inconvenience of another. So, from a systemic standpoint, perhaps there would be no rationale for convenience. Yet, from the selfish perspective of each individual, what matters is his or her convenience. Each individual could be a maestro in his or her own opinion, valuing the service provided by an assistant. Getting an assistant would be anyway extremely difficult since everyone is overburdened. If the self-styled maestro has a willingness to pay (WTP) higher than the opportunity cost of the assistant, there is a justification for convenience.

The economic rationale for convenience thus depends on the differences in the value of the maestro's time compared to the value of the assistant's, the valuation being done by the maestro. Watson does not charge Holmes for the convenience provided. Commercial ventures exploiting the convenience dimension exploit the difference between the customer's willingness to pay and the cost of providing the product or service. The customer avails the offer if his cost of purchasing the convenience is higher than the perceived benefit in terms of better usage of the saved time and effort in either monetary terms (like better earning potential) or hedonic terms (participation in pleasurable activities).

The dependence of Holmes on the convenience of having Watson by his side is the stuff of dreams for packaged consumer goods and consumer durable firms. They plot to form habits around brands and become familiar fixtures in the busy life of consumers, enabling them to save time and effort in performing daily chores. For service firms, this dependence is more nuanced in terms of opportunities and costs involved. The service firms love the premium that such convenience commands, the deep insights that the customer intimacy promises, but they need to manage the inconvenience that it implies for the employees. Unlike products, service cannot be stored, and hence production and consumption in services happens simultaneously. It may also require the customer and service provider to interact while the service is being delivered. This simultaneity and inseparability of service may expose the service personnel to a diverse range of customers, some of them irritable, grumpy, obnoxious, demanding, angry, uncivil or with criminal intent. Unlike Watson, employees in service firms may not look kindly at being taken for granted by the customer. Unlike Watson, such employees neither have any hedonic interest nor any inclination in developing deep relationships with individual customers. If the customer is too demanding, the service personnel can quit. High attrition rates in mass service firms may simply preclude the opportunity to develop customer–employee relationships at an individual level. In contrast to the individualized service of Watson, delivering service convenience at a mass scale requires a service system design which can simultaneously handle customer intimacy and worker interchangeability.

The task of delivering service excellence through convenience is thus one of balancing the convenience needs of different stakeholders. The convenience of the customer is most prominent, the question of convenience of the service provider is a hidden concern. Holmes articulates his need in a brazen message. The message intrudes upon the privacy of Watson on a Sunday evening. The order cares little whether Watson had a difficult week, whether he is in fine mood or if he is indisposed. Watson does not message back; he silently complies but with perhaps a tinge of disapproval which may turn into bitterness over time. Holmes has scant regard for the convenience of Watson. Apart from these two conveniences, there is a third convenience which is more subtle. There is a third person who is conspicuous by his or her absence. As a medical doctor, Watson may have had patients to attend to that Sunday evening or Monday morning in September 1903. Who cares for the inconvenience caused to such a patient when the doctor rushes to the aid of a detective? While the convenience of Holmes finds articulation and the inconvenience of Watson is suppressed, the inconvenience of the patient who could have come looking for Watson and found a locked house goes unarticulated, unnoticed and unrecorded. The benefit of providing a convenient service to a customer has to be thus weighed against the cost of inconveniencing the service provider as well as other customers who were served and the potential customers who could not be served.

The fundamental question to be asked is thus, *whose convenience is it anyway?* This question is not a rhetorical question, it forces the firm to segment the customers and the service providers and prioritize among the convenience needs of different stakeholders.

Consumers value convenience because they are aware of alternate uses of their time and effort. The value of convenience is thus related to opportunity cost. A hermit, sitting under a tree in the Himalayas having renounced the world, may have little use of convenience. A busy executive may have a secretary to take care of routine work, the CEO may have a few executive assistants to provide analytical and research support apart from a secretary, an industrialist may have the convenience of having a family office headed by a general manager and staffed with a team of executive assistants and secretaries. Each of these secretaries, executive assistants and managers may employ time- and effort-saving household gadgets like washing machines, etc., or engage a maid or occasional help at home to free up time. Consumers thus sell time in labour markets and buy it with time-saving goods and services. A ready-to-eat frozen pizza that just needs a few minutes in a microwave saves a lot of time and effort in ingredient shopping, food preparation and cooking; freeing up the time for working longer hours in office in the hope of a promotion to get a better pay to be able to buy more time- and effort-saving goods and services!

The firms delivering convenience through goods spend their effort in understanding the time- and effort-saving needs of consumers and translating this understanding into better designed products and fine-tuned marketing communications. Convenience could be delivered through varied means like efficient pack sizes (e.g. shampoo sachets), packaging innovations which make it easier to handle the product or design innovations which allow a household equipment to be efficiently stored after use. The major part of the challenge of delivering convenience through goods are in product development and marketing. Once the product is designed, the manufacturing and distribution strategy could be based on cost leadership. In contrast, firms delivering convenience through service face significant challenges in designing the appropriate service delivery mechanism due to the simultaneity of production and consumption in services. While convenience can be designed into a product and then produced on a mass scale; a service needs some kind of interaction between the service producer and the service consumer and hence faces several kinds of variabilities.

Service convenience, as per Leonard L. Berry, Kathleen Seiders and Dhruv Grewal, has been defined as the consumer's *time* and *effort perceptions* related to *buying* or *using* a service. A consumer not only pays a monetary cost for the service but also non-monetary costs related to time and effort in availing the service. A cost leadership strategy focuses on competing on the monetary cost. In contrast, the firm competing on convenience focuses attention on the non-monetary costs. A monetary cost is objectively captured in the price charged to the consumer, while non-monetary costs are subjective as they are based on perceptions. Perceptions are likely to vary across different consumers. The value of convenience is thus subjective, making the choice of consumer segment to target an important decision.

Figure 10: Monetary and Non-Monetary Costs

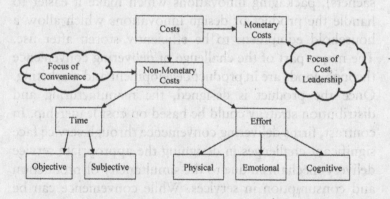

Convenience in the time dimension can be reflected in the reduction of time involved. Residents of top floors of a high-rise apartment block may experience convenience in using a high-speed elevator which skips some of the lower floors. This time reduction can be objectively measured. The same elevator ride may be perceived to take even less time if there are mirrors fitted inside the elevator. Time flies when one is occupied. The perception of time is thus both objective as well as subjective. Similarly, a customer waiting in a checkout queue in a supermarket has both a subjective as well as an objective perception of the time required for the checkout process. In addition to time, the person also needs to expend physical effort in pushing a heavily laden trolley. Children, elderly or infirm customers may face difficulties in standing in queues for a long time. Apart from physical effort, customers may spend cognitive effort in estimating how much more time they need to spend in the queue as well as experience emotions like anxiety, boredom, anger, frustration, etc. They may move from one checkout counter to another with a seemingly shorter queue, only to watch with dismay as people standing behind them in the earlier queue complete the checkout process ahead of them. Waiting does not just involve objective and subjective perceptions of time, but also perceptions of physical, emotional and cognitive effort involved.

The potential for time and effort savings can manifest in any part of the process of purchase and consumption of the product or service. A service providing Decision Convenience reduces the perception of time and effort involved in identifying and evaluating alternatives and in coming to a decision. The value of Decision Convenience increases with product proliferation and pricing complexities. A shopping assistant may present relevant merchandise, thereby decreasing the number of options for evaluation and hence reducing the cognitive effort in coming to a decision. We leave our decisions regarding which exhibits are worth seeing to curators of art in museums and exhibitions. A daily online news digest curates, based on individual preferences, the news that might interest us; thereby saving us the time and effort to decide which items to read. Similarly, a dollar shop reduces pricing complexity by offering all products at a specific price point. A cost comparison website for air tickets, hotel bookings or insurance products reduces the cognitive workload in figuring out the best deal.

Access Convenience reduces the time and effort in reaching the selected service provider. A cold drinks firm may aspire to increase the penetration of its dispensing machines to provide chilled drinks at an arm's length of desire. A hotel inside an airport may charge a high premium for providing Access Convenience even when it offers only basic amenities. A bank may decide to have the largest branch network to reduce the customer's travel time to the branch. Such a large branch network would be very costly unless the firm has sufficient market share and volumes to justify investments. In contrast, a bank which targets high net worth individuals may also provide Access Convenience, but instead of a large branch network, it could have its wealth managers call on clients at home or work, effectively bringing the bank home. A third bank could provide Access Convenience without investing in physical facilities or high-quality service personnel by developing technology like smartphone apps which bring the bank to the customer's fingertips at any point of time, day or night or holiday. Note that these avenues for providing Access Convenience are not mutually exclusive, the same bank which provides an extensive branch network for its regular customers could also provide phone banking or smartphone apps and also provide doorstep service to its elite customers.

Transaction Convenience refers to the time and effort perceptions related to the actual transaction—the process of exchange of goods or service and payment for the same. A retailer may provide Transaction Convenience by investing in more checkout counters or quicker scanning technology like RFID to reduce the length of queues. Quick Service Restaurants (QSRs) may provide Transaction Convenience by reducing the time between order placement and food delivery. Online websites like Amazon may provide one-click checkout to reduce the time and effort needed in providing billing, shipping and payment details. Digital wallets may provide transaction convenience in paying for small-ticket items by eliminating the need to tender exact change, or provide transaction convenience to a group of friends pooling together to pay a bill.

Benefit Convenience refers to perceptions of time and effort reductions in the consumption of the product or service. A red-eye flight operating in the middle of the night may have a lower monetary cost but may be perceived to have a higher non-monetary cost and thus not offer benefit convenience. A flight reaching an airport late at night may be perceived to be convenient for the busy executive with a home in that city while it may be perceived to be inconvenient to an elderly first-time visitor unsure about where to go and anxious about safety. The parents of an unaccompanied child could consider an airline to offer convenience if it offers to guide the child from check-in to the arrival gate, thereby reducing the parent's anxiety levels if not of the passenger. A direct flight between two airports may be considered more convenient than a much lower cost route through hub airports. A long layover between two flights may be considered inconvenient in an airport with little opportunities to keep one engaged and avoid boredom. A very short connection time between two flights may be considered inconvenient if the traveller feels heightened anxiety about missing the connecting flight. Convenience is thus finely balanced, both too much and too little can trigger feelings of inconvenience.

Post-Benefit Convenience refers to perceived time and effort reduction in reinitiating contact after the product or service has been consumed partially or fully. A call centre which answers customer's queries, takes feedback, solves technical glitches, provides replacements or spare parts or schedules a service visit quickly, etc., could be considered to offer Post-Benefit Convenience. A firm may invest in developing competencies in service recovery, not just covering up the initial glitch but imprinting a more positive impression on the customer by reducing anxiety levels.

Convenience, as a concept, is thus rich and varied in connotation and perception. A service which offers convenience in the dimension of subjective time in the Decision Convenience domain is different from one that offers convenience in the dimension of emotional effort in the Benefit Convenience domain. Both these services are convenient in some respects and inconvenient in some other respects. It seems ideal to offer the customer all dimensions of convenience in each and every domain. This could imply a prohibitively large amount of investment and costs in offering such a diverse range of conveniences. Interestingly, one form of convenience can trigger another form of inconvenience. For example, a technology-based solution for Transaction Convenience can trigger inconvenience in the form of increased anxiety for a technophobe. A quicker travel route through a troubled neighbourhood could be convenient on the time dimension but generate higher levels of anxiety. In addition, a convenience offered to one customer segment may inconvenience another segment. For example, a meet-and-greet service offered by an airline can quicken the journey of entitled passengers through immigration counters while others wait in long queues. These kinds of cross-interactions between different kinds of conveniences and perceptions of different customer segments need to be balanced while choosing the basket of convenience to offer. Perhaps instead of providing all kinds of convenience in all domains of customer experience, it may be worthwhile to understand which kind of convenience the target customer segment values most, and if that can be delivered without added inconvenience for everyone. Some of these conveniences could be offered by all competitors, and hence are merely hygiene factors which every firm has to provide. The identification of an unmet convenience need of the target segment is a valuable insight. The operations strategy of the firm would then be tailored to a basket of conveniences that are deemed to be a differentiator.

The basket of conveniences selected for delivery decides the kinds of investments that the firm would plan and the operational strategies it might adopt. Decisions need to be made in capacity (the number and penetration of branch networks and service stations, the staffing levels in call centres, whether capacity strategy should be Lead or Lag, etc.), facility (store layout that minimizes customer travel times, shelf layout which keeps items within easy reach; equipment like escalators, high speed elevators, etc., which reduce objective time, trolleys, comfortable seating, etc., which reduce physical effort; infotainment like TVs, newspapers, etc., which make the wait engaging, displays for service tokens which reduce cognitive load and anxiety; signage which reduces effort in finding the way, etc.), technology (call centres, CRM systems, interactive voice response systems, smartphone apps, chatbots, etc.), planning (availability of adequate service personnel, availability of repair and maintenance related inventory, time-tabling and scheduling, etc.), scope (partnerships with other service providers to provide service outside coverage area, etc.), workforce (skill level of service personnel, training of frontline service personnel as well as back office staff, performance management, incentive system, etc.), quality (monitoring of service quality, quality improvement, generation of ideas for better product design and marketing, etc.) and organization (extent of decentralization of decision-making to handle crisis situations on a real-time basis, extent to which service personnel can deviate from standard protocol to take care of customer needs and requests, etc.).

Since the dimension of convenience is so varied, different firms can provide different kinds of baskets of convenience with customers gravitating towards the basket that suits their preference. This insight may lead a firm to take a supply-driven orientation to the service system design for competing on convenience—build it and they will come. Another firm may take a view that while it is difficult to gather insight on unmet convenience needs it is much easier to just copy the convenience offerings of major competitors. If they offer TVs in waiting areas, so can we. The casualty of these approaches is the potential to truly offer personalized services, which comes from customer intimacy.

Note that there are two different types of convenience needs: universal and personal. Every person who stands in a queue for a long period of time would, to a greater or lesser extent, feel the urge to sit down. A queue management system may provide adequate seating space and issue tokens to incoming customers, thereby converting a physical queue into a logical one. The reduction of physical effort and mental anxiety would be universal. However, the old, the infirm, the sick, the physically challenged, the child, the obese, the pregnant woman, the lactating mother, etc., would have specific needs not shared with the general population. A visually challenged person may be unable to follow the display showing the token number to be served next, and a hearing-impaired person may be unable to hear the announcements. An airline which provides safety instructions to passengers in Braille provides convenience to the visually challenged segment of the population. A safety belt is a universal safety and convenience tool while an extension seat belt or child seat belt serves specific needs not shared by the general population. An airline which announces to passengers the languages spoken by the flight crew provides convenience to passengers who may be more conversant in languages other than English. An airline which mandates all flight attendants to learn sign language could be convenient for the hearing impaired.

It is relatively easier to provide for universal conveniences; the firm need not worry about segment preferences or demand projections. A flight with 200 seats requires 200 seat belts. Providing for specific personalized conveniences requires the airline to have an adequate number of extension seat belts, child seat belts and safety instruction cards in Braille on each flight. One way would be to forecast the distribution of demand for each item, determine a service level and keep adequate inventory on each plane. Another would be to make it compulsory for passengers requiring specialized services to disclose it at the time of booking and act on the information. The first option is static, it neither requires the firm to invest in visibility nor respond to specific needs. The static option can be handled with spare capacity or inventory. The second option is dynamic, it allows the firm to exactly match the need on each flight resulting in lowering of the spare inventory and hence fuel cost of each flight but perhaps incurring higher costs related to IT and logistics.

The static option for providing convenience serves universal convenience better and can be delivered through one-size-fits-all equipment. The static option is thus open to copying by competitors who can simply approach the equipment vendor and buy equipment with similar specifications. Over time, the conveniences delivered through the static option are likely to become standard offerings, and cease to be a differentiator. In contrast, the dynamic option requires the firm to invest in knowing individual customer needs and preferences and invest in internal processes meant to deliver the individual requirements. The dynamic capabilities gained are not really available for a competitor to purchase from a vendor and are a more sustainable source of competitive advantage.

It is only deeper engagement with customers which may reveal unarticulated needs. An airline may not offer a service to guide senior citizens through check-in, immigration, security and boarding formalities in the same way it provides the service for an unaccompanied minor. The senior citizen may feel so overwhelmed and confused about where to go and what to do inside an airport that he or she feels compelled to request for wheelchair assistance even when fully capable. Wheelchair assistance offers physical, cognitive and emotional effort reduction while the real need was perhaps only for a reduction of cognitive load in terms of better direction of next steps. In the absence of a deeper understanding of customer needs, the airline would invest in a static strategy of having more wheelchairs and unskilled personnel for pushing those wheelchairs rather than a dynamic strategy of technology-based identifying and tracking of senior citizens through airports.

Knowledge about customer needs and preferences is at the heart of a strategy to deliver convenience. But how does a firm gather this knowledge about its customer base? Investments in IT, which allow the firm to capture customer requirements and keep a history of previous interactions, are crucial. But more crucial is the clarity of *why* the firm covets the knowledge. IT investments are the tools for realizing the objective of Know Your Customer (KYC). Airlines may provide loyalty cards for incentivizing repeat purchase rather than for better service convenience through information on services requested and delivered. Banks and financial institutions may be carrying out KYC activities because they are mandated to do so rather than because they want to compete on service convenience. Knowing customer identity is just the first step to knowing their needs and preferences, a firm wishing to compete on service convenience must dig much deeper than this superficial characterization.

A firm which does not compete on service convenience would not feel the need to incur additional investments and costs in acquiring related capabilities.

One extreme way to know about customer preference is actually a very age-old one: Serve only one person. Devote your time to understanding the preferences and behaviour of this single person. The size of the customer segment, $N = 1$. This is perhaps the relationship between a master and a slave, an individual and a servant, maid or attendant, knight and his page, boss and secretary, detective and assistant, Holmes and Watson, Don Quixote and Sancho Panza, Wooster and Jeeves, Stevens and Lord Darlington. The institution of the valet or the butler brings this medieval relationship into the modern professional domain. A valet serves an individual, a butler takes care of a household. In the Kazuo Ishiguro novel *The Remains of the Day*, Stevens, the butler, selflessly serves not just Lord Darlington and Darlington Hall but is privy to the backstage political machinations in the run-up to the Second World War. Stevens values his dignity as a professional butler so much that he becomes insensitive to his own emotional and personal needs. Jeeves, the valet in the series of Jeeves novels by P.G. Wodehouse, is not just adept at solving all kinds of difficult situations, but his greatest ability is to correctly anticipate the behaviour of Wooster. Perhaps Jeeves understands Wooster more than Wooster does himself.

Mantra of Convenience: Anticipate Customer Need to Reduce Time and Effort

The institution of the valet or butler is feasible only for the aristocracy, the ultra-rich or the head of state. Can lesser mortals dream about having a Jeeves by their side? The fundamental nature of this need for a Jeeves reflects in the Japanese cartoon series *Doraemon*. Doraemon is a robotic cat from the future who helps young Nobita with all kinds of chores like doing homework so that Nobita can concentrate on more meaningful activities like chatting with love interest Shizuka. Doraemon is convenience personified, reaching into his pocket to bring out just the right tool needed to reduce lazy Nobita's time and effort. The basket of convenience represented by the range of tools emanating from Doraemon's small pocket seems unfathomable. The fact that Doraemon is a robot opens the doors to mass manufacturing of the hardware. The fact that the robotic system is run by a software which has the potential to learn from repeated interactions opens the door to customization. Oh how I wish I had a Doraemon!

Jeeves is aristocratic, Doraemon is plebeian. Jeeves is the past, Doraemon is the future. Jeeves is for the very top of the pyramid, Doraemon holds promise for the middle, if not the bottom. Jeeves is class, Doraemon is mass customization. The Jeeves strategy for delivering service convenience requires utmost care in selecting and training high-quality customer-facing service personnel. Growth of the firm is directly linked to the number of Jeeves-like personnel it has. Attrition of service personnel is the biggest challenge in a Jeeves firm. The Doraemon strategy of delivering service convenience depends on capturing the customer preferences and history of interactions in CRM systems, adoption of data analytics and Artificial Intelligence (AI) to learn patterns of interactions and automating some of the frequent responses in terms of service routines. The more these routines are standardized, the more unskilled personnel can be hired and trained according to a script to deliver a good enough convenience experience. A high attrition rate of service personnel can be managed if knowledge management systems are robust and training of new recruits can be quick and effective.

A firm which wants to be a Jeeves to a niche segment of customers trades off cost for convenience. While it cannot exploit economies of scale, it could reduce the cost somewhat through economies of scope. The small size of the niche segment does not allow large volumes, and hence the Jeeves firm is unlikely to reap economies of scale. Yet, the understanding of the needs and preferences of Wooster allows the firm to offer a range of services and hence spread its cost over a large variety of offerings. There is thus scope economies in gathering customer preference information, a fact that is not alien to social networking sites like Facebook and search giants like Google. Jeeves is perhaps so close to the customer that it does not need social media analytics to understand its customer. In contrast, a Doraemon firm is more likely to see value in Big Data and social media analytics than Jeeves. While the Doraemon firm is capable of achieving mass customization and can reap both economies of scale and scope, the quality of customization perhaps can never rival that of Jeeves, who has access to much richer information. Jeeves is high convenience at very high cost, Doraemon is good enough convenience at affordable cost.

A physical Doraemon for everyone is perhaps a distant future, but a digital Doraemon for everyone is already making its mark. Personal digital assistants like Alexa from Amazon or Siri from Apple lurk in the background listening to all conversations. AI algorithms start looking at patterns in the data and building personalized profiles. Learning from the data, the algorithm mutates and changes from a standard version to one customized for each individual user. The technology is already there, what remains is for us to become slaves to our digital Doraemons.

The ultimate test of whether a firm is successful in competing on convenience is whether the firm has entered the autopoiesis of the consumer. The repeated interactions between the consumer and service provider build trust and dependence and affect outcomes. The real value of Watson would be understood by Holmes if Watson is not around. Can he hire another assistant and be as effective as the Holmes–Watson team? The potential for synergy between Holmes and Watson, the consumer and the service provider, is the true source of value for convenience.

At its extreme, convenience can lead to addiction. Nobita can become so dependent on Doraemon that he cannot perform any activity without support from Doraemon. The existence of Nobita and Doraemon become intertwined, except for the fundamental asymmetry in the relationship. Doraemon can survive without Nobita, electing to serve Shizuka instead, for example. Nobita cannot. Stevens can get addicted to the self-set standard of dignity and professionalism, having no time left for himself and idle banter. Being a butler is so much a part of his autopoiesis that you wonder if he has a self otherwise. Watson too can get addicted to being Holmes's assistant, sacrificing his Sunday leisure for the convenience of Holmes. Convenience is asymmetric in relation—the convenience of having Watson by his side allows Holmes to play the violin while Watson would be left in his spare time to pick up his life in what remains of the day.

CHAPTER 15

Risk Minimization

'I guess the question I'm asked the most often is:
"When you were sitting in that capsule listening to the
countdown, how did you feel?" Well, the answer to
that one is easy. I felt exactly how you would feel if
you were getting ready to launch and knew you were
sitting on top of two million parts—all built by the
lowest bidder on a government contract.'

—Quote attributed to John Glenn, the first US
astronaut to orbit the Earth

'After all, you only find out who is swimming naked
when the tide goes out.'

—Warren Buffett, chairman's letter to
shareholders of Berkshire Hathaway Inc., 2002

THERE IS NO business without risk. That does not mean
that all businesses should focus on risk minimization as
their *main* objective. It is only in certain cases where the
risk of a catastrophic failure becomes predominant that
there is a need to explicitly focus on risk minimization.

Risk reduction entails additional costs. Carrying these additional costs would affect the cost-competitiveness of the firm in normal business scenarios. Not carrying these additional costs would render the firm fragile under extraordinary situations. So, for most businesses, risk management takes the form of a cost–benefit analysis where the additional cost of risk reduction is compared to the expected value of the benefit. For example, a firm is well advised to take fire insurance. The Insect focused on cutting costs may save the small amount in the insurance premium but risks closure of business if a fire devastates the factory. For more established firms, fire insurance premium may be a standard operating procedure and does not even merit a managerial decision. Hedging risks related to foreign currency exposure or input price volatility using forward and futures contracts may similarly be a standard operating procedure for treasury departments.

Risk is multidimensional. The first step in risk management is the identification of sources of risk. A firm is exposed to marketing risks that the consumer behaviour would suddenly change, rendering a mismatch between the customer needs and the products or services the firm offers and the resources it has invested in. A firm is exposed to production risks that the budgeted production quantity may not be produced due to breakdown of machinery or a strike called by the labour union, etc. A firm is exposed to project execution risks due to delay in land acquisition, granting of environmental clearance, etc. A firm is exposed to supply chain risks that its suppliers may default due to sudden shortages of raw materials, its distributors or wholesalers may default in paying on time, or it is hit by a bullwhip effect, etc. A firm is exposed to inventory risks related to low shelf life, obsolescence, theft, pilferage, etc. A firm is exposed to cyber security risks related to ransomware, theft of intellectual property, corporate espionage, etc. A firm is exposed to financial risks related to working capital management, foreign exchange exposure, loan repayment, etc. A firm is exposed to regulatory risk arising from sudden changes in rules of the game, alteration of taxation and depreciation-related rules, imposition of retrospective penalties, etc. A firm is exposed to political risks, civil unrest, geopolitical risks associated with working in a diverse set of countries, and outbreak of war. A firm is exposed to acts of God like accidents, extreme weather situations, spread of epidemics and natural disasters. The list is endless.

The first reaction to this endless list is a feeling of numbness. If we have to minimize risk, where do we start? We begin by understanding that whatever be the source of risk, the nature of risk can be classified in terms of Subway, Coconuts and Black Swans.

Spyros Makridakis, Robin Hogarth and Anil Gaba introduced us to Subway Uncertainty and Coconut Uncertainty. Imagine you travel by the suburban transport system to reach your office every day. The transport system could be a metro train or a carpool or any other means of transport. Since the origin and destination locations are fixed, over time you develop a good idea of the time taken by you to reach the office, say an hour on average. You should then start an hour before office time. But wait, one hour is just an average estimate. Sometimes the train is late, sometimes the tracks are waterlogged, sometimes there are malfunctions in the coach, sometimes there is so much rush that you are unable to board, sometimes trains are cancelled, sometimes there are suicide attempts, sometimes the journey is uneventful and on time. The commute time as a result is thus perhaps best described by a normal probability distribution with one hour as the distribution mean rather than a point estimate. Since the normal distribution is asymptotic, it implies that on most occasions the commute time is between 3 sigma limits, but there is a non-zero probability that you might be extremely late. This risk of reaching office late due to uncertainty inherent in using the subway is a Subway Risk.

Let us say you have worked diligently in the office for a year and plan a vacation in a seaside resort. Imagine yourself relaxing by the seashore and sipping coconut water. And suddenly a coconut falls on your head. Didn't see that coming, did you? Well, that's what is called Coconut Risk. It doesn't happen every day that a vacationer relaxing under a coconut tree gets hit on the head. But can it not happen? Coconuts do fall to the ground. And they fall to the ground every day. It just so happened that your head was in the way. Tough luck.

Subway Risks are fundamentally different from Coconut Risks. Coconut Risks exist when the underlying event is a rare event best described by the Poisson distribution. An earthquake striking a specific place at a specific time is a rare event. Modelling it as a Poisson event implies that the probability of the earthquake occurrence is constant over every time period (t, t+Δt), and the probability of a second earthquake within the same time period is zero. This gives rise to the memoryless property of the Poisson distribution. The fact that an earthquake has not happened for the last one year does not make it more or less probable than if it has not happened for the last century. Subway Risks, in contrast, are not based on rare events. The normal distribution does not model rare events; it models—surprise, surprise—'normal' events.

The differentiation of risk based on normal or rare conditions is very insightful. The tide goes out twice every day. The tide also goes out just before a tsunami hits the shore. The way we should react to these two situations is quite different. We may have a hearty laugh when the tide goes out under normal conditions and reveals a naked swimmer. If the tide goes out at an unnatural time and the sea recedes to the horizon, naked swimmers should be the least of our preoccupations. We should warn all swimmers, clothed or naked, to run for their lives towards high ground. You are a fool if you have not taken precautions about Subway Risks and choose to go swimming naked. You are a fool to think you have adequate protection due to your swimming costume when the sea recedes abruptly. You must be quick to scamper to safety when the Coconut Risk emerges without bothering if either you or others are naked.

To manage Subway Risks, firms resort to keeping a cushion as buffer from the uncertainty. This buffer may take the form of safety time. In the subway example, you might start from home one and a half hours before the start of office. The extra thirty minutes is the safety time to cover uncertainties. The buffer may take the form of safety stocks to cushion against variabilities of demand and supply. The buffer may take the form of safety capacity like an IT services firm keeping engineers on the bench to serve sudden requirements. How much safety time or stock or capacity needs to be maintained depends on the service level desired by the firm. Techniques of cost–benefit analysis like Implied Backorder Costing allows firms to compare the cost of stock-outs with the benefits from stocking an additional unit to evaluate the service level to operate at, and the resultant safety stock to maintain. Risk is traded off with cost to arrive at an agreeable risk at an agreeable cost to the firm.

Keeping safety stock may not be the right approach to managing Coconut Risks for two main reasons. First, the nature of the rare event implies that there would be a large number of time periods where there would be no instance of the event and only a few time periods which require safety stocks. *When* it rains, it pours. An average safety stock calculated as an expected value may be too small to serve the needs of the rare rainy day, while burdening the other days with unnecessary safety stocks. Second, there are far too many Coconut Risks. You may take protection against a fire but get hit by a cyclone. You may take protection against fire and cyclone and get hit by an earthquake. You may take protection against fire, cyclone and earthquake and get hit by a meteorite. How many Coconut Risks would you cover? And if you need to keep safety stocks for each independent rare event, you may be burdened with so much safety stock that it affects your cost competitiveness.

The way to handle Coconut Risks is best illustrated with the story of the old Japanese man who saved his villagers from a tsunami following an earthquake. The old man had a farm located on a hillside overlooking the village by the seashore. He felt the earthquake and saw the villagers venturing into the exposed seabed as the sea receded to the horizon. He had never experienced this earlier but remembered an old story. The old man quickly set fire to the rice fields and the villagers rushed back on seeing the flames from a distance and were saved from the tsunami.

Notice several elements of this story. The old man was situated at a height and could see further than the villagers. While he had not experienced a tsunami himself, he remembered a story about a previous tsunami. He could sense an anomaly and realized the need for a quick response. He understood that a fire potentially devastating the village was a greater pull than the curiosity of exploring the receding coastline.

Sensing the anomaly is the first step and may seem trivial. An anomaly is apparent only in contrast to the normal. The sea recedes during low tide twice every day, but the sea receding significantly before a tsunami is an anomaly which is apparent only to those who have experience of the normal receding. The problem is compounded if the picture of normalcy, and hence an anomaly, is fragmented due to the presence of multiple observers, each privy to only a small part of the bigger picture. One malfunctioning valve or inactive sensor in one section of a plant or one faulty gauge in a control room or one novice or overworked or distracted operator can have cascading effects with disastrous consequences. In High Reliability Organizations (HROs), investments in processes for sensing an anomaly and effective communication are perhaps the most important part of risk reduction.

An upstream supplier in a supply chain may serve demand from firms which are competitors. The demand from these suppliers could be uncorrelated under normal circumstances but could be highly correlated during rare boom and bust periods. In addition, supplier capacity shortage may result in shortage-gaming, and disconnect ordering quantities of downstream firms from real consumer demand. The upstream supplier is thus similar to the old man who is in a vantage position to understand that the increased ordering from downstream firms is not normal; it is an artificial demand which can collapse any time. But merely sensing the anomaly does not imply the disaster can be averted unless the risk is mitigated. If the upstream supplier does not take adequate precautions in terms of insisting on advance payments from customers or tightening contract terms to pass on the inventory risk to downstream firms, it can go bankrupt when the bust hits the downstream firms, unleashing an enormous bullwhip effect. But should the upstream firm just be content with reducing its own risk or does it have a moral obligation to communicate to downstream firms that the extent of over-ordering may not be justified by consumer demand growth and hence a bust is expected anytime soon?

The way to handle Coconut Risks is through quick response rather than safety stocks. Quick response is possible when the firm is able to anticipate the impact of the rare event even though it may not anticipate *when* the rare event would occur. Quick response implies a clear understanding of the steps to be taken in preparation or during the aftermath of the rare event. These steps could be based on learnings from previous occasions of effective or ineffective handling of the rare event. The learnings could be distilled formally as standard operating procedures or informally as organizational storytelling. Stories of how seniors handled different kinds of rare events should thus be an important part of management training. When a coconut hits you on the head, there is little capability left to think. The thinking about what to do when a coconut hits has to be done prior to the event. A rare event may also temporarily cut off communication between the different parts of the firm and hence the knowledge of steps to be carried out has to be decentralized rather than centralized at the headquarters.

Keeping safety stocks or detailing standard operating procedures to handle rare events are both ineffectual when it comes to handling Black Swan events, a term coined by Nassim Nicholas Taleb. Black swans are not rare events. A meteorite hitting the earth is rare but meteorites are known to hit the earth. It is a known unknown since the event is known but its occurrence details are difficult to predict. In contrast, a Black Swan event is an unknown unknown. How can we prepare a standard operating procedure for an unknown unknown? Since human beings have not experienced it before, there is no possibility of storytelling either. You are thus completely exposed to the risk of the Black Swan event. The good thing (for you, but bad for the economy) is that all your competitors too are equally exposed. However, a firm with a rich repository of standard operating procedures or stories related to handling Coconut Risks may be in a better position to evaluate the impact of the Black Swan event once it happens. While the event itself is unknown, the kind of impact it creates could be similar to a known Coconut Risk, allowing a firm to take appropriate risk mitigation steps. So, instead of worrying about Black Swans, we can better prepare ourselves for Subway and Coconut Risks.

For each of the sources of risk identified earlier, we should evaluate if the risk emanates from normal conditions or from rare events. Risk of civil unrest may be a Coconut Risk in a developed country with stable economic and political conditions, while it may be a Subway Risk in an underdeveloped country with deep racial, political or ideological fault lines and a history of uprisings. An inventory risk faced by a firm could be a Subway Risk for a commodity supplier in a stable demand context and a Coconut Risk for a firm selling high-fashion fads. A coconut hitting your head is not a Coconut Risk if you had selected to sleep under a coconut tree during high winds.

The risk mitigation strategy would vary depending on the kind of underlying condition from which risk emanates. For Black Swan events and extremely rare Coconut Risks perhaps the best strategy is to ignore the possibility. For standard Coconut Risks like fire, the mitigation strategy may be to instil standard operating procedures to minimize occurrence, and quick reaction in case of occurrence, as well as taking an insurance policy to compensate for the loss, if any. For company- or sector-specific Coconut Risks, there may be no firm offering insurance, making it necessary to build a culture of risk avoidance and quick response. For Subway Risks, investments need to be made in safety stocks, safety capacity or safety time to balance cost of disruption with cost of investments.

Mantra of Risk Minimization: Invest in Redundancies, Train for Contingencies; Just in Case . . .

The risk minimization exercise till now is indistinguishable from cost minimization. The reason is that the premium paid for insurance is commensurate to the expected cost of a rare event. The investments in safety stocks are commensurate to the cost of a lost sales. What we are essentially doing is replacing a low-probability, high-impact event by a certain but low-cost option. This is still the language of the Elephant. The Elephant de-risking its operations is fundamentally different from the risk-reduction initiatives of a Tortoise.

A Tortoise carries its home on its back all the time. Its operations surely could have been much more efficient if that load was off its back. The Tortoise is not time responsive. Instead of trying to outrun its predators, the Tortoise retreats into its shell. The shell of the Tortoise does not allow efficient or time-responsive operations and is essentially a risk-reduction tool.

Who is a Tortoise? Risk minimization is essential for firms which handle extraordinary situations on a day-to-day basis. A firm generating nuclear power, a department handling the cyber security of a large bank, a counterintelligence unit or an organization launching a manned mission into space have a much more heightened risk profile than ordinary businesses. Risk minimization in such circumstances is much more complex than hedging the risk or taking an insurance. A firm may face a sudden rise in raw material prices due to a demand–supply imbalance caused by a natural calamity hitting its suppliers. The firm can financially hedge the risk by writing suitable contracts in forward and futures markets, but these contracts do not solve the supply chain manager's problem of sourcing raw materials to

keep the factory running. The contract size in forward
and future markets may be quite small compared to the
monthly raw material requirement, since the markets are
meant for managing price risk rather than supply volume
risk. The firm which has no option but to keep its factory
running, perhaps because it supplies an essential product
during a war, and simultaneously faces high volatility in
raw material availability, needs to behave as a Tortoise.
Similarly, insurance is just a financial tool to compensate
the firm. It does not alter the activities and processes
that either give rise to or affect the risk. Insurance as a
concept is meaningless for the manager of the nuclear
power plant since failure is not an option. A manager of a
normal business who has taken fire insurance may order
immediate evacuation in case of a fire, the commander
of a nuclear-powered submarine could sacrifice lives in a
desperate bid to contain a larger civilian fallout. Tortoises
are the firms which have no option but to sleep under a
bunch of coconut trees in a windy location.

The heightened risk perception means that Tortoises
take precautions which may be deemed unnecessary
by Elephants. The safety precautions are not based on
cost–benefit analyses but on making the risk as low as
possible, even if that means incurring significant extra
costs. The Tortoise system is built to have redundancies.
The Tortoise would have not just a back-up generator
to reduce a risk of a power outage but even a back-up
generator of the back-up generator. If a subsystem fails, the
containment mechanism has to be in-built so that overall
system performance is unaffected. Individual parts of the
system may have performance, reliability and durability
specifications which are excessive for an Elephant. These

parts may require to be individually tested and certified for operations in extreme environmental conditions. The employees may need background checks and pass physical and emotional stress tests at regular intervals.

A Tortoise may reduce risks by risk-sharing. A large financial risk may be divided between a set of partners who share the risks and rewards. As a result, the stress on an individual firm's balance sheet can be reduced. Different firms may have different capabilities of handling risks of different kinds. So, by prudent selection of partners in a coalition, the marketing risks can be transferred to a partner more capable of handling marketing risks while production risks remain with the partner who is strong in handling production risks.

A Tortoise firm has a culture which is distinctive. This may include a companywide attitude towards risk reduction. The firm may adopt proactive tools like Failure Mode and Effects Analysis (FMEA) to identify potential risks and take pre-emptive actions. It may also encourage reactive tools like early detection of mistakes so that corrective actions can be quickly performed. The more complex the product or service, larger the number of inter-departmental linkages, and hence the cost of hiding a mistake is higher. Bad news needs to percolate quickly across hierarchy and departmental boundaries rather than be confined in silos. This is all the more challenging as the highly sensitive nature of work may require sharing of information on a need-to-know basis. The Tortoise needs a problem-solving orientation rather than one of shooting the messenger. It may require designing a reporting structure such that there are checks and balances so that an individual or a specific group cannot run amok. Audit functions may be strengthened to perform not just cost audits but also technical, quality, security and forensic audits. The Tortoise cannot take a transaction orientation to vendor management and award supply contracts on lowest cost basis. Instead, they need to prune their vendor list and develop a partnership orientation towards a select group of capable suppliers and instil a culture of risk reduction. At the other end of the spectrum, the Tortoise partnering with a single supplier for a critical component could de-risk itself by adopting dual sourcing.

The culture existing in a Tortoise system is different from the culture existing in a bureaucratic system where each and every employee acts like a Tortoise. Government organizations may go overboard in their bid to reduce corruption and install very strict and widespread vigilance systems. Corruption can potentially thrive in any nook and corner of a government department and hence the vigilance department can have sweeping visibility and jurisdiction. At its worst, the vigilance department may degenerate into vigilance terrorism, instilling so much fear in the mind of employees that no one wants to try anything new in the fear that some stupid bureaucratic rule may be deemed to have been violated. Who wants their pension to be withheld at the time of retirement and an inquiry commissioned for a supposed innovative experiment which was attempted by a young, idealistic employee decades ago? Would the old man in the tsunami story take the risk of setting fire to the rice fields if he was likely to be served a show cause notice after a few years for the destruction of property? Every employee may wish to reduce perceived risk and sacrifice initiative and innovation in the process. The saddest part of this culture is that the risk reduction orientation of a collection of employees in a bureaucratic organization does not result in risk reduction for the organization. A collection of Tortoise employees may not be a Tortoise system.

Learning from past mistakes and innovating based on these learnings is very important for a Tortoise since mistakes are very costly. Instead of mere organizational stories in Elephants, Tortoises need formal studies to document and learn from mistakes. In many cases, the failure of a Tortoise is analysed by industry watchdogs to generate learning for all firms in that industry. Airline mishaps are analysed by specialized agencies to derive the root cause and suggest precautionary measures for all airlines. The search for the black box of a crashed aircraft holds no prospect for the passengers of the ill-fated flight but is invaluable for future air safety. The design of the black box is also a very good example of a Tortoise design as it ensures that precious data can be salvaged even under extreme conditions. In some cases, learnings from disasters have implications not just for the specific industry but also for all organizations. The pioneering study by Karl Weick of the Mann Gulch fire disaster helped in a better understanding of the breakdown of sense-making in an organization. The analysis of the launch decision leading to the Challenger Space Shuttle disaster threw light on group processes.

A fundamental insight in handling risks is that risks can be transferred from one dimension to another. For example, sharing financial risk among partners may reduce financial risk but increase coordination risks among partners. Marketing risks can be reduced by offering multiple product options to customers but this increases manufacturing and supply chain complexity and risks. Since business is essentially risky, there is an irreducible amount of risk that a firm has to carry. If a marketing manager keeps on reducing marketing risks, then after a point this is only possible if some other dimension of risk goes up. Even worse, the marketing manager may not even know which kind of risk is increasing and in which functional area. Thus, instead of individual functional managers reducing risks in their own silos, risk reduction needs a systemic approach at an organizational level.

The phenomenon of transfer of risk from one dimension to another is both a challenge and an opportunity. Think carefully. If risk can be transferred, why don't we *choose* which kind of risk we would like to manage? The strategy of the Tortoise is to invest in risk mitigation for the *chosen* dimension.

A firm which has invested in redundancies and risk management practices in the manufacturing department may thus take a strategic call to transfer the financial and marketing risks to manufacturing risk. As a result, the firm does not need to build redundancies and risk reduction practices all over the firm but concentrate them into a part that it feels is strong enough to bear the risk. A firm may choose to manage market risks through a highly capable sales and marketing organization and outsource production. However, note that since the risks are being transferred and concentrated in one or a few functional areas, investments in risk reduction need to be scaled up in the chosen areas so that any catastrophic failure is avoided.

Each of these risk-reduction initiatives has a time and cost implication. It would be a crime to benchmark the cost efficiency of a Tortoise with that of an Elephant or its time responsiveness with that of a Cheetah. The project manager in a space programme tasked with launching an astronaut into orbit has a responsibility to launch on time and within budget but also a greater responsibility to bring the astronaut safely back. Time overruns or cost overruns cannot override safety concerns, even if they are deemed inconsequential. In case of failure, no one would appreciate that the launch was as per schedule or laud the manager on cost efficiency. A failure may be catastrophic not just for the crew but also affect public opinion, jeopardize government funding, demoralize the workforce and push back future projects. It is only by being a Tortoise that the manager in such a firm can have a clear conscience and sleep peacefully at night. So, while superpowers may engage in a race to explore space, instead of the Cheetah it is the slow and steady Tortoise that wins this race. If you had earlier marvelled at the beauty of the Cheetah, appreciate the beauty of the Tortoise too.

CHAPTER 16

Flexibility

'And on the pedestal these words appear:
"My name is Ozymandias, king of kings:
Look on my works, ye Mighty, and despair!"
Nothing beside remains. Round the decay
Of that colossal wreck, boundless and bare
The lone and level sands stretch far away.'

—*Ozymandias*, Percy Bysshe Shelley

'A cat has nine lives.'

—English Proverb

A CAT HAS just one life. It also has the capability to land on its feet while falling from a height. The cat accomplishes this through a well-developed vestibular system allowing it to make gyroscopic movements whereby it is able to orient its feet towards the ground whatever be the initial orientation at the start of the fall. It anticipates the impact of landing and arches the back and flexes the muscles of the back and feet. It is not that cats are never injured or never die from a fall. They may suffer shock, thoracic injuries and broken bones but the injuries are spread across all limbs rather than concentrated in the head and legs like in human beings. A human rarely escapes death if falling from more than six storeys on to a concrete surface, but cats are known to survive falls from skyscrapers. Our intuition says that the greater the height, higher should be the incidences of injury and mortality. This intuition is correct for humans but not for cats. The injury and mortality rates for cats are an inverted U-shape with a peak around seven storeys and they decrease with increasing height after the peak! That is eerie. How is that possible?

A cat reaches terminal velocity of 60 miles per hour much earlier than a human attains terminal velocity of 120 miles per hour. During the initial acceleration stage of the fall, the cat spreads its limbs downwards but then relaxes and spreads them horizontally after terminal velocity is reached. The fluffy cat thus increases drag and acts like a natural parachute if it is falling from a greater height. A fall from a smaller height is comparatively riskier as the cat may not have had adequate time to react.

A cat can walk away from a fall which other animals cannot survive. It is this survivability from a fall that credits a cat with nine lives. Business firms, whether Elephants or Cheetahs, need to be flexible to survive drastic changes in business environment and a fall in their fortunes. A firm which has flexibility is likely to survive from firm-specific issues or industry-level challenges or global economic downturns.

Survivability is an aspiration for any business. The hallmark of a good business is that it should stand the test of time. Test of time—oh, what a beautiful idiom.

Immortality is the nectar that we humans have always thirsted for. Faced with the bitter truth of our mortality, we strive relentlessly to create something of value that would outlive us. A poet strives through poetry, an artist through art, a king through empire-building, an industrialist through an industrial empire and the ordinary manager, let us not forget him, through a flexibility strategy! Don't laugh at the manager for trying to join an august group. Don't laugh at the august group as they earnestly try to mock the divine with their aspirations of creating something timeless. Leave it to Mighty Time to laugh at Ozymandias.

Reciting *Ozymandias* to investor queries regarding survivability is ill-advised. I therefore ask you to take inspiration from Sisyphus, eternally repeating the act of pushing a large boulder up a steep hill only to have it roll down again. Invest in building flexibility in the system, knowing fully well the futility of it all. In the long run, all our efforts would be laughed at by Time. In the short run, we develop our vestibular systems, fine-tune our gyroscopic movements, fatten the pads in our feet, and flex our muscles in anticipation and hope of surviving a few falls.

Flexibility is one of the four major performance dimensions of a system, the others being cost, time and quality. It is also the dimension that is least understood. The difficulty stems from the fact that the dimension of flexibility differs from the others since it is rarely a dimension of competition. A firm may win customers by offering a lower cost or by delivering on time or by offering a better product. In all these three dimensions, the firm competes with other firms based on its cost, time or quality performance. In contrast, flexibility allows a firm to respond to uncertainties in business environment. In a sense, it is fighting more against changes brought about by Time rather than competitors. The same changes may not equally affect all competitors. The flexible firm outperforms the competitors since it adapts better to changed circumstances. While this may outwardly reflect in better value proposition to the customer relative to competition, the source is not an external competitive benchmarking but an assessment of impact of potential shifts in business environments on internal processes and proactive investments in capability to handle the impact.

What could be some of these changes? Consumer behaviour may change over time, either increasing or decreasing substantially the volume of products to be produced. The consumer may have earlier been happy with uniform, standardized products but may start valuing the ability to choose from a larger and larger assortment of products customized to her needs. The pace of introduction of new products may quicken due to technological progress. The extent of product proliferation can change as products move through their life cycles. The product characteristics may need modifications as consumer preferences change. The raw material inputs may require to be changed as technologies evolve, demand–supply equilibriums shift and farming practices change in response to climate change. The supply network could change as upstream suppliers and downstream distributors experience temporary or permanent disruptions in their own business.

It is not really change that is the main challenge here, it is the uncertainty regarding the change. Projected changes in consumer behaviour or technological progress may not fructify. Surprises could be both positive or negative. The economic environment may suddenly deteriorate, resulting in an unforeseen credit squeeze and hurt capacity expansion plans. A technological progress in a related field may spill over to a new industry sector, resulting in disruption of the existing players. A change known with certainty is easier to plan for than changes brought about by uncertainties.

Flexibility is the investment in a system needed to respond to external and internal uncertainties. Each of the different types of uncertainties requires the firm to strive for different types of flexibilities. Seven different types of flexibilities have been identified in literature, as outlined by Donald Gerwin. A firm needs Volume Flexibility to respond to uncertainties in quantity of customer demand and needs Variety Flexibility to respond to uncertainties regarding changes in customer expectations about the variety available to the customer to choose from. A firm needs Changeover Flexibility to stop producing a product and retool and develop suppliers to change over to a new product. A firm needs Modification Flexibility to change design specifications and add features. A firm needs Material Flexibility to handle temporary and permanent sourcing disruptions. It needs Rerouting Flexibility to reallocate work if a machine breaks down, a supplier goes bankrupt or a distributor ceases operations. The need for each of these six types of flexibility may also change over time, resulting in the need of a meta-flexibility called Flexibility of Flexibilities.

Table 2: Dimensions of Flexibility

Type of Uncertainty	Strategic Objective	Flexibility Dimension
Market acceptance of kinds of products	Diverse product line	Mix
Length of product life cycles	Product innovation	Changeover
Specific product characteristics	Responsiveness to customers' specs	Modification
Aggregate product demand	Market share	Volume
Machine downtime	Customers' due dates	Rerouting
Characteristics of materials	Product quality	Material
Changes in the above uncertainties	Strategic adaptability	Flexibility responsiveness

Source: Gerwin, D. (1993). Manufacturing Flexibility: A Strategic Perspective. *Management Science*, 39(4), 395–410.

To illustrate how a firm uses flexibility to handle uncertainties, consider the design philosophy of Cellular Manufacturing. A Nagare Cell design allows a firm to handle Volume Flexibility. Consider a product which requires three activities of duration 2 minutes, 3 minutes and 5 minutes in three workstations. If 1 worker is assigned to do all three activities, then the cycle time is 10 minutes, resulting in an output rate of 6 per hour. If 3 workers are assigned, then the cycle time is 5 minutes, resulting in an output of 12 per hour. With 2 workers, the cycle time is dependent on the assignment of workers to workstations, and could be 5 minutes, 7 minutes or

8 minutes. The resulting output rates are 12, 8.57 and 7.5 units per hour respectively. Thus, the output rate of the cell can be varied from 6 to 12 units per hour with intermediate steps of 7.5 and 8.57 units per hour by simply adding or removing workers to the cell and changing their work assignments.

I have found students to instinctively try to design the cell to maximize output from the cell. For the two-worker situation, the students would discard the cycle times of 7 and 8 minutes as inefficient use of resources since they can achieve a lower cycle time of 5 minutes with the same amount of resources. This is the fundamental difference between an output maximization mindset and a flexibility maximization mindset. The objective of the cell design is *not* to maximize output, if we wanted that we could have simply designed a traditional assembly line. The objective of cell design is to *match* the demand rate of the customer with the supply rate of the factory. When the demand falls, the output rate is brought down by reducing workers from the cell. When the demand rate goes up, the output rate is increased by assigning more workers to the cell. The closeness of the matching depends on the number of intermediate steps of output that the cell can produce. A cell with a higher number of intermediate output rates would be able to closely match the demand and supply rates.

Think of the cell as performing the function of the regulator of a ceiling fan. The regulator controls the fan speed over a range of speeds and can have discrete intermediate settings. Why do we need a regulator for a fan? If the room temperature is constantly high, then we can remove the regulator and always run the fan at a constant high speed. The need of a regulator comes from the inherent fluctuations in room temperature between day and night and across seasons. The regulator makes the fan flexible to uncertainties of ambient temperature. The need for a regulator is directly connected to the volatility of the environment. The value of flexibility is similarly related to the extent of uncertainty in the business environment. It would be foolish to invest in flexibility if the environment is certain and foolish not to invest if the environment is uncertain.

What have we achieved by the cell design? We have invested in flexibility to match demand between 6 and 12 units per hour. We may not be able to accurately predict or control the uncertainties in the business environment, but whatever be the changed demand we would be able to match it *as long as* it lies between 6 and 12 units per hour. Whatever the initial orientation of the cat, the final condition is that it always lands on its feet, *as long as* it has enough time to reorient. A system is flexible within a boundary. Comparing systems on flexibility requires a comparison of the boundaries. It is easy to see that a system flexible over a wider range of parameter values is more flexible. A cell which can be designed to match demand between 4 and 16 units per hour is more flexible than a cell which can handle demand between 6 and 12 units per hour. However, range is not the only measure of flexibility. How quickly the firm can move from 6 to 12 units per hour and whether the quality defect rate increases when output rate increases are also measures of flexibility.

On each of the seven dimensions of flexibility, the performance of the firm can be evaluated on three sub-dimensions: Range, Mobility and Uniformity. A firm investing in the Range sub-dimension of Variety Flexibility implies that the firm chooses to offer the customer a large range of products to choose from. A firm offering a choice of ten varieties is more flexible than a firm offering five varieties. The firm choosing the Range sub-dimension of Variety Flexibility would need to invest in machines which can produce a large number of product variants. It cannot afford to invest in dedicated machines or facilities which produce one or only a few products. It needs to hire manpower with higher skill levels or train operators to produce a wider variety of products. Such a firm would value economies of scope more than economies of scale. Another firm may choose to be flexible on the Mobility sub-dimension of Variety Flexibility. This firm may produce only five variants but may have invested in machines with smaller set-up times and trained its workers to reduce set-up times. A firm with a set-up time of five minutes is thus more flexible than a firm with a set-up time of ten minutes. To achieve Mobility, a firm may invest in Single Minute Exchange of Dies (SMED) practices and divide the set-up time into online and offline set-ups and perform the offline set-up in parallel while the machine is producing the earlier batch. A third firm may choose to value uniformity of yield across variants more than either range or mobility. A firm with a lower rate of quality defects across a given range of five varieties is more flexible than a firm which can produce the ten varieties but struggles to do so, resulting in higher defect rates. Uniformity on quality may require purchasing machines and equipment with invariant quality characteristics over a large range of operating environments and raw material inputs.

Suppose there are three firms, A, B and C. A chooses to produce ten varieties but needs ten minutes to change from one variety to another and has a defect rate of 10 per cent. B chooses to restrict to five varieties but needs only five minutes to change from one variety to another and has a defect rate of 15 per cent. C produces four varieties only and needs seven minutes to change from one variety to another, but its defect rate is only 2 per cent across all varieties. Which firm is more flexible? Confused?

David M. Upton pointed out that managers may understand they need to be flexible but may have no idea which kind of flexibility they need to invest in. In our example, all three firms may believe that they are flexible. Firm A has chosen to be flexible on the Range sub-dimension of Variety Flexibility while firm B has chosen the Mobility sub-dimension of Range Flexibility while firm C has chosen the Uniformity sub-dimension of Range Flexibility. All of them are flexible, but in different ways. All of them are inflexible, but in different ways.

Seven dimensions of flexibility and three sub-dimensions for each dimension imply that there would be a total of twenty-one different kinds of flexibility. The investments needed to be flexible in one type of flexibility may not deliver another kind of flexibility. For example, to improve the Range sub-dimension of Rerouting Flexibility, the firm needs to add suppliers, while to improve the Range sub-dimension of Volume Flexibility, the firm needs to add capacity to handle an increasing peak requirement. Even worse, increasing flexibility in one sub-dimension may impede flexibility in another sub-dimension. For example, a modification made to a machine to produce a product with specifications outside the range specified by the machine tool manufacturer may result in increased defect rates for all or some of the products. The firm has sacrificed Uniformity in its effort to increase Range in Variety Flexibility.

Investing in flexibility is thus a strategic call. It is very important for a firm to determine what kind of flexibility is more important to the firm rather than indiscriminately invest in flexibility. The choice of flexibility dimension needs to be based on changing trends in external or internal environment. Note that four of the flexibility dimensions are related to the demand side (Volume, Variety, Modification, Changeover) while two are supply side (Material, Rerouting). The demand-side flexibility dimensions require an understanding of uncertainties related to the changing needs of the customer and differentiating between the order winners and order qualifiers in the most likely changed scenario. The sales and marketing functions are best placed to answer what kind of demand flexibility would be best appreciated by customers. The supply-side flexibility dimensions require an understanding of potential volatility of input price and availability due to demand–supply imbalances, technological changes and capacity additions or deletions in upstream supplier industries. The operations and supply chain functions are best placed to answer what kind of supply flexibility would be essential in the future. The flexibility strategy of a firm is thus cross-functional in nature. There is little value in investing in supply-side flexibility which does not support the changed customer needs, and there is little value in investing in demand-side flexibility if the firm and the supplier base would not be able to respond to requirements due to changed circumstances.

The flexibility strategy needs to also be forward-looking rather than a strategy for meeting current customer needs and dealing with competition. Understanding the current needs of current customers may not necessarily provide insights on who could be the new customers in the future or what could be new needs of existing customers. Understanding the current capabilities of the supply chain may not necessarily mean that the firm has insight on how new technologies may render obsolete the capabilities. The flexibility strategy needs the top leadership to engage in horizon scanning and spot trends in advance, deduce the key dimensions of those uncertainties that seem to stand out against the innumerable uncertainties that a future holds, and invest in equipment, processes, training, collaborations, etc., to build capability to effectively respond in case the anticipated scenario unfolds.

Mantra of Flexibility: Anticipate Key Future Uncertainties and Build Requisite Capabilities

---

Till now, we have looked at flexibility as a response to environmental uncertainties. A firm can itself be the source of environmental uncertainty for its competitors by bringing about disruptive changes through pioneering new technologies and innovations. These innovations could be product related, process related, supply chain related or related to business models. Innovations by pioneering firms further accelerate investments in new technological domains by competitors and new entrants and change consumer expectations. Innovation is a prime source of uncertainty and the innovative firm keeps the competitors in catch-up mode while itself having a better visibility of the internal product development pipeline. For example, firms in the high-fashion garments sector may be more concerned about reacting to fashion trends and would benefit if the uncertainties regarding fashion trends reduce. In contrast, a firm which uses its internal capabilities to quicken the fashion trends by launching new trendsetters at regular intervals actually increases uncertainties for everyone else.

It is very difficult to discern if a firm has enough flexibility. Benchmarking with peers may be erroneous since the real test of flexibility is the test of time. The extent of difficulty is palpable when you examine the Flexibility of Flexibilities dimension. This meta-flexibility dimension aims to handle the uncertainty about the kind of uncertainties that would bother the firm in future. The term 'Uncertainty of Uncertainties' sounds kind of cute, but it may be difficult to comprehend. I am uncertain about my ability to explain 'Uncertainty of Uncertainties' in the environment that requires the firm to have Flexibility of Flexibilities, but let me try.

First, we need to understand the difference between risk and uncertainty. Risk is measurable, uncertainty is not. In risk, the possible outcomes of an action (or inaction) are known; in the case of uncertainties, the outcomes are unknown. If a fair coin is tossed, the outcomes (head, tail) and the associated probabilities are known. There would be a known risk associated with calling 'head'. In contrast, in uncertainty, since the outcomes cannot be predicted, the underlying probability distribution of the outcomes is unknown.

In the chapter 'Risk Minimization', we discussed the differences between Subway Risks and Coconut Risks and how firms can deal with such risks. Subway Risks are based on an underlying normal distribution, while Coconut Risks are best described by distributions like the Poisson distribution which model rare events. Thus, both for Subway and Coconut Risks we have some idea about the underlying probability distributions of the outcomes. In contrast, in this chapter on flexibility, we have no knowledge of the underlying probability distribution of Volume Flexibility or Modification Flexibility. We just know that the firm faces uncertainty on volume and at best we can specify a range over which the volume may fluctuate. Of course, specifying a range implies that some knowledge of or practical limits to the maximum and minimum values is possible even when we admit that we have no knowledge of the underlying probability distribution. A cellular design allows a firm to handle any volume uncertainty as long as the demand fluctuations fall within the range for which the cell is designed. But, the ability to handle volume uncertainty may not allow us to handle other kinds of uncertainties.

The Uncertainty of Uncertainties situation is thus a very broad set of uncertainties where very little is known about the kind of contingency the firm has to handle in future. It may suddenly have to move from an environment characterized by high demand uncertainty but low supply side uncertainty to one with low demand uncertainty and high supply uncertainty. The situational context may be such that there is so much confusion around that nothing is known with certainty. The situation could be changing very quickly and could affect the firm, its customers, suppliers, and even larger ecosystem players like bankers, regulators, governments, etc. At its extreme, sense-making may disintegrate and the firm may face an existential crisis.

What exactly is an existential crisis? Consider a group of smokejumpers—able-bodied fearless firefighters who fight forest fires after parachuting into the area. Consider the group walking in a line towards the forest fire in a mountainous region with deep ravines. They had a bumpy plane ride and a hard landing where the radio set got smashed on impact. The forest fire seems like any other fire they have handled, one of the team members is seen taking photos of the landscape like a tourist. As the men walk down the steep ravine, through the crackling noise, dense smoke and heat, the leader spots the fire jumping from the other side of the ravine to the one where the firefighters are situated. The tall grass on this side of the ravine and an upwards wind direction imply the firefighters are directly in line of a suddenly very fast-moving fire. The leader recognizes the threat to the life of firefighters and asks them to drop their equipment and run. The progress is difficult due to the tall grass and the need to move quickly up the steep mountain slope. As the fire gains on the firefighters, the leader makes an escape fire by burning the vegetation ahead of the retreating firefighters and shouts, 'This way, this way', signalling the team to join him inside the escape fire. The team had no prior experience of complex and difficult forest fires and had no knowledge of the technique of escape fires. They thought the leader had gone crazy and ran straight upwards for the ridge. Thirteen of the sixteen smokejumpers died that fateful day in August 1949 in Mann Gulch, Montana. The leader survived inside the escape fire. I recommend that you study the masterly work of organizational theorist Karl Weick to know about the Mann Gulch disaster in detail and understand the breakdown of sense-making and the role of enactment in contexts where uncertainty is significantly high.

A firefighter is supposed to *fight* fires, not *run away* from them. Firefighters are supposed to *carry* their firefighting equipment rather than to dump it. The worldview of what a firefighter is supposed to do collapses in the face of a sudden turn of events which threatens their existence. Nothing quite makes sense in this changed world. It is difficult to comprehend what is happening when the leader, instead of *extinguishing* the fire, *starts* a new fire, that too *ahead* of the men who are running from a fire rushing at them from *behind*, instead of running *away* from a fire, asks the men to join him *inside* a fire circle. Nothing seems impossible in this changed world, the unthinkable and the unthought suddenly materializes.

A firm experiencing such a level of uncertainty may face an existential crisis as its earlier forecasts are junked, plans devolve, markets vanish, employees stop reporting for duty, suppliers crumble and cash streams dry up. All its strategies for growth or consolidation or turnaround make little sense when the need is for a strategy for survival. In this primal world, the objective functions of cost minimization or time responsiveness, etc., are thrown away in favour of sufficiency. Do what is sufficient to stay alive. If that means dropping your firefighting equipment or protective gear so that you can run faster, do that.

The protective gear for fighting fires may not protect you while fleeing fires, instead only weighing you down.

The fundamental disruption caused by the extreme uncertainty surrounding an existential shock is thus at the level of objective function or the performance dimension. In a normal situation, flexibility is defined as the ability to minimize the effect of perturbations/fluctuations of inputs (demand side or supply side) on the output (the performance measure[s] that the firm deems important). In a situation of extreme shock resulting in an existential crisis, the flexibility requirement changes as the earlier performance measures lose relevance. The flexibility that the firm needs to survive an existential shock includes the flexibility to move away quickly from the earlier performance dimension (cost or time or quality, etc.) to one of sufficiency. The shock may render annual targets related to revenues, profitability, market share, cost reduction, quality improvement, etc., so meaningless that it may be worthwhile to first survive the shock by junking those targets and performance dimensions and switching to a sufficiency framework. The targets can be reset at a later date when the storm has blown over and there is more clarity about the new environmental context that the firm finds itself in. The firm can then go back to the earlier performance dimensions or review the strategic choices. The sufficiency framework is thus a temporary objective to weather the extreme event.

What exactly is this sufficiency mindset? The film *Dunkirk* is a vivid portrayal of the evacuation of allied troops from Dunkirk during World War II while the Luftwaffe and the U-boats target the retreating soldiers. When the soldiers finally land on home soil, dejected that they fled from the enemy, volunteers offer the soldiers soup and blankets. A soldier murmurs, 'All we did was survive.' A blind elderly man replies, 'That's enough.'

Sufficiency does not focus on any grand plan, neither does it aim to maximize or minimize any objective function. It gives up the superfluous to preserve the essential.

The escape fire is a very interesting scorched earth tactic. The escape fire is supposed to clear a portion of the vegetation, so that when the main fire reaches the spot, it finds nothing left there to burn while there is plenty of inflammable material around. The escape fire thus diverts the flow of the fire around the cleared spot. Is it a fool-proof strategy? Surely not. The diameter of the spot could be so small that the person crouching to the ground in the middle of it can get roasted or die of smoke inhalation. The chances of survival increase with the increase in diameter of the escape fire.

The chances of survival for a firm weathering an extreme shock increase with the cash runway (number of days/months/years for cash to run out) and decrease with the rate at which the firm is consuming cash. To survive inside the escape fire, the firm has to hibernate like a bear. The fat reserve built up for the winter must be enough so that the bear does not awake mid-winter as this can be fatal given the lack of food sources. This fat reserve is the equivalent of the diameter of the escape fire, bigger the fat/cash reserve, the better. In addition, the bear slows down its metabolism during hibernation to conserve the fat reserve; all bodily activities deemed inessential are slowed down to the bare minimum. To survive the existential shock, a firm needs to relook at everything from the lens of essential/non-essential. Anything deemed non-essential needs to be pruned quickly. It could be employees, products, customers, markets, plants or even whole business units. An existential threat is thus a great time to differentiate between the core and the flab that has been added over time. For the activities deemed essential, expenses are monitored closely, all discretionary expenses curtailed, austerity measures put in place, capex plans shelved, marketing budgets downsized, trainings postponed, business development takes a back seat and cash-flow-related metrics gain prominence at the expense of profitability or market share.

Would all these activities be enough to weather the storm? No one knows, and there is no guarantee. We can take some precautions, but the best-laid plans of mice and men often go awry. It is certain that the future is uncertain. A firm which is certain about the success of its Flexibility of Flexibilities strategy needs to be reminded of Ozymandias. The cat has nine lives *only*.

CHAPTER 17

The System Designed to Fail

'There is but one truly serious philosophical problem and that is suicide. Judging whether life is or is not worth living amounts to answering the fundamental question of philosophy.'

—*The Myth of Sisyphus*, Albert Camus

'We are doomed to failure without a daily destruction of our various preconceptions.'

—Taiichi Ohno, architect of Toyota Production System

NOTHING SUCCEEDS LIKE success, goes an English proverb. It is tempting to add, nothing fails like failure. Well, *almost* nothing. What would you consider a failure to fail to be?

Who wants to be a failure in life? Not me. I guess if you have come thus far in reading this book, neither do you. I may be a failure in many pursuits like sports or singing, but I did not will it. I *tried* to be successful. With my track record of success, I might fail if I tried to fail. Would my failing to fail make me a success? Surely not.

Human beings want to succeed in whatever they do. Systems designed by humans reflect this yearning for success. Systems are designed with certain objectives, and system performance is determined in terms of how well the objectives are met. The focus on success is so pervasive and taken for granted that the contemplation of suicide is shocking. Condemned by most religions, discussions regarding suicide are a taboo. It is only rarely that suicide occupies centre stage in a philosophical debate. Even much rarer is a view which calls suicide as the *only* true philosophical question. You may not agree with Albert Camus in *The Myth of Sisyphus*, but you cannot brush away his arguments without further scrutiny. From a systemic perspective, suicide corresponds to a system killing itself. A wayward missile which self-destructs if it deviates from the intended trajectory is an example of homicide rather than suicide. The target for a missile could be very well-defined, and mission control decides if and when the missile needs to be destroyed. In contrast, an AI system which activates a kill switch once it considers itself to have gone rogue requires the AI system to ask philosophical questions regarding the purpose of existence. The stuff of science fiction, apparently far removed from the practical world of business.

Business organizations are built for not just success but sustained success. A death wish is not what you would associate with purpose-driven organizations unless a manager wants to purposively destroy value for reasons other than economic ones. If a firm experiences success, the natural tendency is to not tinker with the system, arguing that we should not fix a system if it ain't broke. In contrast, Taiichi Ohno, the architect of the Toyota

Production System (TPS), believed that progress requires breaking the status quo. Seems innocuous advice till you ask if the status quo should be broken when the system is already successful. The answer to that question is the key to understanding Lean philosophy. The answer to that question is Kaizen or continuous improvement.

Kaizen is just one of a large number of tools and practices that constitute the potpourri that is Lean philosophy. The centrality of this concept is not immediately apparent to the student or practitioner who is hit by a barrage of Japanese terms in the quest to understand Lean. Consider a small list: Jidoka, Heijunka, Andon, Muda, Poka-yoke, Kaizen, Kanban, Genchi Genbutsu, etc. My objective here is not to either delve deeper into each technique or provide a comprehensive listing of all techniques. There are many books on Lean which provide a detailed understanding of the tools and techniques. My intent is to understand the soul of Lean. The essence of Lean is not in any specific technique per se, it is in the synergies that result from the integration of these techniques. Lean is a system. It is a system like no other. You could work in a Lean organization, be aware of and master each of the techniques, and yet never really see the whole. In this respect, there is a striking resemblance between Lean and any religious order. Just like a religion has clearly laid down rules, principles and rituals that are to be followed, Lean too specifies a long list of dos and don'ts and ritual practices. You could practise this religion without ever doubting it, never really questioning its tenets. The more time you spend in this Lean religion, the more convinced you become of the superiority of this religion over the non-believers. The casualty of this orientation is the spirit of inquiry. Religion accepts, philosophy doubts. The doubt about Lean does not originate from whether it works but whether it works in all situations.

A simple example of the doubt concerning Lean is expressed by many students when they ask whether this philosophy has been successful outside Japan. Is Lean essentially Japanese? To some extent, the question arises from the plethora of Japanese terms. In no other domain of Operations Management are you likely to see as many non-English terms. The adoption of a new word implies that the scientific body of literature on Operations Management, traditionally codified using the English language, did not have a word to sufficiently describe the TPS phenomenon. The adoption of so many new words implies that non-Japanese researchers experiencing Lean for the first time found the paradigm so alien that they were forced to adopt native Japanese words rather than explain the phenomena using existing words and terms in the English language. This hard coding of Japanese terms into Operations Management terminology naturally gives an exotic flavour to Lean. This is a blessing and a curse. It is a blessing because it draws the attention of the student towards a *different* system. It is a curse because the student may focus more on using these exotic Japanese terms as jargon without ever understanding the fundamental paradigm shift that Lean philosophy entails.

What exactly is this paradigm shift? Most students would identify Push vs Pull as the paradigm shift. Yes and No. TPS is a Pull system while traditional factory models like Henry Ford's assembly line were built on the Push system. In fact, we never really understood the Ford system as Push till TPS came along and showed us what Pull is. So, even though Push preceded Pull historically, Push has been defined retrospectively after witnessing Pull. In Push, the manager *schedules* production by telling the worker each day what is to be done, when and in how much quantity. In Pull, the manager *authorizes* production to be done under certain conditions. To simplify matters, consider a worker at a workstation with an inbox containing raw materials and an outbox containing finished products. Two consecutive workstations in a line are linked by the fact that the outbox of the upstream workstation is the inbox of the downstream workstation. Pull specifies the maximum number of units in the outbox of each workstation and authorizes the worker to take raw materials from the inbox and produce as long as the number in the outbox is less than the specified quantity. Notice that in Pull the manager does not specify the time or the quantity to be produced explicitly, instead couples the factory to the demand in the marketplace and allows the customer demand to dictate the time and pace of work in the factory. Push is proactive, Pull is reactive to customer demand.

Push and Pull also differ very substantively in their orientation towards inventory. In Push, the manager controls the output rate by increasing or decreasing raw material availability. In Pull, the manager controls the outbox inventory ceiling to regulate the output. As a result, the Push system may experience high WIP inventory congestion at times when capacity utilization increases. In contrast, the inventory in Pull systems is bounded due to the ceilings imposed on the outbox. The Push system argues that to pump higher volumes of water through a pipeline we need a bigger diameter of pipes. The Pull system argues that a higher volume can be pumped by keeping pipe diameter unchanged by increasing the pressure differential. Push looks at inventory as stock, Pull as flow. Push uses warehouses for storage, Pull uses warehouses primarily as a staging point for further movement. Push orientation leads to a firm offering trade discounts to dump stocks with distributors and wholesalers, while Pull orientation leads to a firm offering consumer promotions to influence the demand rate.

TPS is a Pull system, but not all Pull systems are TPS. Systems like CONWIP (short of CONstant WIP) aim to put an upper limit of inventory not at individual workstations but on the total inventory in the system. Systems like Drum-Buffer-Rope (DBR) scheduling in Theory of Constraints (TOC) aim to limit inventory in the system by connecting the rate of raw material release into the system with the bottleneck rate. By equating Pull system with TPS, the student ascribes the paradigm shift in TPS entirely to the paradigm shift involved in moving from Push to Pull. TPS is much more than Pull. It will blow your mind when you realize the entirety of this paradigm shift.

Hopefully, by the end of this chapter, you will get the insight. But I have already given you the key to the insight—Kaizen. First, note that in contrast to all other terms in Lean which are embedded in a particular production context, continuous improvement is a universal concept. It has as much relevance in production as in service, as much relevance to a spiritual quest as in a material quest for wealth, as much relevance in statecraft as in a pursuit of happiness. Not everyone can relate to Heijunka or Kanban, but everyone can understand what the concept of continuous improvement wants to achieve. Or so it seems.

On the face of it, continuous improvement seems like a nice concept. It is a relativist concept rather than an absolutist one. Consider a classroom full of schoolkids, some gifted in mathematics, some gifted in specific art forms, some yet to find their gifts. An absolutist performance standard compares each child with an externally set standard of success or failure. Such a standard of success is likely to be based on the expected performance of an average child, neither the top performer nor the underachiever. In contrast, continuous improvement only requires each child to develop further from the last assessment. Nice concept, isn't it? If we translate this to business firms, it essentially means that benchmarking of performance is not competitive benchmarking but related to historical performance of the firm. Can a firm really ignore competitive benchmarking? Not usually, but there are exceptions. Note that the internal focused measure of performance inherent in continuous improvement makes sense for the development of overachievers. Comparing a gifted child, excelling in an art form, with the rest of the batch does a disservice to the gifted child. Athletes who are head and shoulders ahead of their competitors and win every time are not driven by the act of winning, but the wish to better their own records. They compete against themselves. At the same time, continuous improvement becomes that much harder to achieve the more you excel. There is a decreasing return to scale in continuous improvement.

It may be much easier for an amateur to achieve a one-second reduction in time for a race than for the world record holder.

Continuous improvement is thus applicable for all but most challenging for the overachiever. It is not a nice, feel-good concept; it is a brutally purposive ideology which strives for perfection. How does a firm adopt continuous improvement as an ideology? Just telling people to continuously improve is not going to make them continually improve. Neither would it help to coin slogans or organize Zero Defect days. Drastic measures are needed.

For Lean, progress *is* continuous improvement. To improve, Ohno requires us to destroy our preconceptions. The word 'destroy' has a tinge of violence, but we would set that perspective aside for the moment. It seems intuitive that constraints in the form of preconceptions need to be lifted for progress to happen. Questioning of preconceptions like 'the Earth is flat' or 'the sun goes around the Earth' have indeed resulted in spectacular progress. But Ohno is not referring to these kinds of preconceptions which can only be broken one time. Read his prescription closely—he advocates destroying preconceptions *daily*. *Continuous* Improvement requires *daily* destruction of preconceptions. A continually improving system would thus require a *daily* supply of preconceptions to break! Preconceptions that can be broken every day are most likely regenerated every day. Preconceptions like 'We have made enough improvements in quality and there is little left to improve quality' or 'We have reduced set-up times enough and there is very little left to improve changeover times' or 'We have reduced waste and there is very little waste left to reduce costs.'

Lean is a mix of idealism and pragmatism. It takes an extreme, idealist stand of Zero Defect or single-piece flow but recognizes the pragmatism needed to take the existing state of the firm into consideration. Continuous Improvement is the journey from the pragmatic to the idealistic condition. Some students have a romantic view of Continuous Improvement. From a distance, it seems to be one of those warm, fuzzy concepts which would be nice to have. Far from it. Continuous Improvement involves a continuous stressing of the system. Every time the system improves quality by identifying a root cause and taking remedial actions, the hunt begins anew. Every time the system reduces production lot size, the effort renews to achieve an ideal lot size of one. There is no end state when the firm may declare, 'We have arrived. We have succeeded. Now we can celebrate.' The firm which is forever and *continuously* improving is also *forever* dissatisfied with its status quo. Being *forever* dissatisfied is not everyone's cup of tea. The relentless pursuit of improvement may take its toll on employees and cause depression and stress. A status quo of daily incremental inconsequential improvements could also be as numbing as a status quo of no improvement.

Continuous Improvement is central to Lean. Take, for example, the Lean practice of standardized work processes. The concept of standardization of work is nothing new, it was one of the earliest initiatives that scientific management focused on in the days of Frederick Taylor. The assembly line of Henry Ford had taken this idea to its logical conclusion. Successful standardization of work means all work processes have been standardized. From now on, workers can just follow the laid-down procedure. This orientation makes standardization a one-time affair. Set a standard and then follow it forever. Toyota started off from where Ford left the idea. It not just standardized work but also valued the breaking of the standard. As soon as a standard is made, efforts start in finding a better way to perform the task and hence improve the standard. Set a standard and follow it while simultaneously experimenting on ways to improve and rewrite the standard. The traditional mindset encourages a deviation-counteracting mindset in following set standards. Lean encourages deviation-counteracting behaviour in following set standards and deviation-amplifying behaviour in the experimentation needed for improved standard-setting.

Adoption of some Lean principles without adopting Continuous Improvement is a recipe for disaster. Take, for instance, the concept of Just in Time, or JIT. Lean systems wish to reduce the waste of inventory and hence vendors are required to produce and transport parts to the assembly line just in time for the assembly. To witness this JIT supply is nothing less than magical. The sense of wonder increases as the gap between the arrival time of a part and the use of the part in the assembly operation narrows down. The most important word in JIT is 'just'. Neither too early, nor too late, *just* in time. A novice taken in by this masterful demonstration by the magician may not necessarily understand that the gap was earlier several days which was progressively reduced to a few hours over a long time period through a process of Continuous Improvement. JIT delivery has to be *achieved* through Continuous Improvement, not by *decreeing* that suppliers should deliver JIT one fine day. This achievement includes rigorous assessment of all that can go wrong at the vendor, during transportation and at the factory, and taking countermeasures to increase reliability of supply. It requires investments in more reliable machinery, reliable transportation assets, close proximity of vendors, collocation of vendors, real-time tracking and, above all, assurance of high-quality and quality checks at the vendor.

The adoption of Heijunka similarly requires a Continuous Improvement mindset. Heijunka aims for levelled production, levelled in terms of both volume and variety of products. Consider a firm which has to meet a monthly demand of 400 cars of Type A, 200 of Type B and 100 of Type C. Levelling on volume implies that the production rate would be constant, resulting in the same daily output throughout the month. The levelling on variety implies that the number of cars of Type A, B and C produced in a time period should be in the ratio 4:2:1. At one extreme, the time period can be taken as the month with the firm first producing a lot of 400 As followed by 200 Bs and 100 Cs. This would have been the traditional approach. The time period could be reduced in a Lean system to a fortnight with lot sizes of 200 As, 100 Bs and 50 Cs. As the firm successfully handles the transition challenges, the system could be further stressed by moving to a weekly and then a daily cycle, thereby reducing the lot size even further. What could be the end point of this journey? The smallest cycle would be of 7 cars, with 4 As, 2 Bs and 1 C, perhaps sequenced as AAAABBC AAAABBC . . . But this is not the ideal Heijunka. In the first part of cycle AAAABBC we are producing only As. We are closer to true Heijunka if we adopt a sequence like ABACABA ABACABA . . . The As are equally spaced out as far as possible and so are the Bs and the Cs.

By traditional standards, this is nothing but utter foolishness. ABACABA implies a production lot size of 1. Each time you set up, produce one unit and then set up again for another variety. The set-up cost would be extremely high since the number of set-ups would match the number of units produced. The firm can bring down the set-up costs by trading off set-up costs against inventory holding costs. As the production lot size increases, the set-up costs decrease while the inventory holding costs increase. The resultant U-shaped total cost curve is minimized at the Economic Production Quantity (EPQ). The Economic Order Quantity (EOQ) and its derivative, the EPQ model, are the foundations of inventory modelling. The EPQ model suggests that adopting a lot size of 1 would be extremely costly for the firm. On the other hand, Lean philosophy is supposed to reduce costs by eliminating waste. Is there then an apparent contradiction between the EPQ model and waste reduction through Heijunka? Is the EPQ model flawed in predicting a huge increase in costs at a lot size of 1? Is the Heijunka model flawed in predicting reduction of cost through reduction of wastage at a lot size of 1?

To resolve this conflict, we examine the structure of the EOQ or EPQ formulation. Consider an item with annual demand D, cost of a set-up C_s and the inventory holding cost being C_h per unit per year. Let quantity Q be produced every time the item is set up for production. The annual set-up cost is $\frac{D}{Q}C_s$ while the annual holding cost is $\frac{Q}{2}C_h$. The annual total cost $TC = \frac{D}{Q}C_s + \frac{Q}{2}C_h$ is a U-shaped curve which is minimized at $Q^* = \sqrt{\frac{2DC_s}{C_h}}$, the point where the annual set-up cost intersects the annual holding cost. The optimal total cost incurred at optimal lot size Q^* is given by $TC(Q^*) = \sqrt{2DC_sC_h}$. The traditional mindset looks at the cost per set-up C_s as a given constant, Lean looks at it as a parameter that can be reduced by investing in initiatives like SMED. As the C_s values decrease, the annual set-up cost curve shifts leftwards and downwards. Since the annual holding cost curve remains unchanged, the annual total cost curve also shifts leftwards and downwards; resulting in lower Q^* and $TC(Q^*)$. This is also apparent from the Q^* and $TC(Q^*)$ formulas where C_s appears in the numerator.

Figure 11: Reduction in EOQ as Cost per Set-Up Decreases

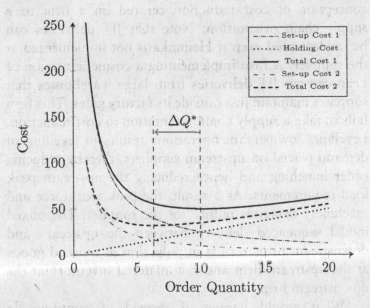

The parameters are D = 50, C_h = 5. Reduction of C_s from 5 in scenario 1 to 2 in scenario 2 reduces the Q^* from 10 to 6.32 and the total cost curve shifts downwards.

Note the cause and the effect. Reduction in C_s is the cause, reduction in Q^* and $TC(Q^*)$ are the effects. It is through continuously improving (that is, reducing) C_s that we obtain continuously improving (that is, reducing) lot size Q^* and continuously improving (that is, reducing) total cost. There is thus no contradiction between the EPQ model and Heijunka. The difference lies in the way of looking at parameters—in one case (traditionally) taking the parameters as given constants and in the other case (Lean) as preconceptions that can be continuously questioned, attacked and broken.

The practice of Heijunka breaks away from a conception of cost reduction centred on a firm to a supply chain orientation. Note that JIT deliveries can be implemented even if Heijunka is not implemented at the supplier. A firm implementing a cosmetic version of Lean can get JIT deliveries from large warehouses that suppliers maintain just outside its factory gates. This firm fails to take a supply chain orientation to cost reduction. Levelling downstream operations results in levelling of demand placed on upstream suppliers, thereby reducing order bunching and hence reducing the upstream peak load requirements. As a result, the peak workforce and machinery demands reduce for the supplier. The mixed model sequenced delivery between the upstream and downstream firms results in reduction in finished goods at the upstream firm and raw material inventory at the downstream firm.

What would happen if instead of continuously improving the system a firm attempts to jump straight to the end state? A firm can always decide one day that production lot size should be 1 and all vendors should supply JIT. The firm would be committing suicide. Lean is nothing short of a death wish if not preceded by investments in set-up cost reduction, vendor development and a plethora of other initiatives aimed at process and quality improvements. Death due to a sudden Lean implementation would not be prolonged, it would be immediate. The drastic stress on the system due to the attempt to reach the end state would likely give rise to quality issues. These quality issues would trigger pulling of the Andon Chord. The Andon Chord would be the final instrument of death though the foolishness of the amateur in playing with fire would be the root cause.

The Andon Chord is a constant reminder of death on the Lean shop floor. It is a remarkable piece of process innovation, simple in its form yet profound in its implication. It is a piece of chord hanging over the workstations that the worker can pull whenever there is a quality issue which needs to be resolved. Jidoka is the philosophy to make a problem self-evident. If a worker is fatigued or observes a quality issue, the worker pulls the Andon Chord to bring the problem to the notice of the supervisor so that corrective action can be taken. The management *authorizes* the worker to pull the chord in the event of a quality issue and thereby trigger a series of activities. Immediately, lights start flashing and music starts playing to bring the quality issue to the notice of the line supervisor. If the supervisor thinks the problem can be handled then he pulls the Andon Chord a second time and proceeds to take remedial action by bringing in reserve workers if needed. The assembly line stops at the end of the assembly cycle time if the chord is not pulled a second time.

The Andon Chord is nothing short of a revolution on the factory shop floor. It takes away the decision regarding starting and stopping the line from managers and gives it back to the worker. Decision-making related to line stopping moves from centralized top management to real-time, decentralized decisions at the level of the shop floor personnel. Evaluation of quality moves away from inspectors in the quality department to the line worker in the production department. Production targets a move away from output orientation to quality-output orientation which puts quality at the centre of the production process. In the traditional system, the production-at-any-cost orientation gives rise to a Garbage-In-Garbage-Out situation. In contrast, Lean is a Garbage-In-System-Fail system. The worker pulling the Andon Chord initiates the system tripping. To restart the line, there is no other option but to identify the root cause of the quality issue and take remedial action for removing the root cause. If not, the system remains in a failed state.

Many students think of the Andon Chord only in the context of quality issues. The Andon Chord had been primarily designed for productivity improvements through waste reduction. Waste related to defects are just one of seven different kinds of waste that Lean strives to reduce. The Andon Chord could thus be pulled for a variety of reasons. It could be assembly-related issues like proper fitment of parts, it could be quality-related issues related to an upstream operation like defects in a paint job, it could be difficulties related to handling of machines, it could be worker-related like the inability to adhere to cycle time due to fatigue, etc. The Andon pull results in Jidoka—the problem becomes evident to all and presents an opportunity for improvement. Andon pulls could as much highlight opportunities for productivity improvement through waste reduction or improvement of machine tools as improvement in product quality.

The aspect of machine maintenance is frequently overlooked by the student. Lean philosophy requires a strong maintenance department which goes much beyond mere maintenance activities to understanding the machine so thoroughly so as to make changes to augment functionality or improve reliability. Note that any changes made to the machine means the manufacturer's warranty would be void, and the modifications would mean there is no point in expecting external help in case of a machine breakdown. Lean expects the maintenance department to be self-reliant and undertake preventive maintenance to minimize machine-related Andon pulls.

In most cases, the line stops only briefly as the supervisor makes a note of the improvement areas. The idealistic nature of Lean stops the line, the pragmatic nature of Lean restarts the line as it sees little value in keeping the line in a stopped condition while the improvement activities are underway. This pragmatism is a strength and a weakness. If the improvements do not fructify, then merely pulling the Andon Chord serves no purpose and the workers and supervisors may over time start to view the defect as normal, thereby risking abandoning the central philosophy of Kaizen.

It is equally important to note the kind of causes for which the Andon Chord would not be pulled. A worker in an assembly line has a limited time to observe and identify quality defects and is most likely to use eyesight and tactile capabilities to do so. Not all quality defects are easily observable. A defect in design which results in a car experiencing increased vibrations at high speeds is not likely to be observable by an assembly line worker. Neither can the assembly worker observe issues related to heat treatment, reliability of components, safety or emission norms. The bottom-up, decentralized, emergent, process-oriented Quality Circle thus does not obviate a need for top-down, centralized, directed, project-oriented quality improvement paradigms like Six Sigma. Total Quality Management orientations allows Quality Circles in assembly to coexist with Quality Function Deployment in design and engineering. In reality, TQM and TPS are two foundations of Lean. While TPS originated in Toyota, TQM was implanted into Toyota. TQM broadened the scope of quality from the traditional manufacturing function to other functions like design, engineering, sales, service, etc. To its credit, Toyota extended TQM activities to its upstream suppliers and downstream distributors, thereby improving quality across the entire supply chain. While TQM is widely adopted outside Toyota, the defining characteristic of the quality dimension of Lean remains the Andon Chord which originated in TPS.

Death by Andon Chord seems a wholly unnecessary innovation from a traditional mindset. Systems are built to last, not to be fragile. Instead of adopting the philosophy of avoiding anything that could stop the line, the Andon Chord makes the system more fragile than is necessary. Could we not have solved the quality issue without resorting to shutting down the line? Why play Russian roulette? Why play this game of brinkmanship on a daily basis? Why shift power away from management to workers on such an important decision as shutting down the line? Why design a system that threatens itself? Why commit suicide?

You would see this aspect of brinkmanship in pushing the boundary of the possible and impossible in many Lean practices. It is present in the 'just' of JIT delivery, in decreasing lot size in Heijunka all the way to 1, in the gun-to-the-head approach inherent in Andon. Lean is never happy with the considerable achievement already attained, it is ever-ready to stake everything for the sake of further improvement. Is this violence towards the self really required? Could we not design Lean with all the wonderful process innovation *except* Andon? Could Lean survive if it does not threaten itself? What if we rescue Lean from this Andon Chord? Or is the Andon Chord so central to this philosophy that rescuing the system from the means of suicide is nothing short of destroying the system itself?

We are now very close to the heart of the Lean philosophy. Every system is designed to achieve something. The default orientation is that systems are designed to succeed. When would we consider a system to be successful? Now let me pronounce the first part of a great mantra: 'A system designed to succeed, succeeds if it succeeds.'

Nothing succeeds like success. I know you are feeling a great urge to beat me up with a broom for offering such an amazing pearl of wisdom, just hold that broom for a moment. Complete the following mantra for yourself: 'A system designed to fail . . .'

When I ask students to complete the sentence, I get a variety of responses. A system designed to fail, fails if it succeeds; a system designed to fail, succeeds if it fails; a system designed to fail, fails to succeed; a system designed to fail, fails, etc. All these statements miss the mark. Now let me pronounce the great mantra:

A System Designed to Succeed, Succeeds if It Succeeds.
A System Designed to Fail, Fails if It Fails to Fail

Lean is a system designed to fail. It is the first, the one and the only management system that is designed to fail.

I am not joking. Read the mantra again slowly and try to understand. Else you might read tons of books on Lean or work in a Lean organization your entire life and yet never get an insight into Lean.

Can a system be designed to fail? Should a system be designed to fail? It is very difficult for a management practitioner to accept that a system can be designed to fail. It goes against everything that management teaches. Managers aim for success, not failure. They design the organization to achieve success, endure shocks, ensure business continuity and have a sustainable competitive advantage. Investors evaluate firms on the success achieved and the sustainability and future growth in earnings. Who wants to be a failure? Who in the right frame of mind would even think of designing a system to fail?

While Lean is the first use of this design philosophy for management, there are several examples of products designed to fail. Think of the design objective of the electric fuse wire. The fuse is a fine strand of wire designed for a specific purpose. While it conducts electricity during normal situations like any other conductor, its raison d'etre is its behaviour under abnormal situations. In the event of a voltage fluctuation, the wire heats up and breaks, disconnecting the internal wiring of a house from the external grid. The fuse wire is a system designed to fail. It must break (and hence fail in conducting electricity) when the voltage fluctuation in the external grid crosses a limit. If it fails to fail (that is, fails to break, that is, continues to conduct electricity) then a bigger failure occurs as the internal household appliances are exposed to the voltage fluctuation. We essentially sacrifice the fuse wire in order to save the much more valuable appliances. Now think of the fuse wire and repeat the mantra: A *system* (fuse wire) designed to *fail* (fail to conduct electricity in the event of voltage fluctuation), fails if it *fails to* (does not) *fail* (break). Got it?

Nowadays, you rarely encounter a fuse wire because of the increasing adoption of miniature circuit breakers (MCBs). If the MCB trips, it is very easy to just pull up the switch to reconnect the circuit again. Earlier, you had to replace the broken fuse wire with a new one. Sometimes the fuse blows out again and again resulting in frustration. Then inevitably someone gets the brilliant idea. Why not use two or three fuse wires? The diameter of the connection would thus increase, resulting in a much more stable fuse wire which does not trip easily. Brilliant, isn't it? People with such brilliant ideas need to be recognized by keeping them as far away as possible from messing with operations. Instead of sacrificing the fuse wire, such an approach sacrifices household appliances. A fuse wire which fails to disconnect in the event of a voltage fluctuation may live but fails to fulfil its destiny. It's a sad existence.

An Andon Chord which is not pulled has not fulfilled its destiny. The purpose of its existence is to stop the line in the event of a quality or process issue. Any effort in bypassing the Andon and trying to keep the line from stopping is foolish because it focuses on the Andon Chord and not the root cause. The focus should be to find the root cause of the process or quality defect and take measures to eliminate the root cause. Lean places a premium on improvement and the Andon Chord is the discipline which Lean imposes on itself in this pursuit of improvement. If the time lost due to Andon-triggered line stoppage reduces to a low level, it is time to stress the system by reducing in-process inventory, reducing manpower or decreasing the cycle time. Potential process improvements which were being overlooked could now surface, leading to the next round of Andon pulls. Since the potential for improvement is limitless, the absence of Andon pulls means the management has slackened in its quest for improvement and hence compromised on Kaizen. A traditional factory manager dreads a line stoppage; a Lean factory manager dreads the absence of line stoppage! There cannot be a more absurd idea than rescuing Lean from the Andon Chord. The centrality of suicide, represented by the Andon Chord, defines Lean.

Mantra of Lean: Improve or Die

Who would find the root cause and how? Lean places the responsibility for debugging the process or quality issue squarely with the shop-floor-level Quality Circle made of experienced line operators and supervisors, not the quality department, managerial staff or outside consultants. This builds ownership of quality and process improvements within the production function. The philosophy is that people closest to the problem, in terms of both space and time, are best placed to identify and solve the problem. Instead of waiting for outside help, Lean makes the production worker self-reliant in problem-solving. Lean trains the Quality Circle in several tools to aid the process. Line workers are to be taught to interpret statistical control charts. (Control charts were originally designed in a way so that relatively unsophisticated workers could comprehend the concept. Control charts are meant to be used by production workers rather than an analyst sitting in an air-conditioned office. This is why R Charts [Range Charts] are used to check variation in dispersion since a production worker is more likely to understand the concept of range rather than the concept of standard deviation. Control charts which are used by workers are likely to be dirty and smudged; if you see pristine-looking control charts on factory floors, be very wary—these may be only for visitor consumption.) Problem-solvers are required to move out of offices and visit the site (*gemba*) of the quality defect and have direct experience of the issue at hand. Ishikawa diagrams allow the worker to systematically think of underlying causes. Why-Why analysis teaches the worker to look beyond the superficial symptoms and understand the chain of causality going back to the root cause.

Improvement due to elimination of root cause differentiates Continuous Improvement from improvement based on suggestion schemes. In suggestion schemes, employees provide suggestions for improvement and may receive a part of monetary benefits. Suggestions could be regarding any activity or process and it is up to the management to decide whether to act on the suggestion. Suggestion schemes and Kaizen both harness the curiosity and problem-solving capabilities of the employees. However, the Quality Circle works on ideas related to the immediate work environment and the responsibility for identifying the root cause and eliminating it rests with it. The familiarity with the problem context and intensive nature of the Why-Why process allow Quality Circles a better ability to identify the root cause than suggestions offered by a casual observer. The activities of the Quality Circle are part of the employees' work, and there are no monetary benefits to employees. Improvements in suggestion schemes originate from individuals; Quality Circles in contrast are group processes. Suggestion schemes are a nice add-on, Quality Circles are systemic. A system designed to succeed can forget the key to the suggestion box, a system designed to fail dies if the improvements do not materialize.

Are you able to now understand the totality of the Lean system? Are you able to grasp the insight? If you are still unable to see the beauty, the fault lies with my ability to explain. I am sorry for my incompetence as a teacher. I can only create the build-up to the enlightenment, I cannot cause it. There is but only one way to achieve enlightenment. Human beings have to keep going at it, keep trying, keep trying. And one day the whole thing comes to you in a flash.

For me, that moment arrived when I was in the third year of my doctoral studies. I had been exposed to Lean thinking in engineering college, in the shop floor, in the business school. I had read books, a lot of them, and thought that I knew what Lean is. Then one fine day, after several hours of discussion on an unrelated topic with my thesis guide, we took a coffee break. Standing side by side in a first-floor corridor with coffee cups in hand and staring at nothing in particular, Professor Ashis K. Chatterjee said, 'By the way, do you know Professor Russell Ackoff has said that Lean is a Safe-Fail system?'

And the world melted away from my consciousness in a flash. I saw her beauty for the first time. What a beauty!

Every engineer is taught to design systems with a factor of safety. A bridge being erected at a location which experiences maximum wind speeds of 100 kmph should *not* be designed to withstand 100 kmph but a higher speed. If the bridge is designed to withstand 200 kmph winds, then the design has a factor of safety of 2. The design principle underlying the use of factor of safety is the Fail-Safe orientation. We do not want the bridge to fail even under extreme situations. Similarly, Fail-Safe orientation pushes the designer to idiot-proof a product so that any untoward incident can be avoided. For example, the product could be designed in such a way that a battery cannot be inserted unless it is properly aligned. Fail-Safe orientation in system design is so widespread that we take it for granted.

Safe Fail is a paradigm shift. It shifts the focus from failure to recovery from failure. Safe-Fail systems are designed without a factor of safety, exposing the system to environmental uncertainties. The fact that a Safe-Fail system would fail at some time or the other is not just a certainty but a desired goal. The most important part of the system design is thus designing what happens after failure. The fragility of the system is compensated by building processes aimed at quick recovery from a failure. It creates a sandbox within which failure occurs. The MCB or fuse box is the sandbox within which the failure happens in the example we discussed earlier, ring-fencing the failure site from the expensive appliances. Recovery from failure is as easy as pushing up a switch or replacing a fuse wire. In Lean systems, the sandbox is the Quality Circle which immediately attends to the failure, making it an internal failure rather than a potentially much messier and costlier external failure. The recovery from failure consists of two main activities: learning and shaping. First, the system focuses on uncovering the root cause behind the quality or process issue which triggered the Andon pull. For Lean, being a learning organization is not a fancy management concept but a necessity for survival. It moves away from treating the environment as a black box and strives to know more about itself, its suppliers, customers and the environment. Lean aims to be self-aware. After the root cause is identified, the second step involves shaping the environment by removing the root cause. By shaping the environment, Lean reduces the variabilities and uncertainties in the environment and thereby reduces the requirement for buffer inventory.

Lean is a Safe-Fail system. It abhors the factor of safety and aggressively reduces inventory, which is the prime tool used in a traditional system to buffer it from uncertainties in the demand and supply environment. Reliance on the inventory buffer for all kinds of uncertainties results in a bloated inventory. The buffer inventories also hide quality issues and hinder process improvements. The movement from Just-in-Case to Just-in-Time is thus a movement from Fail-Safe to a Safe-Fail system As the buffer inventory is progressively removed, quality and process issues surface and failure is a certainty. It is the investments in a host of quality improvement tools which enable Lean to recover from the failure. Andon triggers the failure, Kaizen recovers from the failure and the cycle keeps on repeating as inventory buffers are progressively reduced, quality control is tightened, production lot sizes are reduced, and the system is progressively stressed. The system moves from one failure to the next, not in circular fashion but spiralling towards Zero Defect. The success of this system is in its progress from one failure to another failure; one recovery to the next recovery. Its failure lies in either failing to fail or failing to recover. Its beauty lies in the acceptance of transience. What a beauty!

Did this beautifully synergistic system originate in Toyota from a grand design to build a Safe-Fail system? Most likely not. The history of TPS introduction shows that Lean is an emergent strategy rather than a directive one. TPS emerged through a process of trial and error, and several concepts were named after they had been implemented and fine-tuned. Ohno has stated that an initiative as central as Kanban actually developed quite late and may never have happened if computers were introduced in the factory earlier. However, there is one overarching framework which supported the evolution over several decades. It is the spirit of Kaizen, the spirit to continuously question work practices and improve them. Many years before the birth of Lean, when Eiji Toyoda joined the family business, one of his earliest stints was in the Audit and Improvement department. Every firm has an audit team, large organizations may have an audit department, but have you ever seen an Audit *and* Improvement department? The spirit of improvement predates the particular form of Continuous Improvement which Taiichi Ohno formalized several decades later.

What are the boundaries of a Lean system? Does it work equally well in all contexts? To answer this, we need to answer a more fundamental question. Should all systems be Safe-Fail system? If you examine the features of the original Lean system implemented in Toyota Motor Corporation, you would see that it was intended to handle high-inventory cost structure in a high-volume repetitive manufacturing context. The Andon Chord is strung over the assembly line. Lot sizes can be progressively decreased only if there is a significant lot size to start with. The progressive improvement of quality presupposes a long product life cycle. The focus on inventory cost reduction presupposes a cost structure where cost of holding inventory is significant, perhaps due to high cost of product or high warehouse rentals or high credit costs, etc. Lean may have reduced effectiveness if the product is inexpensive or if the opportunity cost of lost sales due to unavailability is significantly high or warehouse rental charges are low, and credit is easily available at low rates. Lean implementations result in duplication of machines and lowering of machine capacity utilization. This may have negative implications in those firms which use very specialized machine tools requiring high investment costs. While Lean can handle demand fluctuations within a reasonable band, products having high demand volatility with sudden peaks and troughs become difficult to handle.

Difficulties in application of Lean increases as we move from a high-volume-low-variety environment to a low-volume-high-variety environment. Many of the Lean concepts like standardized work and Heijunka lose their relevance in the make-to-order context of Job Shop and Project environments. Product proliferations increase the manufacturing complexities, making coordination through Kanban difficult, increasing the potential for quality defects and spreading thin the bandwidth of the Quality Circle. Safe-Fail systems cannot be employed if the event of a failure is not acceptable. If you are sending a man to the moon or operating a nuclear power plant or running a bank you are likely to find more comfort in the redundancies and buffers in Fail-Safe system design.

Lean systems are organic in nature and need time and sustained effort to build. If this Lean system grows very fast, then the investments in training and culture-building may lag behind the increase in workforce or the demands on Lean experts and mentors. Firms experiencing high worker turnover would find it more challenging to build a culture supporting Lean. Similarly, firms expanding globally may be hampered by culture and language barriers between Lean mentors from the home country and employees hired in new markets. The influx of new managers and workers and suppliers during high growth phases or as a result of mergers or acquisitions may dilute the quality orientation. New employees may not fully understand the need for the Andon Chord and proceed to achieve short-term 'success' through initiatives equivalent to increasing the diameter of an oft-tripping electric fuse. The short-term 'success' ultimately leads to the much bigger failure of the entire Lean philosophy.

The culture of the organization is thus an important determinant of the success of a Lean implementation. Lean requires a culture which values continuous improvement and forever questioning of the status quo. The firm has to build up this culture through manpower development and discipline over a long time. Of course, it helps if the employees come from a regional or national culture which not just values discipline and hard work but also a curiosity regarding the surrounding reality. Would it work if employees are culturally accustomed to taking shortcuts or relying on stop-gap arrangements? It also perhaps helps if the employees have religious or philosophical beliefs where continuous improvement is embedded.

An opportunity to align the work life and the spiritual life is perhaps the ultimate potential of a Lean system. Practising Continuous Improvement in the workplace could align with the aspiration to move from Untruth to Truth, from Darkness to Light, from Death to Immortality (*Brhadaranyaka Upanishad*). Buddha used to end his sermons with the words '*Charaiveti Charaiveti*' (Keep moving, keep moving). The refrain '*Charaiveti Charaiveti*' finds mention in the *Aitareya Brahmana* of the *Rig Veda* where the example is given of the unrelenting motion of the honeybees, the birds and the sun in order to motivate the seeker to keep moving. Similarly, Kaizen at the workplace could harmonize with the Protestant orientation of questioning what-is in order to move to what-should-be, and the Confucian orientation of striving for moral perfection.

I may be completely wrong in my assessment, but I find a trace of Buddhist, if not Zen Buddhist, philosophy permeating the Lean practices. The Why-Why practice to identify root cause harks back to the spiritual search of the Buddha which ultimately led to his expounding on the concept of *pratītyasamutpāda* or the theory of dependent origination which is the bedrock of Buddhist philosophy. Just as breaking the endless cycle of causation allows liberation from rebirth and suffering, the elimination of root cause solves the quality problem. The principle of Genchi Genbutsu parallels the Zen focus on observing reality as it is. The truth is not to be found in the lengthy reports or statistical analysis but in the reality of the workplace, just like Zen abhors scriptural learning and prefers direct realization. The fanatical focus on waste reduction aims to cut down work to its barest essence, like Zen-inspired calligraphy or poetry. The beauty of the Lean workplace is not in the Platonic conception of timeless perfection but in the Zen orientation of *wabi-sabi*, finding beauty in impermanence. And above all, Taiichi Ohno resembles to me a Zen master, a strict disciplinarian who rarely explains himself but pushes supervisors and workers towards achieving what seems impossible at first. Yet, in the recollections of compatriots like Michikazu Tanaka, he also comes across as a compassionate person who cares for workers very deeply, basing productivity improvements on improving work practices rather than speeding up the line. And it is in the Heart Sutra (*Prajñaparamita Hridaya Sutra*) of the Mahayana Buddhist tradition that I find the closest parallel to the journey of Continuous Improvement. The Heart Sutra aims to provide the key insight about Emptiness, the insight which is claimed to be capable of taking us to the other shore of enlightenment. The message that Form does not differ from Emptiness seems

apt for the Safe-Fail system for what traditionally is
considered Success leads to Failure and what seems to be
a Failure leads to Success. The Heart Sutra is translated
into various languages but ends with a mantra in Sanskrit.
If ever there was a description of the seeker's progress
towards enlightenment and the moment of its fulfilment,
this is it. If ever there was a hope of enlightenment in
the unending cycle of death and rebirth, Andon pulls and
Kaizen, perhaps this is it.

गते गते पारगते पारसंगते बोधि स्वाहा

> *Gate, Gate, Pāragate, Pārasaṃgate, Bodhi Svāhā!*
> (Going, going, gone to the other shore,
> Altogether gone to the other shore,
> Enlightenment comes in a flash. So be it.)

I wish you that flash, no less.

CHAPTER 18

Multiple Paths

'Oh, East is East, and West is West, and never the
twain shall meet,
Till Earth and Sky stand presently at God's great
Judgment Seat;
But there is neither East nor West, Border, nor Breed,
nor Birth,
When two strong men stand face to face, though they
come from the ends of the earth!'

—*The Ballad of East and West*, Rudyard Kipling

ONE OF THE persistent questions I have been asked is
whether an organization can be both an Elephant and
a Cheetah. Yes and no. Elephants are Elephants and
Cheetahs are Cheetahs and never can they meet in the
same organization unless enlightenment strikes. And
when they meet, they meet as equals under the gaze of an
enlightened management and maintain their distinctive
differences, each recognizing and appreciating the
strength of the other.

291

Before I describe the enlightened situation under which multiple paths can coexist, we need to understand the source of confusion. Fundamental to the existence of this confusion is the notion of trade-offs. The objectives of cost minimization and time responsiveness are different. The decision choices which minimize cost are different from the decision choices which minimize response time. An Elephant targets full capacity utilization to reduce cost, a Cheetah targets a much lower capacity utilization to ensure a strategic buffer capacity to ensure responsiveness. A firm cannot simultaneously operate at full capacity and spare capacity. There exists a trade-off.

Why is it so difficult for firms to realize the existence of this trade-off? This is because they can see from their own experience that there have been times when the firm could advance simultaneously on cost and time dimensions. They read in the business press about firms which have come up with a new technology whereby performance on both dimensions improve. This experience seems to be a contradiction at a first glance. What are we missing?

Figure 12: Trade-off and Efficiency Frontier

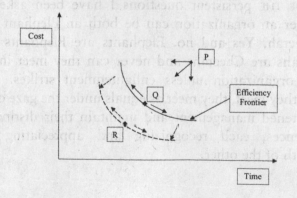

The notion of trade-off exists only on the efficient frontier. A firm at P, which is not on the efficient frontier, can always improve on both dimensions. This firm has so much slack and inefficiency in its operations that simultaneous advance on multiple dimensions is possible, till it reaches point Q on the efficient frontier. After this, the trade-off curve becomes a reality; the firm can reduce cost or time only at the expense of the other. Achieving improvements on both dimensions is not possible unless there is a technological shift. Innovations in product technology or process technology or business models result in shifting of the efficient frontier. Due to the shift in the trade-off curve, firms can enjoy improvements on multiple dimensions as they adopt and adapt to the new technology and move from Q to R. However, after the process of adoption of new technology is complete, the new trade-off curve requires firms to decide whether they want to excel in one dimension or other. A trade-off curve can be shifted; it cannot be obliterated.

Only firms which have had to confront the trade-off curve and decide a strategic positioning can recognize and appreciate the strengths and weaknesses of alternate strategic choices. They know that East is East and West is West and have had to make a choice between East and West. Their quest for having both East and West under the same firm is different from the inefficient firm gleefully announcing that they have proven the pundits wrong by simultaneously improving on multiple dimensions or the quest of the technology leader furiously investing in product- or process-related R&D that would shift the trade-off curve.

We return to our original question with greater clarity. Can a firm excel on both cost and time dimensions when it has reached the efficient frontier and there are no technological advances? Yes and no. A specific path can help the firm excel in a chosen dimension and not the other as trade-offs exist. So a specific path can be either cost-efficient or time-responsive, not both. But the firm can maintain two separate paths, one focused on cost, the other on time.

First of all, why should a firm aspire to be simultaneously handling multiple paths when excelling in any specific path is in itself very difficult? The reason is that each path serves a specific segment of customers with varying needs. Multiple paths thus increase the revenue of the firm as they allow differentiated offerings to serve differing needs of diverse customer segments. Sometimes multiple paths are mandated by design, for example, when a large general hospital needs to provide both affordable out-patient services to cater to a large patient volume as well as emergency services to cater to critical or trauma patients where time of response is crucial. But is there a cost to having multiple paths within the same firm?

The benefits and costs of having multiple paths depends on economies and diseconomies of scope in shared resources. Each path may use certain resources which are shared with other paths. Multiple paths may enable the firm to harness better economies of scope as the fixed costs of the shared resources are spread over a larger volume aggregating over multiple paths. Sharing of resources over multiple paths may also result in diffusion of learning and best practices from one path to another.

As a result, the marginal cost of producing a product belonging to a specific path may decrease as the variety of paths increases, resulting in strengthening the economies of scope. Higher the value of the cost of the shared asset and stronger the learnings, more meaningful would be the economies of scope gained.

In contrast, the sharing of resources between paths may also lead to competition between the paths for the use of shared resources. These competitions can turn ugly and degenerate into turf wars and game playing. Such competitions are likely to intensify as the demand for the shared resource outstrips its availability. Sharing of resources may also give rise to confusion if the operating policies in the management of the shared resource differ between the Elephant and the Cheetah. Even worse would be a situation where the different paths think their own policies and cultures to be superior to the competing path and strive to impose them on the other. An Elephant trying to teach a Cheetah the importance of cost efficiency while catching deer, or a Cheetah extolling the virtues of responsiveness in hunting grass would generate bad blood and confusion at the least and disaster if the suggestions are actually implemented. There are significant chances of diseconomies of scope existing in handling multiple paths where the paths are continuously fighting against each other internally rather than focusing on the real competition in the external market. The costs of settling these disputes and handling the infighting include not only the time and effort of senior management but also negatively affect the workforce morale and company culture.

Handling multiple paths is thus an opportunity as well as full of potential for disaster. Synergies between the paths

are not automatic; they have to be striven for. The plan for
handling multiple paths has to start with the fact that these
paths are distinct, and their distinctiveness needs to be
maintained. One way to maintain the distinctiveness is to
make sure that the two paths do not bump into each other
any more than required. This requires the decomposition
of a system into two or more sub-systems in such a way
that most of the interactions happen between parts of
the same sub-system and very few interactions happen
between parts of different sub-systems.

There are several ways in which the firm can attempt
this decomposition. A space-based decomposition
separates the two sub-systems into two different
locations. This may mean that the Elephant and the
Cheetah divisions are located in two different plants
or business units (BUs). Each of the plants could have
their own equipment, workforce, processes and culture
with little need to interact with the other plant except
through the corporate headquarters. However, the
duplication of equipment and workforce at each location
would result in a higher cost than if they were shared.
The only shared resources here are the staff functions
located in the corporate office like legal, accounting
and corporate finance, corporate brand management,
etc. The organization structure resembles a diversified
conglomerate with decentralization of decision-making
at BU level.

A second type of space-based decomposition occurs
when the two sub-systems are located inside the same
plant or BU. The management may demarcate certain
departments or production lines within a factory
location for each sub-system. The operating policies

of each sub-system would be unique, the structure resembling a factory-within-a-factory, also known as Focused Factory, first described by Operations Strategy pioneer Wickham Skinner. The shared resources in this case are not just the corporate support functions but also the plant-level functions including sales and marketing, accounting and HR.

A third kind of space-based decomposition can be observed in cases where the supply chain is designed with a strategically placed buffer between upstream and downstream operations. This buffer inventory divides the supply chain into two parts, a downstream portion which works on a Pull mode with Make-to-Order or Deliver-to-Order based policies; while the operations upstream of the buffer inventory work on a Push mode with Make-to-Stock based policies. Such a decomposition allows the firm to produce as an Elephant upstream and a Cheetah downstream with the buffer inventory absorbing the demand fluctuations and allowing the upstream Elephant to produce efficiently without unnecessary changeovers.

A time-based decomposition can be attempted when the shared resources are so costly that duplication of resources is not possible as in space-based decomposition. The high cost or unavailability of the resources may mean that two sub-systems are forced to coexist in the same space. Each sub-system may be earmarked certain times of operations, thereby segregating the different operating policies. For example, the segregation could be shift-wise or according to different days of the week.

A different kind of time-based decomposition can occur in firms facing seasonal demand. The year could be divided into peak and off-peak periods and the firm can employ different operating policies during different times. For example, the firm may behave like an Elephant during off-peak, producing long production runs in a Level production strategy operating at full capacity utilization along with FTL deliveries using the most cost-effective delivery mode (like sea shipment). The firm could then shift into Cheetah mode during the peak season, chasing demand with short production runs and quick changeovers enabled by spare capacity with flexible workforce and LTL delivery with higher frequency of delivery using speedier delivery modes (like air shipment or express cargo movements). Such a firm alternately shifts from an Elephant to a Cheetah and then back into Elephant.

An even more evolved kind of firm can employ both space-based and time-based decomposition. The firm can have an Elephant supply chain with manufacturing and distribution technology, processes and policies designed to minimize cost and a separately located Cheetah supply chain with manufacturing and distribution technology, processes and policies designed for time responsiveness. The firm then uses the Elephant for the off-peak and Cheetah for the peak season. What happens to the Elephant sub-system during peak and the Cheetah sub-system during off-peak? You may think that the sub-system not in use would be shut down as the firm alternately behaves like an Elephant or a Cheetah. Herein lies the beauty. Note that the peak is followed by the off-peak period which is followed by the peak again. Thus, during the peak season, the Cheetah would be chasing the demand for the current season while the Elephant would be producing for the next season. The Elephant would thus continue producing throughout the year while the Cheetah would chase intermittently during the peak season. Even this idleness of the Cheetah during a large part of the year can be reduced if the product is such that there are two or more peak seasons in a year. This may happen in fashion goods with spring–summer and fall–winter seasons or in the Indian agricultural context which has two main cropping seasons (Kharif and Rabi) in a year. The firm would then have both the Elephant and the Cheetah operational over the year, each bringing distinct operational competencies and benefits resulting in the firm reaping low costs for a large proportion of the produce, and low opportunity loss during the peak season albeit at a higher cost.

Handling multiple paths requires clarity of purpose, not just at the operational level, but also among the shared resources working at a different plant, division or corporate level. Take for example a dispatcher working in the logistics department who must differentiate between a consignment from the Elephant supply chain which needs to be sent through the lowest cost mode in contrast to another consignment coming from the Cheetah supply chain which may need to be sent through express cargo. This clarity is not automatic. The logistics function may experience high labour turnover and a new worker or supervisor may not immediately grasp why two consignments are treated differently.

Similarly, a newly recruited HR manager tasked with designing or fine-tuning the incentives schemes may feel confused about why there is a need to differentiate between the Elephant and the Cheetah in measuring performance. In fact, the Key Performance Indicators (KPIs) tracked for an Elephant are likely to be different from a Cheetah's; the Elephant KPIs giving more importance to efficiency- and productivity-linked parameters like high capacity utilization while those of a Cheetah would prioritize customer-service-linked parameters like low response times, high on-time delivery and high service levels. Imposing an incentive scheme which values and rewards high capacity utilization is as disastrous for a Cheetah as one which rewards high responsiveness for an Elephant.

In those cases, where an Elephant and a Cheetah share the same sales and marketing function, there is a heightened requirement on having clarity on questions like 'Who is our customer?' There may exist a need to design advertisement and sales promotion tactics differently for each of these multiple paths. Consider a firm with a legacy division selling high-volume low-variety products which over time has built a strong distribution network with deep penetration in a dispersed market. This firm may realize that it can use its distribution muscle to sell not just its original products but also other related and unrelated products. The distribution network is the shared resource but, for historical as well as reasons related to size of business, the new divisions may have little say in how sales promotion is designed. These new divisions may have much higher product variety with high volatility and seasonality, which are not present in the legacy division. They would have ideally liked a Cheetah sales organization but are saddled with a legacy Elephant. A successful Elephant sales manager may not automatically be successful in handling a Cheetah sales force. Ambidexterity is not automatic; it has to be striven for.

The concept of an ambidextrous organization has been discussed in innovation literature by Charles A. O'Reilly III and Michael L. Tushman to describe an organization which is as adept at exploitation as in exploration. Ambidexterity has been cited to be useful in innovating for the future while simultaneously being efficient and effective in its current businesses. Managing multiple paths requires an ambidexterity of a different kind, not in handling the present and the future, but in handling two distinct operating sub-systems in the present. To successfully manage multiple paths, each of the shared resources must develop ambidexterity. In normal usage, ambidexterity implies that the person is able to use both hands with equal ease. The ambidexterity implicit in managing multiple paths is different. The senior management must understand that they have an Elephant hand and a Cheetah hand, and they must know the strengths and weaknesses of each and when and where to use each hand and for what purpose.

The traditional view of ambidexterity has correctly underlined that the structure, processes and culture involved in exploration are different from those of exploitation. However, it has not considered whether the discontinuous innovations being pursued under exploration are in the same operations strategy domain as the incremental innovations being pursued under exploitation for current operations. Consider an Elephant which is evaluating two innovation ideas—one involving exploring a new business model which essentially requires itself to behave like a Cheetah, and a second one involving a discontinuous technology shift which would help it become a better Elephant. Both innovation choices are discontinuous changes, but they are different in terms of the fit with the existing operating model of the firm. The discontinuity in sync with the current operating strategy has a much higher chance of being chosen rather than the one which requires the entire organization to disrupt itself. Disrupting oneself implies fighting against one's own autopoiesis; it is possible but very difficult to achieve. An Elephant is likely to adopt incremental innovation arising from exploitation and discontinuous innovation arising from exploration to become an evolved Elephant while a Cheetah is likely to adopt incremental innovation arising from exploitation and discontinuous innovation arising from exploration to become an evolved Cheetah. An Elephant evolving into a Cheetah or vice versa is perhaps a much more challenging kind of ambidexterity to handle.

Changing paths is thus perhaps a much more difficult proposition than handling multiple paths. Changing paths implies an Elephant morphing into a Cheetah or vice versa through disruptive innovations. The change management process would have to fight the deviation-counteracting mutual causal processes inherent in the autopoiesis of the firm. Every small change attempted during the change process risks being reverted since the intermediate states are unstable. The intermediate states would see a huge amount of flux regarding operating policies and are likely to generate confusion within and across functional boundaries. If disruptive change of this kind has to succeed, multiple changes across functional boundaries need to be orchestrated simultaneously so that the system can move from one stable autopoiesis to another stable autopoiesis avoiding the intermediate unstable conditions as far as possible. It may be much easier if the top management starts from a clean state and sets up a separate BU and runs multiple paths for some time and eventually closes down the BU that has outlived its utility.

Managing multiple paths is not the same as the job of a traditional corporate office managing a diversified set of businesses. Diversity in this context traditionally means diversity in terms of sectors or geographies or technologies; for instance, a diversified firm could be operating separate BUs related to mining, upstream metal production, downstream manufacturing, financial services, IT, etc., located in different countries. The corporate office of a diversified group performs the role of capital allocation and tracks financial returns to its investments while allowing each individual BU to have independence in decision-making under an overarching corporate philosophy and identity. The complexities of each BU are encapsulated, and the corporate office need not worry whether they are Elephants or Cheetahs or Artists or anything else as long as financial return expectations are met.

The benchmarking of individual businesses is primarily on financial metrics, not operational ones. Traditional measures of diversity thus are not based on diversity of Operations Strategy. A diversified corporate may indeed be managing a collection of Elephants across different sectors of the economy and different geographies. It may have developed competencies in managing a collection of Elephants but may not realize that its competence in managing Elephants may not automatically extend to managing Cheetahs or Artists or other souls. Such a firm may fail miserably if it chooses to add a Cheetah or an Artist to the portfolio and benchmark its processes, policies, performance and culture against the rest of the portfolio BUs.

In contrast, the top management of a firm handling multiple paths must be acutely aware of the operational and cultural distinctiveness of each of the sub-systems. Each sub-system is autopoietic and has its own soul. The two sub-systems, each a Level 8 autopoietic system, also interact with each other, demonstrating structural coupling between two Level 8 autopoietic systems. A corporate handling multiple paths is thus at a level higher than single-path Level 8 firms under its management. Note that Level 9 originally was reserved for transcendental system in Table 1. We perhaps need to push transcendental systems to Level 10 to accommodate structural coupling between Level 8 organizations as Level 9. Does it have a soul of its own different from the souls of the individual paths constituting it? We can take inspiration from the biological concept of symbiosis.

Symbiosis refers to biological interactions between two organisms and has been described by Heinrich Anton de Bary as 'the living together of unlike organisms'. The managing of multiple paths can similarly be seen as the living together of unlike/dissimilar strategic choices. Biologists use multiple terms to classify symbiotic relationships based on the outcome of interactions. The interaction with another organism could have a positive, negative or a neutral effect on a particular organism. A symbiotic relationship where the outcome is positive for both is called mutualism (like the pollination of a flowering plant by a honeybee); if it is positive for one and neutral for the other it is called commensalism (when small mites attach themselves to bigger insects for transport, or when spiders use branches of trees for building their webs); if it is neutral for both it is called neutralism (such as different ant colonies living side by side and sharing the same nest); if it is negative for one and neutral for the other it is called amensalism (like the inability of new saplings to grow in the shade of large trees); if it is negative for both it is called competition (like two species of predators competing for the same prey in a particular location); and if it is positive for one and negative for the other it is called parasitism (like endoparasites such as roundworms living inside the human body and ectoparasites like ticks living on mammals).

The structural coupling between an Elephant and a Cheetah could result in mutualism if the Elephant is used upstream to replenish a buffer inventory at the lowest cost, which is used by a downstream Cheetah to respond quickly to volatile demand. Structural coupling could result in neutralism if, for example, the emergency department of the general-purpose hospital is in a location or building different from the main hospital and shares little except the hospital name. Structural coupling could result in competition if the Elephant and Cheetah share a very high-cost scarce resource like the operating theatres in a hospital. The competition could be reflected in ideological battles regarding whether the shared resources should operate at full capacity utilization or have spare capacity, apart from regular on-going battles regarding garnering a major share of the scarce resource. Structural coupling could result in commensalism if a new fast-track delivery service is offered at additional cost to a customer using an e-commerce site offering affordable merchandise with free delivery for the standard delivery mode. Structural coupling can result in amensalism at best and parasitism at worst if the dominant Elephant imposes its operating policies like full capacity utilization on the smaller Cheetah sub-system.

However, there is a crucial difference between symbiosis in the biological world and symbiosis in handling multiple paths in a Level 9 corporate. In the biological world, no one actively manages the interactions between the two species; while there are senior managers in the Level 9 corporate whose job description would include the management of multiple paths. It is up to these senior managers to achieve the promise of mutualism while limiting the diseconomies of scope and ensure that East and West coexist peacefully and strengthen each other while retaining their distinctiveness. The biggest resource of this Level 9 firm is the dynamic capacity in handling the tension between divergent sub-systems and the learning gained over time. And in the process, the managers have the opportunity to create a soul for the Level 9 corporate—a soul which has balance as the essence.

Mantra of Multiple Paths: Balance

PART IV: THE BEAUTY

CHAPTER 19

The Beauty of Operations

'Everything has beauty, but not everyone sees it.'

—Confucius

'Beauty is the illumination of your soul.'

—*Anam Cara: A Book of Celtic Wisdom,*
John O'Donohue

THE BEAUTY OF OPERATIONS! You must be kidding me! Operations is about rolling up the sleeves and getting your hands dirty in bringing something into existence rather than pontificating from the ivory towers. Not for nothing do you roll up the sleeves—the work environment could be dirty in a literal sense of the word, a far cry from the spic and span air-conditioned office cubicles populated by strategists. Dirt originating from the metal cutting through metal, from the fuel burnt to power the factories, from the smoke billowing out of the furnace. Dirt and soot cover every possible surface, surfaces which are drab and gloomy except for the bright yellow lines signifying danger. To a casual visitor, the yellow lines demarcate a safe zone for walking inside the factory; for the workers, crossing the yellow lines are a daily part of the regular job. They undertake these risky jobs wearing garish fluorescent jackets and colour-coded helmets meant not just to protect but also to identify and rescue in case of any eventuality. You can sniff danger everywhere.

You may not need to sniff to get an aroma of the place. Pungent chemical scents may waffle through the air or the smell of the sweat and grime coming from a large number of workers huddled together in small, inadequately ventilated, dimly lit, hot and humid rooms. You suddenly realize that the term 'sweatshop' has an olfactory connection. Sweat pours out from the human bodies working under tin roofs of factories during the oppressive summer heat and high humidity. Big industrial fans blow the heated ambient air at workers, leaving one to wonder if it would be better to switch the fans off. The lone water cooler could be the most prized asset on the shop floor. These workers may have a blessed life compared to the workers in steel mills who handle molten metal. Not for nothing are plants named Hot Strip Mill or the even more aptly named Heat Treatment Unit, they handle products which are, well, hot and are not partial about meting out this treatment to products and workers alike. As a young engineering student visiting an integrated steel plant during a summer internship, I remember standing on top of a continuous casting machine and watching a worker stand close to the molten steel being poured from the ladle into the mould. The worker must insert a thermocouple inside the flowing metal to record the temperature. It was so hot inside the control room that I shuddered to think about the worker who was standing a few feet away from the molten steel, covered in protective clothing from head to toe. Later, when I stepped out of the plant into the blazing mid-day summer sun, the weather outside actually felt pleasant.

And then the noise. The constant hum of heavy machinery, the periodic clanking of metal presses, the intermittent hammering of the sheet metal work, the jarring sound of the electric saw, the high-pitched whirring of engines. The extent of noise becomes apparent only when there is a sudden power failure or when a shift ends. If the noise, heat and humidity seem a nuisance in a factory located on the surface, they are unbearable in the claustrophobic confines of the tunnels being bored under the earth or inside mines or inside engine rooms of ships and submarines. The faces of the coal miners tell the story of their workplace. Heat, humidity, dust, noise, harsh lights, stench, etc., are the reality, to a varied degree, of different workplaces. The other extreme of this reality are the sterile work environments of pharmaceutical, bio-medical, nuclear or electronics manufacturing, the clean rooms populated by workers covered from head to toe in protective clothing. The absence of colour, sound and smell is overpowering. The workplace is essentially functional in design, not meant to be aesthetic.

Operations textbooks rarely mention workplace aesthetics. It almost seems that the Operations world is devoid of the sensual. Perhaps the visual, auditory, olfactory worlds are too stark and too inconvenient to merit mention on the pristine white pages of a textbook. Whatever little focus these worlds get are more from the orientation of handling occupational hazards and improving workplace safety or an orientation of handling

pollution. These are more in the spirit of reducing or
removing ugliness rather than appreciating beauty.

The situation improves markedly when we move from
manufacturing to services. Service workplaces are more
aesthetics-oriented perhaps due to the presence of the
customer in certain parts of the service workplace. Still,
aesthetics, it seems, is for the appreciation of the customer,
not the service provider. The two worlds are separated, for
example in a restaurant, by the revolving door demarcating
the air-conditioned, scented and aesthetically designed food
consumption area with its soothing music in the background
and comfortable seating from the food preparation area
witnessing shouting and frenetic activity in a much more
confined standing space with a potpourri of smells, smoke,
heated ovens and even more frayed tempers.

Tempers run high on a factory shop floor. The
inhuman working conditions and the long hours of work
create frustration and helplessness which erupts in fits of
rage at the slightest provocation. Men fighting against
men. Men fighting against the system. Men fighting
against the union. Union fighting against the management.
I have purposely used the word 'men'. Gender diversity
on the shop floor could be highly skewed unless the work
involves dexterity where women have an advantage. The
survival of workers on the shop floor could boil down to
questions of physical prowess, stamina and endurance.
While physical violence could be rare, verbal abuse could
be more commonplace. Such a primal landscape devalues
aesthetics, survival is the prime motivation, not the
appreciation of beauty.

The survival-related challenge does not limit itself
to the factory, it permeates the living spaces of workers.

I challenge anybody who sees beauty in the industry to read the seminal work of Friedrich Engels on the working conditions of English workers in the textile mills in and around Manchester. Written during 1842–44, it describes in gruesome detail the dehumanized working conditions in the mills which extended to the widespread misery, malnutrition, disease and death in overcrowded living spaces. The industrial revolution had created the conditions suitable for the communist revolution. Thanks to the threat of revolution, the factory also changed in response to the critique, becoming progressively more labour-oriented, albeit sometimes changing only when faced with violent resistance from labour unions. Still, the conditions have indeed changed considerably. Today's workplaces are a far cry from the exploitative practices of yesteryears.

My friend, you might wonder if I have deliberately painted a very grim picture of the Operations world. Indeed, I have overstated the ugliness case for a large number of progressive organizations around the world who value workplace conditions and maintain safety, cleanliness and environmental standards as well as maintain cordial work relationships. But there are still some firms where the work environment leaves a lot to be desired in terms of pollution and safety standards, leaving any talk of aesthetics redundant. The maintenance of safety and cleanliness are hygiene factors, these need to be addressed before we claim to see beauty in Operations. We must start this journey by first making sure we do not see Operations through rose-tinted glasses. We need to see reality as it is. The reality is that there are still vestiges of the ugliness that Engels described in 1844. As managers

we need to eradicate this ugliness by bringing in the
hygiene factors of safety, cleanliness and a non-polluting
environment before we talk of lofty ideals of beauty. We
need to see the ugliness; only then would we know when
we see true beauty. We are Operations folks; we roll up
our sleeves and get on with the work of improving work
environments. But at the same time, we should not get
demoralized that what we do amounts to just removing
the ugliness. We have the potential to not just remove the
ugliness but also see the true beauty of our beloved. But
I would prefer if you accord the highest priority to the
removal of ugliness than deriving joy from understanding
the beauty of Operations. Removal of ugliness benefits
the workers and hence must have higher priority than the
philosophical discussions of beauty inherent in strategic
choices which provide joy only to you and me.

We all need beauty in our life, else we live lives no
different from an animal. This sense of beauty can come
from our work or from our family and friends or from
the pursuit of a hobby or perfection of a craft or an
appreciation of art or appreciation of nature. A manager
or a consultant may appreciate the beauty inherent in
music or painting or a novel but these are sources not
directly related to the chosen field of managerial or
professional work. You may ask, what is the need at all
to see beauty in Operations? I just perform my role as a
manager for which I get paid and then I use my free time
to delve into my chosen hobby or interest. Fair enough.
But this means that for a substantial part of your working
life you will have no connection to beauty except perhaps
humming a tune under your breath and hoping that the
boss will not notice. It divides your day into two parts—

one in which you suspend your sense of beauty to earn a living and another where you retreat into art or nature to recover from the ugliness of the other. How much better would it be if you could fill up your life with different kinds of beauty, appreciating the beauty of organizations as much as you appreciate the beauty of a work of art?

The beauty of an organization is not based on the aesthetics of the architecture of the corporate office or the work environment. If it was, it would be very easy to beautify any organization by painting the workplace in bright, vibrant colours or arranging neat rows of potted plants to hide the rust or redesign and rearrange the furniture or hang large oil canvases in corporate headquarters located in architectural marvels. Such cosmetic changes are as beautiful as lipstick on a gorilla. A firm which believes in the philosophy that the only purpose of business is to make money, and harms consumers, stakeholders and the environment in its dirty pursuit, may try to hide behind aesthetic facades but no amount of perfume can hide the stench of the blood on its hands. True beauty is not skin deep.

True beauty is the beauty of the soul.

True beauty is when a manager working in an organization sees a glimpse of the soul of the system she is managing. True beauty arises when the manager gains clarity on existential questions like 'Who are we?', 'What is the purpose of our existence?', 'Why should we exist?' And most importantly, from an Operations standpoint, how should we structure our existence? True beauty arises when a leader closes doors to alternate forms of existence and is conscious of what she wants the organization to become. True beauty is in the becoming of the organization and the awareness of that becoming in the consciousness of its managers. True beauty is when employees and customers have a sense of what the firm stands for and what it strives to become.

The beauty of Operations is that this process of becoming can be manifested not in terms of abstract ideas but in terms of concrete choices made on the dimensions of Operations Strategy. The capacity strategy of an Elephant could be quite different from that of a Cheetah or an Insect or an Artist, and so too the production strategy, quality strategy, etc. These strategic choices exist because of the existence of hard constraints. A firm cannot simultaneously operate at full capacity utilization and keep spare capacity, it cannot simultaneously have a Lead capacity strategy as well as a Lag capacity strategy, it cannot simultaneously have a post-facto, inspection-based product quality orientation as well as an a-priori process quality-based orientation, it cannot simultaneously operate a continuous review as well as periodic review-based inventory control for a particular product, it cannot simultaneously run a truck on FTL as well as LTL basis, it cannot simultaneously send a consignment by air shipment and sea shipment, it cannot simultaneously be capital-intensive as well as labour-intensive, it cannot simultaneously take a transaction orientation as well as a partnership orientation in dealing with suppliers, it cannot simultaneously deliver a product as per MTS as well as MTO, push as well as pull, etc. Some of these hard choices have to be made because trade-offs are real, some hard choices have to be made since there are limiting constraints like budgets, some hard choices have to be made because the competencies in excelling in one dimension may not just be unhelpful but actually hinder the development of competencies in another dimension, some hard choices have to be made since the enabling cultures are different.

What is clear to any student of Operations is that hard choices exist. Hard choices exist not just on one dimension or sub-dimension of Operations Strategy, but across so many dimensions that there are a very large number of permutations possible of the various doors that can be closed. As a result, you don't close one door, you close a *set* of doors. Some of these door closings are coordinated, some are jarring. Some of these door closings give rise to synergy, some of them are just the sum of the parts and some lead to friction. The beauty of Operations is figuring out the synchronization of the door closings across a large number of hard choices which are synergistic in nature. The beauty of Operations is to make the system work as a whole, not just the sum of the parts. Systems have the potential to have soul; the beauty of Operations is to create synergy, create the soul.

The beauty of Operations is to understand that there exists no one best set of door closings. Instead, there are patterns of door closings which can be observed across diverse sectors of industry and technology. I want you to see these patterns. I have tried to present some of these patterns, perhaps there are many more that I haven't seen. These patterns are what I am calling Elephant, Cheetah, Artist, Insect, Conductor, Composer, Praying Mantis, Tortoise, etc. I would fully understand if you disagree with the names of the patterns, call them what you want. But see the patterns. These patterns exist, whether you are able to observe them or not is your challenge.

The ability to see patterns has major implications for a practising manager, leader or consultant. First, it means that you can intuitively make sense of a large number of door closings and check if the resultant pattern matches closely or to some extent one of the known patterns. If so, some of the knowledge, insights and best practices in managing the known pattern could be adopted or adapted to the context at hand. Second, the manager or consultant must be acutely aware of the existence of alternate patterns representing alternate existences and hence guard against becoming colour blind and seeing everything from the viewpoint of a specific pattern. Each pattern has its beauty; each pattern has its reason for existence. The beauty of Operations is the beauty of patterns, not one pattern. Third, the pattern of door closings observed in a context may not reflect any known pattern. New patterns come into existence as technology and society develop and organizations evolve. When I started teaching Operations Strategy, there were no multi-sided platforms or online marketplaces acting as digital matchmakers. Would it be right to force-fit existing patterns prevalent in factories and service shops on these new platform businesses? Instead, we should study each new business model in terms of the constraints and the hard choices and start seeing the patterns of door closings that emerge. If these patterns match existing patterns, then so be it. If not, we need to describe these new patterns and perhaps coin new metaphors which succinctly reflect the essence of this new form. The metaphor is just an evolved kind of label. Time responsiveness is a label; Cheetah is a metaphor. The label is fundamental; we human beings need a name to refer to something. The metaphor is a matter of choice.

As you immerse yourself in the world of patterns you start seeing more patterns. Instead of Elephants and Cheetahs you start differentiating between manufacturing Elephants and distribution Elephants and R&D Elephants. You see how a Cheetah competing on on-time delivery has similarities as well as differences with a Cheetah competing on delivery reliability. The more you observe patterns, the broader metaphors used like Elephants and Cheetahs seem inadequate to represent the finer differences in patterns. Create more refined metaphors if you like, the added metaphors add beauty to the language of Operations. But each new metaphor needs to be grounded in terms of hard choices in dealing with operating constraints. Each new metaphor should represent a new pattern of door closings. Each new metaphor should present the beauty of an alternate existence.

While our understanding of patterns originates from the hard choices inherent in operations, patterns are not exclusive to the field of operations. The pattern in operations does not stand alone, it supports and is in turn supported by the patterns of door closings in sales, marketing, HR, finance, etc. The pattern is ultimately a pattern of the business model. An Elephant pattern business model as opposed to a Cheetah or an Insect or an Artist pattern business model, etc.

Who can see this beauty? An operations manager whose entire career has been in Elephant firms can appreciate the beauty of Elephants but may stumble at appreciating the beauty of the Cheetah. An operations manager whose entire career has been within the operations function may not be exposed to the hard choices in sales, marketing, HR, finance, etc., to appreciate the beauty of the business model and not just the operations aspect of the business model. Conversely, a sales manager whose entire career has been in a Cheetah sales function may neither appreciate nor understand the hard choices faced by operations managers working in an Artist. Thus, the true beauty of a pattern inherent in a business model is perhaps apparent only to those managers and consultants who have been exposed to a variety of functions across a variety of firms having diverse strategic positioning. At the same time, the patterns I have discussed all emanate from the hard choices faced in operations and hence need senior leaders to have an understanding as well as appreciation of Operations Strategy even if their functional expertise lies somewhere else. The beauty of Operations is perhaps most accessible to those managers who have risen to general management positions and have experience of handling operations contexts.

There is beauty in every organization, but not everyone can see it. To see beauty in patterns requires exposure to diversity—sectors, contexts, operating philosophies. Not everyone gets this exposure, unless one works as a consultant helping diverse organizations or moves across leadership positions in diverse organizations. But just exposure to diversity is not enough. To see beauty in patterns one needs to cultivate acceptance of diversity rather than focus on one best way, whatever that may be. Acceptance of the pattern is the key. The challenge is to have acceptance of diversity as well as an improvement orientation.

Why is acceptance difficult? The moment we see an Insect, we may start thinking of how this Insect can break the vicious cycle and become an Elephant. However, this change requires first an acceptance by the firm that it is behaving like an Insect. It is difficult to appreciate the beauty of Cockroach or a Leech. Yet, there is a beauty in the illumination of the soul. The beauty when a Cockroach understands the Cockroach pattern and looks at its own organization and gasps, 'Oh, I am a Cockroach!' There is a separate beauty in its trials and tribulations in trying to become an Elephant. An Insect which understands that it is an Insect is as beautiful as an Elephant or Cheetah or Artist which gets an insight about its own soul. As a consultant, your job is to enable this soul searching. Oh, what a beautiful job you have.

A metaphor representing a stable set of door closings implies that there are basins of attraction towards which the decision choices gravitate. There is beauty in gravitating towards a known pattern. Yet, this basin of attraction may also imply that there would be a huge amount of struggle inherent in trying to move out of this basin. Merely changing one or a few decisions regarding hard choices in operations may not be enough to escape the basin; it may need simultaneous changes to a large number of decisions across not just various operations dimensions but also sales, marketing, HR, finance, etc., to make sure that the firm moves from one stable pattern or basin of attraction to another. There is beauty in such a transformation. The struggle to change is really a struggle against oneself, a struggle against the firm's autopoiesis. It is through this struggle that the beauty of autopoiesis becomes more apparent.

To see beauty in Operations, you must appreciate beauty in the first place. A person who sees no beauty in the natural world or the world of arts is unlikely to see beauty in Operations. To see beauty in nature, you need to stand and stare. To appreciate beauty in art, you need to go to the gallery and study paintings or go to the theatre to immerse yourself in drama or cinema or a musical performance. Where do you go to see beauty in Operations? The simplest way is to visit as many organizations as you can, take up as many diverse consulting assignments as feasible. But this approach has limitations. Not everyone can visit an organization or a workplace; organizations are secretive by nature, fearing copycat competitors and industrial espionage. And a casual visit does not allow deeper discussions about hard choices made by the firm. In contrast, a case study allows us to peek into a firm at a particular point in time and understand the decision dilemma arising out of the hard choices before it. Competitor analysis can throw up important external manifestations of the underlying business model employed by a competitor. Industry analysis allows us to understand the strengths and weaknesses of the different business models existing in a specific industry at a specific time. Each of these businesses has a beauty of its own, a soul it calls its own.

A manager or consultant who sees the beauty in Operations can appreciate the collection of Elephants, Cheetahs, Insects, Artists, etc., which populate an industry ecosystem. Each has a pattern of its own and is at the same time part of a bigger pattern. Each competes against the other patterns and also enables them. The value of an Artist is seldom appreciated till the consumer has had enough of cheap Insects and standard Elephants. A standard delivery mode offered by an Elephant creates the background for a Cheetah to create value by offering an express delivery service. Without the Elephant as a benchmark to differentiate its service, the Cheetah may lose its reason for existence. A pattern cannot exist without its complements. We can only discern a pattern against the background of other patterns and the ultimate background of the random pattern.

It may be difficult for you to see the beauty of a Leech or a Praying Mantis. You may recoil at the understanding that the Leech is designed to defraud customers, employees, partners, banks, etc., and just vanish with their money. A Praying Mantis tracks its Composer prey to illegally copy its innovations. You may think of them as ugliness rather than beauty. This is the biggest test of your acceptance of diversity of souls. I want you to see the beauty of these patterns too. Your recoiling from them is emanating from your value judgement about the unethical nature of their business. You are perfectly within your rights to have this value judgement; in fact, I would be worried if you agreed with what they are doing. But this value judgement belongs to the realm of the observer, not the object being observed. The beauty lies in the Leech or the Praying Mantis pattern being part of the collection of patterns. A Leech or Praying Mantis is an alternate existence which an Elephant or Cheetah or an Artist has chosen not to be. Without the Leech pattern, we cannot appreciate the true beauty of the other alternate patterns. And remember, if you are not going to judge a Leech pattern, neither can you say that an Elephant or a Cheetah or an Artist is a better existence than a Leech. Patterns do not exist in a hierarchy in terms of beauty or values, each one is incomparable. I am using this Leech example for you to get out of judging alternate existences. Patterns exist and their existence is beauty. Period. It is for the autopoietic Leech to have a value judgement and decide if it wants to continue with its wretched existence or shift to a more ethical one. For you, all patterns are beautiful, the collection of patterns is beautiful. At the same time, you need to have an ethical position to decide whether you want to work for or associate yourself with a Leech who may or may not know that it is a Leech. By taking your own value judgement you define yourself, your own autopoiesis, which has nothing to do with the beauty of the Leech pattern. Your ethical decision to disassociate from a Leech illuminates your soul.

Sometimes a pattern is conspicuous by its absence. When we identify the absence of a pattern in an industry ecosystem, we should ask why the ecosystem does not support that pattern. Maybe there are specific constraints, maybe the industry is still maturing and customers are not demanding the value offered by the missing pattern, maybe the regulatory environment or technological landscape are not supportive. Things change. Maybe technological breakthroughs or changes in customer expectations would tomorrow provide an opportunity for a known pattern to incarnate for the first time in this industry. Maybe an entrepreneur would feel the absence and strive to change consumer perceptions and bring the pattern into existence.

And finally, does a pattern exist at all? Is there anything called an Elephant or a Cheetah? An Elephant is an idea, just like a circle is an idea, an abstract form. There exists no perfect circle in reality, yet we instinctively call something as circular when we see an approximation. Circles are different from triangles, even though there does not exist in reality either a perfect circle or triangle. Elephants are different from Cheetahs, even though there does not exist in reality either perfect Elephants or Cheetahs. An Elephant is ultimately an idea—a firm competing on cost leadership. A Cheetah is ultimately an idea—a firm competing on time responsiveness. A Tortoise is ultimately an idea—a firm intent on risk minimization. A business unit may implement these ideas in a specific social and environmental context using the technology available to it. What we see in the physical world are these implementations. The beauty lies in observing existing reality to comprehend the realm of ideas, the realm of forms which lie beyond.

What a wonderful world is this world of Operations. What a beauty it is for those who can see the different patterns of existence, different patterns of becoming. I am reminded of the song 'What a Wonderful World' sung by Louis Armstrong.

> I see trees of green, red roses too
> I see them bloom for me and you
> And I think to myself what a wonderful world

If I were a singer, I could have sung: 'I see Elephants and Cheetahs, and Artists too' . . . but I would rather prefer if you, my friend, sing that for me. Sing it when you recognize the patterns and see the beauty of their coexistence. Oh, what a wonderful world, isn't it, my friend? Fill up your life with a sense of wonder, a sense of beauty. When you see an Elephant, you see beauty, when you see a Cheetah, you see beauty, when you see an Insect, you see beauty. Each and every pattern of Operations Strategy is a beauty. You get drunk on this beauty and extoll like the Rig Vedic seer, '*Madhu vātā ṛitāyate madhu ksharanti sindavah*'. There is honey in the breeze, there is honey in the rivers . . . The whole world of Operations, which lacks aesthetic sensitivities, is now beautiful honey for you!

CHAPTER 20

Consciousness of Systems

'*Aniccā vata sankhārā, uppadavaya-dhamminō*'
(Impermanent truly are compounded things
[conditionings], by nature arising and passing away.]
—*Mahāparinibbāna-sutta, Dīgha-nikāya*

'Out of the night that covers me,
Black as the pit from pole to pole,
I thank whatever gods may be
For my unconquerable soul.
. . .
It matters not how strait the gate,
How charged with punishments the scroll,
I am the master of my fate,
I am the captain of my soul.'

—*Invictus*, William Ernest Henley

WE HAD STARTED with a working hypothesis—systems have souls. It is now time to review our understanding based on what we have discussed so far. A system has the capability to be more than the sum of parts. This is achieved through synergy, when the parts interact in a manner where each is supported by some of the other parts and in turn support others in achieving their objectives. These interactions are not standardized, there are stable and distinct patterns of interactions in different competitive contexts. These interaction patterns are created through the closing of doors in various dimensions of operations strategy and related financial, sales, marketing, HR strategic choices, etc. The synchronized door closings across various strategic choices result in stable patterns of interactions in the business model which give rise to distinct cultures. These distinct patterns of doors closings, interaction between parts and organizational culture give rise to the distinct souls that I have described so far. I reiterate my belief that organizational systems have souls.

However, it is not as simple to simply declare that systems have souls.

Can a pattern exist without an observer who can discern the pattern? Darkness covers darkness in the absence of an enlightened observer—we do not know that we do not know. The organization would be busy with the daily activities—understanding markets and competitors, forecasting sales, planning operations, estimating financial impact, etc., without once pausing to ask existential questions like who are we, who are we not, what is our purpose, why do we exist, how are we structured to accomplish what we want to achieve and how our daily routine contributes to becoming what we want to become, etc. The sole purpose of existence is to go through a treadmill to meet ever-expanding financial targets. This system too has a soul, but it is not aware of it. It is not that this organization does not have sensory capabilities or intellect, the firm may be stuffed with the most capable managers who watch customer behaviour and analyse competitor moves diligently. Yet, they are blind about themselves as they have not turned their attention inwards at their own operations, their own autopoiesis. They are ignorant of the existence of patterns and hence are ignorant of the specific pattern that describes their business. They are ignorant about their ignorance.

This ignorance about the soul of a system is not a competitive disadvantage if every firm is ignorant. But the moment a competitor is able to see its own pattern, it must be able to distinguish one pattern from another, and hence start understanding the set of patterns. This competitor can then not only understand its own autopoiesis as well as observe from outside and guess the pattern being employed by other firms while the ignorant firm continues to not know that it does not know.

To know a single pattern is not possible since there would be nothing to distinguish the pattern from. Knowledge of a pattern is thus contingent on knowing what it is not. An Elephant knows it is not an Insect or a Cheetah or an Artist. The more the number of patterns that it knows it is not, the more sharply it understands what it is. The knowledge of a pattern is intricately linked to the knowledge of all patterns. To understand the soul of a system, we must necessarily be conscious of the existence of other systems. My friend, I have not seen all the operations systems. I have described the few that I have seen. As you see more patterns, you would understand the soul of a system much better than the hazy view I have described.

How can an organization become conscious of its own soul? Does an organization have a consciousness in the first place? An organization is a Level 8 system populated by Level 7 human beings who have a consciousness of their own. The pattern can be discerned by a single employee or a collection of employees of an organization. Not all employees are equally capable of discerning a pattern as they may not have knowledge of the doors closed by strategists. A worker may not be in the least interested in strategic choices while a lower level or a functional manager may have knowledge of a partial set of door closings and the rationale and thinking process behind them but be unaware of the bigger picture. The consciousness of a strategy thus becomes stronger as we move from functional managers to general managers and CXO positions. Consciousness emanating from knowledge of strategic choices is concentrated in top echelons while consciousness emanating from experience of culture has the potential to permeate every part of the organization. The existence of a distinct culture is contingent on distinct patterns of door closings and the consciousness of the soul is contingent on becoming conscious of the distinct culture and the underlying distinct pattern of door closings. The culture can be experienced by not just employees but also the customers and the suppliers, though external observers would not be able to discern fully the strategic choices. While it is desirable that the entire organization be conscious of its own soul, it is absolutely necessary that the top leadership be conscious of the soul it is nurturing and aware why it is not nurturing some other soul.

It is also necessary that the leaders enlighten the rank and file about the organizational soul they are part of, what that soul is and what it is not. I do not use the word 'enlighten' lightly. The moment is magical when a Level 7 part becomes aware of a higher-level system it is part of. The part becomes aware of the whole of which it is a part. Not all parts have the opportunity to know the whole that they are part of. Individual atoms constituting a cell do not know differences between cells, individual cells constituting an organ do not know the differences between organs, different organs constituting a human being do not know the differences between one human and another nor can they contemplate the soul of the human that they constitute. Yet, different humans constituting an organization hold the *potential* to know the differences between one organizational soul and another. It is the challenge of senior leaders to enable this potential to translate into reality, the magical moment when the part contemplates the whole and sees the soul infused in the system and becomes thankful to the leadership for creating the conditions for the realization to happen. As a senior leader, you have the potential to inspire the rank and file to realize the soul of the whole.

The Gayatri Mantra, the invocation with which we started this book, is a very ancient mantra appearing in the Rig Veda, which is supposed to provide deliverance. Read the mantra carefully. It is nothing short of deliverance when the Level 7 human being senses the brilliance of The Soul permeating everything, and realizes that this act of contemplation itself is part of the same spiritual whole that he or she is able to contemplate as a part. The inspiration to realize the whole comes from the whole.

As a senior leader in the organization, can you create a whole which inspires a part to contemplate the whole? It would be nothing short of deliverance from the inanities of modern organizational life.

To develop this shared consciousness about its organizational soul, the senior leaders may use strategy retreats to stand back from day-to-day operations and discuss the purpose of the organization and how it is structured internally in terms of door closings to achieve this purpose. These deliberations could be used not just for alignment of functional strategies with the overall organizational strategy but also for communicating the vision of the soul that the top leadership wants to nurture. This kind of reflection on an organization system is episodic. Instead of an episodic reflection process, there is a need for a systematic process for reflecting on systems!

In most organizations, even the annual strategy retreat is dispensed with. These organizations schedule quarterly or annual business review meetings where the focus is on reviewing the performance achieved and setting future targets. Such meetings mostly focus on individual or departmental performance rather than reflections on systems. The meetings end in finding scapegoats for poor performance, or raucous celebrations and parties for achieving milestones. The ends justify the means and there is little interest in pondering over existential questions. Achievement of targets is the only reason for existence, consciousness is of targets, not the soul.

Consciousness of a system is too valuable to be relegated to an annual event. An organization system is in a constant state of flux. New employees join, others retire or move elsewhere, customer behaviour changes over time, technologies move from cutting-edge to mature know-how, organizational priorities change as CEOs depart and new leadership takes charge. The strategic choices need to be constantly reviewed to handle the changed reality, requiring a continued consciousness of what we are becoming. At each such recalibration of the strategic choices there is potential for a move away from the current pattern of existence. Sometimes these moves are deliberate strategic moves, at other times these are quick fixes that are not thought through and result in confusion and conflicts with other strategic choices. The system loses consciousness of what it is supposed to be. Entropy is the constant enemy of a strategist. Things fall apart.

It should not come as any surprise to us that all man-made things are impermanent. Impermanence is the dharma of conditioned existence—phenomena whose existence depends on the existence of other phenomena. A production planning strategy does not exist in a vacuum, it has interactions with the capacity strategy, inventory strategy, sales promotion strategy, etc., and vice versa. The door closings are interrelated and hence conditional. And as with all conditioned phenomena, the interrelated strategy too is fragile and prone to disintegration. It is the role of management to continuously be mindful of the overall pattern and undertake repair and maintenance activities.

A lack of consciousness about the soul can lead to a gradual degradation of the cultural environment of the firm. It is easy for an Elephant to gradually turn into an Insect. All it has to do is neglect its consciousness. It starts with a shifting of focus from investing to squeezing profitability by obtaining more and more from the existing assets, which progresses from gradual constriction of investments to explicit focus on cost-cutting and finally degenerates into cutting corners. A different kind of

change process is involved when an organization is
conscious of its soul and decides to become something
else. An Insect may realize the futility of living from one
day to another and start investing. Change processes
can thus arise both from a lack of consciousness of who
we were and from a consciousness of who we want to
become. Both result in an alteration of the soul.

This raises serious questions regarding the assertion
that systems have souls. Is this soul permanent or does
it change? If an Elephant changes into a Cheetah, is its
soul that of an Elephant or a Cheetah or both or neither?
And if impermanence is the dharma of conditioned
phenomena, should not the soul also be impermanent?

The soul of an organizational system is neither
Elephant nor Cheetah nor both nor neither. Patterns
are ever changing. The pattern of existence we become
conscious of and call an Elephant (or any other name) is
a set of interrelated strategic choices which give rise to a
distinct synergy and culture. While this pattern continues
to hold, we call it an Elephant, and when the pattern
changes to that of an Insect we call it an Insect. The soul
is in a constant process of becoming. Even when there is
no change in its strategic choices, its becoming lies in its
reaffirming the doors closed. The closed doors reaffirm the
patterns of interaction happening within the organization
every moment. In a way, an organization is continuously
dying and being reborn. I want you to be conscious of this
continued fading away and becoming again. Is there at
all an unchanging soul of a system? Or is it that a system
neither has a soul nor does it not have a soul?

To me, the consciousness of a continued fading and
becoming of a system is the consciousness of the beauty

of a system. The beauty is in seeing the inevitability of fading away in the becoming and the inevitability of becoming in the fading away.

And if you happen to witness this beauty in the organizational life, what about your own existence? The reflection on the impermanence of a Level 8 organizational system can act as a tool for meditation on your own Level 7 system. Both meditations can go hand in hand, the consciousness of impermanence permeates both Level 7 and Level 8 systems. If you have never asked yourself existential questions like 'Who am I?', how would you see the soul of an organization?

Who am I? I hope you find your own answer to this eternal existential question, I have found mine for the moment. I am a moth attracted to the beauty of my beloved, going round and round the flame, burning away in the quest for greater clarity. Follow me at your own peril.

'Judge the moth by the beauty of its candle.'

—Jalaluddin Rumi

APPENDIX A: CASE ANALYSIS

A1. McDonald's Corporation

'The definition of salesmanship is the gentle art of letting the customer have it your way.'

—Ray Kroc

THE NEXT TIME you visit a McDonald's, bow.

The other patrons may be amused by your bowing before McDonald's. For them, the McDonald's experience is just so everyday 'normal' that they have stopped seeing its beauty. Most of them anyway would only know McDonald's at the level of the products—the burgers and French fries, rather than the business model. For them, the burger and fries are so 'normal' that they would be surprised at your making a song and dance about it. Their eyes are closed. I want to awaken you to the beauty of the everyday normal.

What does McDonald's stand for in the minds of the consumer? 'Pleasant, fast service and tasty, inexpensive food', according to David M. Upton.[2] What does McDonald's stand for in the minds of a student of Operations Management? High volume, low cost, standardized processes offering consistency of product and service at a low price point? Consistency is the hallmark of this business—how boring! If you consider churning out the same products again and again like a robot to be boring, do also consider the excitement among investors about a company which consistently provided 25.2 per cent average annual return on equity and 24.1 per cent average annual earnings growth between 1965 and 1991.

You may or may not consider consistency to be boring but be under no illusion—consistency is very challenging to achieve. McDonald's needs to be consistent, not just in burgers, but also in other products; not just in product quality but also in service quality; not just in company-operated outlets but also in franchise-operated outlets; not just in one retail store, but also in thousands of outlets across countries and continents; not just on a specific day, but every day, day after day, year after year, decade after decade. How challenging is that? Now consider that McDonald's has an annual workforce turnover rate of 100 per cent. That means if you visit the store near you today and visit it again after a year, on an average every worker in that store would be new. Yet, the taste of the products, quality of service, the upkeep of the infrastructure, the cleanliness of the toilets, etc., would remain the same. If

---

[2] This case analysis is based on the Harvard Business School case study 'McDonald's Corporation (Abridged)'. The case study is distributed through the Harvard Business Publishing website. I recommend that you read the case study before you read the case analysis.

you have tried even for a few days to ensure consistency of food preparation in your kitchen, you would know how challenging it is to play at the level of McDonald's. It has achieved consistency in its business model while products change, customer preferences evolve, product and process technologies evolve and mature, workers leave, managers retire, leadership changes, new franchises join and some discontinue, suppliers evolve and change, environmental sustainability challenges evolve, and regulations change. Yet, the burger and French fries taste just the same, the McDonald's Happy Meal brings a smile to a kid's face, just as it did decades ago for the kid's parents.

It hits you like a ton of bricks . . . components do not matter, McDonald's is autopoietic.

Next time you visit a McDonald's, bow.

Components do not matter in an autopoietic system *as long as* the set of interactions and transformations remain unchanged. Interestingly, the set of interactions and transformations are also responsible for choosing the right kind of components—the kind that ensures the continuity of the set of interactions and transformations. Complicated? Let me explain. How does McDonald's achieve a high level of consistency of output? It is by waging a war, a war on variability. A consistent output requires consistent processes to convert the inputs into outputs. The perfect French fries are cooked just right when the 'oil temperature rose three degrees above the low temperature point' and the potatoes are cured for three weeks. But the consistency of the transformation process also requires the consistency of the inputs. 'McDonald's only accepted potatoes with a 21% starch content.' The war on variability requires adherence to a temperature rise of 3 degrees, not 2.5 degrees or 3.5 degrees; a starch content of 21%, not 20.5% or 21.5%. The consistency of output is thus realized by detailing each and every raw material input specification and also specifications of the conversion process. Similarly, consistency in service quality is ensured by 'each of the company's 332 field service consultants visiting over 20 restaurants in the United States several times every year, reviewing the restaurants' performance on more than 500 items ranging from rest-room cleanliness to food quality and customer service.'

The standard operating procedures (SOP) manual was first created in 1957 and had 'reached 750 detailed pages' by 1991. A 750-page manual! Does your firm have one? How many pages? Ever read it? 'It delineates exact cooking times, proper temperature settings, and precise portions for all food items.' It specifies, for example, that the meat in hamburgers should be '83% lean chuck (shoulder) from grass-fed cattle and 17% choice plates (lower rib cage) from grain-fed cattle'. Note the grass-fed and grain-fed parts. Those are specifications of how the cattle need to be fed, not in McDonald's but by cattle ranchers who sell to abattoirs from where the suppliers to McDonald's would be picking up supplies. Thus, McDonald's is specifying practices three steps up the supply chain (McDonald's–Meat Suppliers–Abattoirs–Cattle Ranchers). Why would cattle ranchers listen to McDonald's? They don't even sell to McDonald's.

What is the use of scale in purchasing? The most obvious is that scale allows the buyer to negotiate a bargain from the seller. Lowering the price of purchase is the main—if not the only—objective for most individuals and firms. In contrast, McDonald's is not focused on lowering *price* but on lowering *cost;* not focused on *purchase cost for McDonald's* but on *total cost* in the supply chain. Lowering of price is adversarial—the purchaser wins at the cost of the seller; lowering of price is transactional—the purchaser would buy from whomsoever is offering the lowest price. Lowering the costs in the supply chain is, in contrast, a partnership approach. If costs are lowered (for purchaser or supplier or both), then price (price paid by purchaser as well as the final price to consumer) can be lowered keeping margins intact; while lowering of purchase price through adversarial negotiation keeps costs untouched and reduces the margin of at least one player in the supply chain. A true Elephant uses its scale to reduce costs; lower prices to the end customer would follow. Lower prices to consumers increase the size of the market as the product become even more affordable. A 20 per cent cut in prices in 1991 increased hamburger sales by 30 per cent. Witness the modus operandi of an exemplary Elephant. McDonald's uses scale to impact *practices* in the supply chain. It influences planting practices of farmers to ensure the high starch content of potatoes, cattle-rearing practices of ranchers, food preparation practices at franchise operations, etc., in order to standardize the inputs, processes and outputs at each stage of the supply chain. The cost reduction comes from the standardization which allows the design and deployment of efficient processes and technologies. Variability hurts efficiency and complicates the process technology. By waging a war on variability, not just inside the firm but also across the supply chain, McDonald's brings in standardized practices which allow large-scale efficient technologies to be deployed, leading to the ultimate objective of consistency of outputs. Consistency at a low cost cannot be ensured at a firm level, especially in food products which depend on natural ingredients, if it is not ensured at a supply chain level. Witness an exemplary supply chain Elephant which takes a partnership orientation in standardizing inputs and practices across the supply chain and brings in scale economies. Next time you visit a McDonald's, bow.

Supply chain partners, who accept the standardization requirements and invest in technology, grow with McDonald's. They understand and speak the language of consistency. To grow your business with McDonald's, you do not talk the language of discounts; you show McDonald's how *you* can innovate to help reduce variability and improve quality not just for you but for the other players in the supply chain. Jack Simplot increased his business from 20 per cent to 50 per cent of McDonald's growing requirement of potatoes, not by offering a discount, but by experimenting at his own cost and risk. The Idaho Russet variety of potato is more suited for French fries but they are not available during summer months, when McDonald's has to depend on the less suitable California white potato. Adoption of the Idaho Russet variety as standard holds promise for consistency but requires the development of storage technology. It requires investing in R&D to understand the science behind storing potatoes without degrading the quality characteristics. While McDonald's invested in the R&D, Simplot volunteered to build the initial production line. Similarly, Chicken McNuggets was developed by McDonald's in collaboration with two suppliers—Gorton and Keystone. This kind of collaborative R&D and technology development cannot be nurtured in a transactional and opportunistic buyer–supplier relationship.

This spirit of experimentation and R&D permeates the McDonald's supply chain. This spirit gives rise to process technology innovations like potato-freezing techniques (collaboration between suppliers and McDonald's) and a V-shaped aluminium scoop with a funnel at the end (an innovation by McDonald's) and product innovations like the Egg McMuffin and Filet-O-Fish sandwich (innovations led by franchises). Experiments take time and cost money; experimentation requires an investment mindset. McDonald's took 'five years perfecting its breakfast menu for national rollout, the company spent seven years developing a pizza'. A lot of experiments are required to arrive at the final specification of the 21 per cent starch requirement for potatoes or the three-degree rise in oil temperature for the perfect French fries. R&D requires high-quality trained researchers, equipment and infrastructure and a culture quite distinct from that of a fast food assembly line. In addition, these innovations are not just emanating from the firm, but the supply chain. For the Egg McMuffin being developed by franchisees, McDonald's coordinated with pork processors 'to build equipment that could cut round slices of bacon instead of strips'.

The list of custom-designed equipment, developed alone or in collaboration with suppliers and equipment vendors, includes 'a grill that prepared hamburgers in half the time by cooking them on both sides simultaneously', 'a pizza oven that could cook McDonald's Pizza in under five minutes', 'high-tech temperature and moisture controlled cabinets', grill with a 'cluster of six Teflon-coated rings' for Egg McMuffins, etc. Equipment design is central to ensuring consistency. New product design and new customized equipment design goes hand in hand. Custom-designed equipment means that the technology is not available to competitors off-the-shelf. More capital-intensity ensures that operating complexity is encapsulated in equipment design and even low-skill labour can operate the equipment with little training. The investment in equipment design pays off in terms of reduced wage rate and ability to handle attrition.

Supply chain partners wanting to grow with McDonald's need to speak the language of not just consistency but also innovation. Tell me frankly, if I ask you to name a few innovative firms at the frontier of new product and process technology, would McDonald's pop up in your mind? Most likely not. Yet, witness how McDonald's is partnering with the supply chain in bringing product and process innovations. McDonald's as an innovative firm, McDonald's as an R&D Elephant investing in product and process innovations and recouping the high fixed costs by spreading costs over high volume of sales! Did that thought ever cross your mind?

Wait a minute. Consistency requires deviation-*counteracting* mutual causal processes. Innovation requires deviation-*amplifying* mutual causal processes. If it is difficult to ensure consistency, it is even more difficult to innovate. How difficult is it to ensure consistency in day-to-day operations across the supply chain and *simultaneously* collaborate across the supply chain on R&D and innovation? *Simultaneously* deviation counteracting as well as deviation-amplifying; *simultaneously* consistent as well as evolving? Autopoiesis is an evolving constraint! Next time you visit a McDonald's, bow.

The consistency that McDonald's aims for is the consistency of the processes, it does not mean its product portfolio remains same. The product portfolio has not only evolved over time, McDonald's also serves a differentiated menu across geographies to cater to religious and cultural tastes. So, it is not a puritan in sticking to the original hamburger menu, its puritanism is in insisting that whatever new product or service is introduced, it can be delivered at scale, consistently. It experimented with deep-fried chunks of onion but dropped the product idea since consistency could not be achieved.

Addition of new menu items over time would bloat the menu. Originally, McDonald's offered 10 menu items which by 1992 had increased considerably to thirty-six regular menu items, eleven breakfast menu items and four 'Value Menu Combos' for both regular and breakfast menus (Exhibit 2 of the case). This explosion in variety is problematic from an operations standpoint. Variety sells, but variety also hurts. A high-variety menu offers something for every customer's taste and preferences. A high-variety menu offers only complexity and headache for backend operations, it can increase set-up costs and inventory holding costs and negatively impact efficiency and productivity. How does McDonald's handle this challenge of offering *both* high volume and high variety while ensuring its cost leadership?

The secret is the modularity in the design of the product portfolio. While at first glance Exhibit 2 of the case seems to show a large variety, closer inspection reveals that the kind of variety can be broken down into several types. *Assortment variety* allows bouquets to be made from individual menu items to serve different tastes. *Serving variety* (small/medium/large fries or drinks or 6/9/20 pieces of McNuggets) can offer differentiation based on consumption volume. Since the items and serving varieties are modular, a large number of combinations can be made by the customer. Each of these combinations involve customer choices, including perhaps comparison of the customized assortment and its price against the readymade 'Value Menu Combos' bundles offered by McDonald's. For the customer, this represents variety in terms of choices. For McDonald's, this is delayed differentiation at the very last stage of the supply chain. For example, depending on the order for a large drink and small fry, a store employee would pick up a large cup and fill it from the dispenser and take a small packet and fill it with French fries from a mass of fries stored in the temporary holding bin behind the server. Upstream, there is no difference between large or small fries or an order of nine and an order of twenty McNuggets. A different tactic of variety reduction comes from the commonality of parts. A chicken burger and a hamburger may be designed to use the same top and bottom buns. Thus, at the level of buns, there is no variety in terms of buns intended for chicken or hamburgers. Thus, while McDonald's delivers high variety to customers, the variety in the supply chain upstream of the customer-facing serving station is significantly less, perhaps little more than the original variety of ten items.

Distinguishable variety is simultaneously high for customers and low for McDonald's and its supply chain partners. McDonald's has thus achieved the holy grail of Operations—high volume *and* high variety at low costs; sensitive to variety outside (accommodates variety of customer preferences) while insensitive to variety inside (identical processes across varieties). Decades ago, Henry Ford came across as arrogant in declaring 'Any customer can have a car painted any colour that he wants so long as it is black'. Ray Kroc, the consummate salesman, achieved the same objective of standardization while letting the customers have it their way.

Next time you visit a McDonald's—well, you know the standard operating procedure by now—bow.

A2. ZARA: Fast Fashion

'It's the eye of the tiger, it's the thrill of the fight
Risin' up to the challenge of our rival
And the last known survivor stalks his prey in the night
And he's watchin' us all with the eye of the tiger.'

—*Eye of the Tiger*, Survivor

THE BUSINESS MODEL described by Pankaj Ghemawat and Jose Luis Nueno Iniesta in the case 'ZARA: Fast Fashion', is as beautiful as it is effective in serving its customers (and lethal for its competitors). It stands out against the prevalent business models in the fashion goods segment. For example, the case cites a McKinsey study which identified five major ways in which fashion retailers expanded across borders. Zara defies each one of those recommendations. Instead of choosing a 'sliver of value', it is present all across the value chain; vertically integrated instead of building partnerships; has minimal investments in brands; large investments in tangible assets in retail operations, distribution, manufacturing, information technology and product design; and does not embrace global sourcing to exploit factor-price differences. Zara has clearly closed doors to the business model adopted by most other firms, but the strategic choices made by it are not driven by the need to be different for the sake of being different. Instead, there is a pattern in those door closings which can be traced back to an insight of its founder.

Amancio Ortega Gaona started as an errand boy in the garment industry in 1949, at the age of thirteen. Remarkable for a young boy without formal education, 'he apparently developed a heightened awareness of how costs piled up through the apparel chain'. He started his own business of manufacturing products like housecoats at age twenty-seven; and at age thirty-nine expanded into retailing by opening the first Zara store in 1975. Why get into retailing when the competencies in being a manufacturer in the garment industry are so different from those of being a retailer? There can be so many different reasons for a forward integration, and for Ortega, the reason was to do with his discovery of *where* costs pile up in the garment supply chain and his vision of how to reduce the costs. Ortega was on a quest 'to improve the manufacturing/retailing interface'. He invested in computers at an early age (1976) and soon realized that 'what (other) buyers ordered from his factories was different from what his store data told him customers wanted'.

Why should there be a mismatch between what customers wanted and what factories produced? Isn't it straightforward to just manufacture what the customer wants? The answer lies in the complexity and global nature of the garment supply chain. 'For example, a down jacket's filling might come from China, the outer shell fabric from Korea, the zippers from Japan, the inner lining from Taiwan, and the elastics, label, and other trim from Hong Kong. Dyeing might take place in South Asia and stitching in China, followed by quality assurance and packaging in Hong Kong'. Add to this the Minimum Order Quantities (MOQs) at each stage of production, the transportation batch sizes for each leg of movement, the production lead times, the transportation lead times, differences in quality standards across suppliers in different countries, differences in regulations, customs-related complexities, currency exchange rate fluctuations, changes in tariffs and import quotas, etc., and you start getting an idea of the headache. Note that one way to reduce the headache is to have one large order size compared to breaking up the same order into smaller lots. The global apparel supply chain does a good job of exploiting wage rate and raw-material cost differences across countries but incurs long lead times and stipulates high MOQs.

Long lead times and high MOQs would not be problematic for matching demand and supply if demand volatility is low. Unfortunately, if there is one industry which is the poster child of demand volatility, it is fashion. Fashion trends are hard to forecast, transient and easy to miss. A 'fashion hit' may result in stock-outs and opportunity loss while a 'fashion miss' would result in unsold inventory which needs to be disposed of through clearance sales at steep discounts. Most retailers would try to match supply and demand by taking calculated risks and ordering quantities which minimize the combined cost of overstocking and understocking (the Newsvendor model). But this orientation to handling demand volatility rests on forecasting the item demand months in advance of the selling season and then hoping that there are no fashion shifts in the meantime. It assumes the season as homogenous and bets on the total demand for an item during the season. Yet, fashion changes unpredictably. This betting on the season's demand assumes customer preferences to remain static, the volatility of within-season fashion preferences is wished away.

Zara, in contrast, recognizes the simple fact that its customers are not grass but deer. Elephants thrive on vegetation, cheetahs on fast-moving animals like deer. Grass cannot run away when an elephant approaches, deer run away at the slightest whiff of danger. Zara recognizes its customer as a deer and pursues it to make a sale like a Cheetah, while other retailers treat the customer as grass and approach them as Elephants and initially get away with it. How so? If all fashion retailers were Elephants, the customer has no choice but to shop from Elephants with items designed and manufactured months in advance. The customer has not yet experienced a Cheetah which responds to daily changes in the fashion environment. The dominant Elephant business model suppresses the natural high clockspeed of fashion. In the absence of choice, the deer is made to behave like grass; rooted in terms of preferences during the season with spurts between seasons. And then, one day, a Cheetah emerges, and the deer feels unconstrained by limitations of retailers and realizes the joy of running even during the season. Would you blame the fashion-loving deer for adoring the Cheetah? The existence of the Cheetah is like a tailwind to the fleet-footed deer who realizes the truth of its own identity and sees through the lie of a homogenous fashion season peddled by Elephants.

The choice of the customer is the most important choice that a firm makes. Zara chooses the fastest deer as its target segment, fashion-forward eighteen- to thirty-four-year-old women from middle to middle-high income households. Even though Zara serves other segments like men and children, the centrality of the women segment is unmistakable. For example, the head of the women's section of a Zara store performs the role of the store manager. By building competencies to serve the most demanding fashionistas, the back-end supply chain finds it relatively easy to serve other segments with lower demand volatility.

What does a young woman fashionista from a middle to middle-high income household want? She wants designer clothes and accessories that do not cost a bomb. She wants freshness in the way she dresses, she wishes to try out new fashion trends. She is not interested in and perhaps cannot afford avant-garde high fashion suitable for fashion runways; she looks for fashionable garments and accessories that can be worn on a trip to the supermarket. She is comfortable in being a fashion follower but would like to be a *quick* fashion follower, quick in spotting and trying out the latest trends. She is not looking for long-lasting products, she is anyway not keen on repeating the same outfit any more than necessary.

Zara offers fresh assortments of relatively low-priced fashion products in 'sophisticated stores in prime locations in order to draw masses of fashion-conscious repeat customers'. It offers 'broad, rapidly changing product lines, relatively high fashion content, and reasonable but not excessive physical quality: clothes to be worn 10 times, some said'. Other fashion retailers can

also set up sophisticated shops in prime locations, but
they would not be able to match Zara in the freshness
of the store. What exactly contributes to the freshness of
the store? First, Zara produces annually a higher variety
of items (11,000 distinct items compared to 2000 to
4000 for competitors). Second, each item is produced
in comparatively much smaller lots than competitors,
resulting in very low quantities of a specific item in a
store. Third, the low production quantity imparts a
sense of exclusivity to that design. The probability of the
shopper bumping into another person wearing the exact
same dress is lower than for competitors. Fourth, Zara
operates on a policy of deliberate undersupply, so if an
item sells well it is not replenished. The empty shelf is
filled not by the product which sold out but by a new
item. Fifth, the rapid product turnover at the store level is
supported by 'new designs arriving in each twice-weekly
shipment'. As a result, in three to four weeks almost 75
per cent of the store assortment would have changed.
Any item is removed from the store if it has been on the
shelves for more than a month. A typical Zara shopper
'visited the chain 17 times a year', corresponding to an
average time between visits of about three weeks. This
implies that every time the customer visits Zara, she
finds only a quarter of the items that she saw last time.
The rest of the store is composed of freshly designed and
manufactured items. The focus on freshness of the store
is not limited to merchandise. Store-window displays
and interior presentations in terms of themes, colour
schemes and product presentations are modified every
three weeks. In-store Zara employees are supposed
to wear uniforms like in any other retailer. However,

the difference is that these uniforms are items from the *current* season's collection. The uniform is updated twice during a season and different stores in the same city might mandate different uniforms. Freshness thus permeates even a uniform!

The strategy of offering freshness goes hand in hand with the strategy of creating of a sense of scarcity. If an item stocks out, Zara sometimes deliberately keeps that space empty till a new design is delivered to take its place. An empty space on the shelf implies opportunity loss and mismanagement in any other retailer. Shelf space is the most important asset in retail and utilization of this critical resource is key to retailer profitability. Shelf space kept deliberately empty seems like heresy. Yet, in Zara, empty shelf space communicates something to the shopper—there was an item here which stocked out and there is perhaps little possibility of her purchasing it as Zara produces in small lots and does not automatically make more of the item selling out. The empty space thus communicates a sense of urgency and promotes impulse purchase. If something catches the shopper's eye, she should buy it then and there else it too may vanish. The sense of scarcity impacts consumer behaviour. 'Devout Zara shoppers even knew which days of the week delivery trucks came into stores, and shopped accordingly'.

The fanatic fan following allows Zara to grow through word of mouth rather than media advertising ('Zara spent only 0.3% of its revenue on media advertising, compared to 3–4% for most speciality retailers'). Note that a focus on freshness implies a focus on repeat customers. Repeat customers reduce the customer acquisition cost even further. Every store may seem fresh to a customer visiting for the first time, it is only on repeat visits that the continued freshness of the store becomes apparent, especially when contrasted with visits to stores of other fashion retailers. It is the fashionista and shopping enthusiast who is likely to observe the store freshness differences across fashion retailers than an occasional shopper. Zara is thus able to retain its most demanding customers who make a habit of coming back to the store and purchasing impulsively. The Zara store is thus transformed into the go-to place for fashionistas, increasing the chance that an average shopper is likely to observe not just fashionable store assistants but also fashionable shoppers thronging the store. The fashion runway is not in Paris or Milan, it is right there in the Zara store!

To deliver on its promise of freshness, Zara depends on a high-variety, quick-response Cheetah supply chain. Zara has closed doors on the dominant cost-efficient strategy of outsourcing and offshoring, choosing instead to produce time-sensitive products internally in a vertically integrated manufacturing system located in its key market of Spain. The location of its manufacturing base in Galicia, Spain, enables distribution of finished goods from its warehouse to any store located in Europe within twenty-four to thirty-six hours. Close proximity of factories and markets means not just a quicker response to demand shifts but also better coordination between stores, designers and factories. Onshoring eliminates the time involved in complex cross-border movements of work-in-process and time for shipping from China and the far east. Insourcing eliminates waiting for a supplier to give priority to the firm's order in case a bottleneck led to order pile-up. A common in-house designed custom IT system allows Zara to keep work-in-process flowing seamlessly through the vertically integrated manufacturing system, compared to the lack of end-to-end visibility and control in the multi-firm, multi-country global supply chains. Zara keeps spare capacity in its central distribution centre by operating it at 50 per cent capacity utilization, allowing it to respond quickly to demand spikes. It varies its distribution responsiveness between off-season and peak season by accepting orders from each store 'twice a week during regular periods, and thrice weekly during the sales season'. The distribution centre is focused on movement rather than storage, no package remains there for more than three days.

Reduction of manufacturing and distribution lead time results in an ability to practise the Quick Response (QR) strategy. QR is essentially a Cheetah strategy which 'help retailers reduce forecast errors and inventory risks by planning assortments closer to the selling season, probing the market, placing smaller initial orders and reordering more frequently'. Zara has the ability 'to originate a design and have finished goods in stores within four to five weeks in case of entirely new designs, and two weeks for modifications (or restocking) of existing products'. This contrasts with the Elephant standard of six months and three months respectively. The Cheetah supply chain allows Zara to commit to a season much later than competitors, thereby reducing the demand–supply mismatch. Zara undertakes '85% of the in-house production *after* the season had started, compared with only 0–20% in case of traditional retailers'. Zara watches its prey till the last minute.

The Cheetah strategy is known to incur higher costs than an Elephant, but Zara manages to not only operate a Cheetah supply chain but also sell at prices lower than competitors. How is this miracle possible? First, note that Zara's distribution strategy of operating warehouses with spare capacity, transportation strategy of frequent store deliveries, manufacturing strategy of small batch sizes, location strategy in Europe compared to low wage rate countries like China, etc., are all likely to incur higher costs than a comparable Elephant. However, the Cheetah supply chain also enables Zara to reduce the demand–supply mismatch cost and hence there would be fewer markdowns. Its store managers are incentivized to ruthlessly cull out apparent fashion misses from the store, which are then either moved to other geographies or sold to a separate retail chain.

The quick identification and removal of fashion misses during the season (instead of waiting for end-of-season clearance sales) ensures that Zara has lower percentage markdowns than competitors. The reduction of manufacturing and distribution lead time results in lower inventory carrying costs and hence lower working capital requirements. The freshness of the Zara store results in positive word-of-mouth advertising, obviating the need for costly media advertising. And finally, the Cheetah supply chain, along with freshness and scarcity strategies, allows Zara to increase impulse purchase and reduce opportunity loss when a customer enters a Zara store but leaves without purchasing anything because she did not find the latest fashion. Increasing the sales quantity through impulse purchase also helps in spreading fixed costs over a larger base.

It was during Ortega's early career that he understood that coordination costs in the retailer–manufacturing interface are significantly high in the fashion garment supply chain. The Cheetah supply chain trades off the higher costs of manufacturing and distribution with the lower costs in inventory and better customer response. The result is an ability to price its products competitively while delivering superior responsiveness. Zara can pull this off as fashion is a high-margin business with high demand volatility and a reduction in opportunity loss is more valuable than a comparable percentage reduction in item cost.

Are you starting to see the genius of the Zara business model? An integrated closing of doors across retailing, distribution and manufacturing? A strategy which not just stands out against the outsourced and offshored business models adopted by competitors but also gains from the competitor's strategy since the customer would value freshness more if she is surrounded by staleness? You have seen nothing yet.

Zara stands out from other Cheetah business models in its fanatic focus on supply chain visibility and its strategy of handling fashion volatility. Zara invested in sophisticated but in-house developed IT systems to track customer orders through stores, distribution centres and factories. It developed an ability to track sales and stock positions in each store on a real-time basis, much earlier than other retailers. A highly responsive supply chain needs a high-frequency IT backbone to track and trace each and every finished good, WIP and raw material input on a continuous basis. This level of visibility is difficult to achieve for most multi-firm global supply chains, while Zara not only achieves it but goes beyond it. All that hi-tech IT hardware and software can only tell you what is happening at present or what has happened in the past, it cannot capture what would happen in future. There is a fundamental difference between sales and demand. Sales is the past; it has already happened. *Latent* demand is the future. Who is the person best suited to identify future trends, recognize *latent* demand?

Zara employs a variety of sources to predict future fashion trends like data from fashion shows, trend-spotters on university campuses, etc. But its biggest asset is its store, frequented by fashion-conscious shoppers on a regular basis. It is in these stores that Zara observes how the customer reacts to the merchandise. Does this design appeal to her? If not, what specifically did she not like in the design? What kind of modification of the dress would appeal to her? Conversations like this allow a high-quality salesperson or store manager to glean design insights about the kind of product that might appeal to the target audience. This insight is the holy grail of fashion retailing, the idea about *latent* demand. It elevates the cutting edge of visibility from tracking real-time sales to learning 'what kind of clothes *would* sell if Zara made them'. The insight is shared with designers and product managers who design new products or modify existing designs and manufacture and bring those insights in the form of fashion products back into the store within two to five weeks. The store employees and specifically the store manager are not just hands that stock the inventory, they are Zara's eyes and ears. What is the value of the eye to a predator like a tiger or a cheetah?

Are you starting to get an idea about the genius of Zara? You think so? Let me show you a masterstroke. Sometimes when a person loses one sense organ, the other sense organs become extra-sensitive. Zara intentionally blinds store managers on one dimension to make them sensitive on another dimension. In Zara, 'Store managers determined replenishment quantities by walking around the store and determining what has been selling by counting garments and talking to salespeople. Sales personnel could *not* look up their inventory balances on any in-store computer, so canvassing the store was the only way to learn about stock levels', as reported in another case study on Zara by Andrew McAfee, Vincent Dessain and Anders Sjoman. Can you imagine that a firm which has the ability to track real-time stock and sales of each and every SKU in each and every store from headquarters did not allow the store personnel to find from the computer what her own store has been selling! Why? This intentional blindness of the store manager pushes her out of the manager's cabin into walking the aisles, bumping into customers, checking the buzz with sales personnel and understanding the real action in the trenches. Headquarters does not need her to tell them what customers bought from her store today; they already know. They want her to tell what customers *would* buy if only Zara made it available in that store or designed them. They want the store manager to be entrepreneurial and anticipate not what is selling today but where the fashion is heading.

A salesperson capable of engaging fashion-forward customers from middle to middle-high income households in discussions on the specifics of fashion dressing is not easy to hire. She must be groomed and trained and paid handsomely compared to the industry average. If she leaves Zara, she is difficult to replace. She is the bottleneck in store expansion, it is much easier to purchase and furnish a store in a prime location than fill it with salespersons with the ability to spot latent demand. In contrast, an Elephant may reduce the costs of staffing a store by hiring contractual workers at low wage rates and face high attrition. It uses these low-skill workers essentially as hands rather than as eyes. The Elephant is not just blind, it is blind to its blindness. It does not even care about blindness because anyway it does not have any supply chain capability to react during a season to shifts in customer preferences. A blind Elephant can survive, a blind Cheetah won't. Zara is watching its customers with the eye of a Cheetah. But, if you think Zara is *just* a Cheetah, you are mistaken.

Most firms would look at demand volatility as a problem and take measures to either respond to it (like a Cheetah) or reduce or ignore it (like an Elephant). The beauty of the Zara business model is that it not just responds to demand volatility, but it actually *increases* demand volatility. Now, who in his right mind thinks about adding fuel to the fire? Volatility is a problem, increasing volatility only increases the headache and complexity in the supply chain. Yet, Zara increases demand volatility by deliberate undersupply, by gauging latent demand and designing and selling new products *during* the season. Why does Zara take this approach?

Figure 13: Strategy of Increasing Volatility of Customer Demand

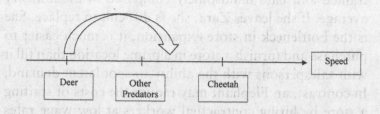

Consider the dimension of speed and the relative positions of the deer, cheetah and other predators in the natural environment. A cheetah has much higher speed than both deer and other predators while other predators can run faster than the deer but not as fast as the cheetah. In such a situation, the cheetah shares the prey with other predators. But consider if somehow the deer could increase its speed to a level higher than other predators but short of the speed of the cheetah. Then the cheetah would be the only predator for the deer as the deer is likely to outrun all predators except the cheetah.

Zara is not a Cheetah; it is a Macho Cheetah. While others struggle to handle demand volatility, it wants more of it. It has realized that it is in its own interest that the deer speeds up rather than slows down. It influences the customer expectation of freshness from fashion retailers and speeds up the fashion volatility because it has confidence that the backend supply chain has been designed to respond much faster than any competitor. The speeded-up deer can never be caught by competitors and becomes a loyal Zara customer. Meanwhile, Zara continues to watch the latent demand with the eye of the master predator.

A3. Jiro Dreams of Sushi

'I don't intend to build in order to have clients; I intend
to have clients in order to build.'
—Howard Roark to the Dean, *The Fountainhead*,
Ayn Rand

JIRO DOES NOT dream of sushi; sushi comes in Jiro's
dreams. No man can will a dream. A man can only
work during the daytime with single-minded devotion
to a cause or purpose he wants to fulfil. And Jiro Ono
surely has worked diligently for his entire lifetime in
the restaurant business, leaving home at the age of
nine, working hard to survive while disregarding the
kicks and slaps from the boss, being paid a pittance
as an apprentice, having ten yen in the bank account
when he got married, eventually becoming a chef, and
at age forty starting Sukiyabashi Jiro in Ginza, Tokyo,
the first sushi restaurant to be awarded a Michelin
3-star. A self-made man from humble origins, at
age eighty-five (when the documentary *Jiro Dreams*

*of Sushi*³ was shot) he has achieved cult status as a sushi chef. In the process, however, he may have sacrificed work life balance. Maybe it comes with the territory. His younger son, Takashi Ono, had once exclaimed as a kid, 'Mom, there's a strange man sleeping in our house!', on a rare occasion that Jiro was at home during daytime on a Sunday. When work takes over your whole life, it consumes the whole day and even seeps into the dreams at night. You cannot control dreams; a dream chooses you to bring itself to life. The sushi-making does not stop when Jiro leaves work, he would make sushi in his dreams; jump out of bed with ideas. The documentary opens with the question 'What defines deliciousness?' For Jiro, the key to deliciousness is revealed in dreams.

And for a 30,000 yen starting price you can taste that deliciousness. Not really. 30,000 yen is just the indicative starting price. Sukiyabashi Jiro neither has a menu card, nor are there prices listed for items. It offers a tasting course of twenty sushi dishes whose composition and prices change daily based on the availability of a fresh catch. 30,000 yen⁴ is not really cheap for a meal that lasts on an average twenty minutes, on a per-minute basis this is perhaps among the most expensive meals in the world.

---

³ I strongly suggest that you watch the documentary *Jiro Dreams of Sushi* by David Gelb before proceeding further. All quotations in this chapter are from the English subtitles of the documentary. The documentary is distributed by Magnolia Pictures and available on streaming platforms. I am grateful to Sumeet Gupta, PGP 2016, and Sandeep Sharma, PGPX 2017, for introducing me to this documentary around 2016–17.
⁴ 1 USD ranged between 80 and 90 yen in 2010.

That is, of course, if you can find a seat; you see, there are just ten of them. Reservations need to be done in advance, about a month in advance when the documentary was made. In a couple of years, the waiting time increased to more than a year.

Any other business might have been tempted to increase the capacity by giving out franchises, opening new restaurants or, at the very least, adding a few chairs. Even adding just one chair could potentially increase revenue by 10 percent! Can you even imagine the return on investment of that one additional chair? But our eighty-five-year-old grandfatherly protagonist would have none of this nonsense; sushi is his passion, calling it a business demeans it. Giving him suggestions is out of the question as his presence may be too intimidating. Even an experienced food critic like Masuhiro Yamamoto feels nervous while dining at Jiro. Takashi Ono, Jiro's younger son, had opened a restaurant in Roppongi Hills which was an exact replica of Sukiyabashi Jiro; except that the layout was a mirror image (to handle the fact that he is right-handed and his father left-handed). Takashi reported that some of his father's patrons prefer to dine at his place just because they feel relaxed and the sushi is the same. Yet, Takashi charges a lower price! Jiro Ono has a presence. He is comfortable with who he is; if his presence makes others nervous, Jiro can only smile at that. Jiro Ono is undoubtedly the master and the market knows it.

Jiro studies the reservations in advance to know whom he would be serving, whether male or female, and decides who would sit where. While serving, he intently watches facial expressions. He observes whether the customer is left- or right-handed and serves accordingly so that it is convenient for the customer to pick up the sushi. So thoughtful. He also serves smaller sushi sizes for women compared to men! He is a blast from the past, perhaps no one warned him about gender discrimination! Perhaps he knows but cares more at a much deeper level about the experience of each person so that he varies his serving for men and women, left-handed and right-handed people. He himself is left-handed, and perhaps has experienced discrimination in a world whose systems are mostly designed for the right-handed male.

He has designed the experience for you very precisely. He needs *you* to adhere to *his* design. No menu cards, no pamphlets, no item prices, no walk-in customers, no choice in terms of seating, no variety (the twenty-item tasting menu is a bouquet, there are no other bouquets on offer and you cannot have your choice of items from the bouquet), no customization (you cannot tell him your preferences. The meal is *omakase*, meaning 'I leave it to you'), no appetizers, no side dishes, no drinks, no green tea, no sauces or condiments for you to sprinkle on the food, no choice in terms of sequence of the twenty items, no refusing one item (folklore has it that when Japanese Prime Minister Shinzo Abe took US President Barack Obama to Sukiyabashi Jiro during a state visit, Obama did not finish half of one item. Jiro apparently put Obama on a blacklist for this sacrilege), no strong perfumes (would interfere with the sushi experience), no relaxed pace of eating (the sushi must be consumed immediately when served, the items are served at a fast pace), no taking photographs of food for uploading on social media (sushi needs full and immediate attention), no whiling away time bantering among friends in the group (the seating is side by side on one side of a table, everyone facing the chef), no elegant restaurant décor to admire (would take attention away from the sushi), no smiling chef engaging you in conversation (instead, a very stern-looking eighty-five-year-old chef observing you intently), the list goes on—and my favourite—no rest rooms (the restaurant is situated in the basement of an office tower with a shared restroom. Anyway, Jiro does not serve beer and the bouquet serving time is about twenty minutes. I am sure you can hold on for that long. A Michelin 3-star categorization means it is worthwhile to visit a country just to dine in that restaurant. When you come from another country and get your reservation after waiting a year, surely you would take care of petty things like relieving yourself before entering the restaurant). Sukiyabashi Jiro is perhaps the only Michelin 3-star restaurant to not have a restroom, even McDonald's has one.

Why on earth would customers willingly subject themselves to such dictates which impinge on personal liberty and choice and moreover pay 30,000 yen for the experience?

It is easy to see that Jiro does not compete on cost or time or the convenience of the customer. In fact, he does not compete at all. He is a master craftsman, an Artist, a *shokunin*, who strives towards perfection. If he has stipulated precise terms of serving a customer, he has stipulated even stricter standards for himself, his employees and his suppliers. Jiro has a fetish for cleanliness. His process innovations result in different standards of work than in other sushi restaurants. The octopus needs to be massaged for forty to fifty minutes—

instead of the earlier practice of thirty minutes—to give it
a soft texture, and served warm to bring out the fragrance.
The shrimp has to be boiled after the customer arrives
rather than being boiled in the morning and kept in the
refrigerator to be taken out before serving. The rice has
to be a specific variety which is cooked in a very specific
way and served specifically at body temperature. Every
item is tasted in different steps of the preparation process,
Yoshikazu and Jiro taste the product before serving. Is
it too tough? Marinated enough? A bit fatty? Does it
taste right? Anything which does not make the stringent
standards of Jiro is thrown away in the dustbin. Jiro is
likely to have high internal failure costs and appraisal
costs in the 'Cost of Quality' framework of Juran. But
he does not care about costs, he only yearns to achieve
better quality: 'I'll continue to climb, trying to reach the
top, but no one knows where the top is.'

It is not easy being a worker in Sukiyabashi Jiro,
attrition is high in the lower ranks, and new hires
sometimes never return after their first day's experience.
A young chef-hopeful joining Jiro would just be cleaning
up or perfecting the hand-squeezing of hot towels
for years before being allowed to touch the fish. After
perfecting the cutting and preparing of fish for ten years,
when he is deemed fit to graduate to sushi preparation,
the apprentice chef starts with cooking egg sushi. He tries
and tries and tries to get the perfect egg sushi, but his work
never seems to clear the high standards of the master. 'No
good, no good, no good', is all that he hears. Jiro is hard
on others not because he is heartless, he is self-critical and
hard on himself too. He is self-disciplined, never satisfied
with his own work, always trying to improve his sushi,

stubborn in terms of having it his way, a perfectionist. But how many failures can an ordinary man take? Why do employees try so hard, working long hours, day after day, for decades, trying to please the master? Daisuke Nakazama, a young chef, recounts how he made more than 200 pieces of egg sushi over three or four months, all of which were rejected, before the master gave his nod. Nakazama was so happy he cried. It took a long time for Jiro to call him a shokunin, but the wait was worth it. *Jiro* called *me* a shokunin!

When does a chef become a shokunin? A shokunin is not a degree that is granted by a university. Being called a shokunin means recognition by peers. What a joy when a peer recognizes you as a master. And if that peer is no other than a living legend, a master craftsman like Jiro; you have arrived. This is the moment for which you worked long hours in search of perfection. *Jiro* called *me* a *shokunin*!

How to become a shokunin? For every wannabe shokunin, Jiro offers simple advice. 'Once you decide your occupation, you must immerse yourself in your work. You have to *fall in love* with your work. Never complain about your job. You must dedicate your life to mastering your skill. That's the secret of success, and is the key to being regarded honorably.' (Emphasis added). Becoming a shokunin means feeling, like Jiro, 'ecstatic all day, I love making sushi'. As Jiro states simply, 'I fell in love with my work and gave my life to it.' It does not matter what the occupation is; even if you are just the cleaning guy in the restaurant, you can be a shokunin cleaner. To me, the key is the *falling in love* part. The rest will fall in place.

Everyone in this place works to please Jiro. Yoshikazu Ono, Jiro's elder son, is in charge of the Sukiyabashi Jiro restaurant. He runs the entire show. Jiro used to go to the market himself earlier, but Yoshikazu has taken up the responsibility after his father suffered a heart attack at age seventy. A unique output requires not just unique processes but also unique inputs. There are fixed suppliers for each kind of supply, relationships are built on trust and are long-lasting. Yoshikazu explains, 'The tuna vendor works exclusively with tuna. Our shrimp vendor only sells shrimp. Each of the vendors are specialists in their fields. We are experts in sushi but in each of their specialities the vendors are more knowledgeable. We've built up a relationship of trust with them.' There is no haggling over prices, any variation in purchase price is simply passed on to the end customer (this is the reason the bouquet does not have a set price). The tuna supplier calls himself anti-establishment, and considers his methods and standards a little unusual, he either buys his first choice or buys nothing. By checking the texture of the tuna with his fingers, he can predict how it would taste. The rice supplier supplies a specific rice variety only to Jiro, refusing to sell to Hyatt. Each of these suppliers are masters in their own areas, and have been doing the same thing for generations with grandfathers who have monikers like 'the god of sea eel'. The octopus seller mentions, 'We are picky about who we sell to. We want customers who appreciate good fish. Even at my age I'm discovering new techniques. But just when you think you know it all, you realize that you're just fooling yourself, and then you get depressed.' The shrimp supplier laments the miniscule supply of wild shrimp in the market, and when he sees some real shrimp, his reaction is, 'This is worthy of Jiro.' Each of these people is a 'Jiro' himself, a shokunin in his own right. We are looking at a supply chain of Artists. Whether supplier or employee, 'Everybody works to please Jiro. All that matters is Jiro's approval. Jiro is like the maestro of an orchestra.'

'No compromise' is the mantra of the Artist, even if that leads to high quality at high costs. Jiro would rather give up the customer than compromise with his art. What does he aim to achieve with his art? *Umami*. Deliciousness. Yoshikazu explains umami as the involuntary 'ahh' that comes out when you have a good beer or get into a hot bath. The dimension of quality that Jiro aims for is not quantifiable performance, numerosity of features, reliability or durability of his produce, serviceability, conformance to other's standards or perceived quality (Jiro has high perceived quality, but that is an *outcome* of his pursuit of something else. Jiro does not 'compete' on perceived quality). Jiro's pursuit is the aesthetics of taste through sushi. That aesthetics of taste should produce the umami in the customer. Note that the way umami is being described, it is not a characteristic of the product, it is the effect that the product produces in a human being. Jiro does not need a feedback questionnaire filled by the customer to know if he has delivered umami, he can see it in the involuntary reactions of the customer. There is no faking it.

Producing umami, customer after customer, day after day, requires perfection to be ingrained in the system, not just in Jiro Ono. While people may think that the sushi is prepared by Jiro Ono, the truth is that 95 per cent of the work is already done before Jiro Ono steps into the picture. When the Michelin inspectors came for the review, it was Yoshikazu who served them. It does not matter who prepared the hot towels or the egg sushi or served the customers, everything is as per the exacting standards of Jiro Ono. Is Sukiyabashi Jiro autopoietic? Does Jiro Ono matter as a component of the Sukiyabashi Jiro restaurant system delivering umami consistently? The documentary asks the fundamental question: What after Jiro Ono? Would Yoshikazu be able to run the place and get the same top billing that his father has achieved?

Opinion can be divided. On one hand, Yoshikazu is already running the restaurant full-time with his father as the figurehead. If it comes down to the ability to consistently deliver umami to his customers, Yoshikazu has already demonstrated that for years for the lay public, food critics and Michelin inspectors alike. On the other hand, people *think* they are consuming the sushi prepared by Jiro Ono. It is Jiro's name which is in the name of the restaurant. Would they be willing to spend such high amounts when Jiro is no more? Impermanence and autopoiesis were never more entwined. Impermanence imbues the restaurant and the food with a joy as well as a sadness, taste it while it lasts.

But why can't Yoshikazu outshine his father when he is already delivering umami consistently? Isn't he an Artist himself? Are we being uncharitable to him just because he is Jiro's elder son, as if he has to prove himself worthy twice over?

To understand the true contribution of Jiro and Yoshikazu, we have to delve even deeper into the essence of Sukiyabashi Jiro.

Jiro's great leap of faith came when he dispensed with every frivolous add-on to focus on the core of the sushi experience. Jiro is a minimalist. Like Steve Jobs, his design philosophy is 'Ultimate simplicity leads to purity'. Jiro's sushi is simple but has depth of flavour. It starts with understanding the natural variability inherent in his ingredients. All tuna is not the same, 'the taste of the fatty tuna is simple and predictable . . . but the flavors of leaner cuts are subtle and sophisticated.' 'Each tuna has its own unique taste. But it is the leaner meat that carries the essence of the flavour.' Jiro accentuates the individual taste and flavour—small tuna are aged for three days, large tuna for ten days. Each of these building blocks of taste and flavour are then arranged as a sequence, like a musical composition. Jiro took his inspiration from Japanese cuisine, which has a progression, an ebb and flow. After contemplating this move for ten years, Jiro, in his late seventies, took a leap of faith in composing a twenty-item sushi tasting course in terms of a progression. There are three movements in this progression, just like a concerto; explains Yamamoto. Classic items are in the first movement. The second progression is an improvisation, 'like a cadenza', with fresh catches of the day and seasonal items. The third movement creates a finale with traditional sushi items. He recreates this progression every day based on the best fish available in the market. Eating this progression is like listening to classical music. This is his big leap in product innovation, a culmination of his design philosophy. With each bite you are experiencing Jiro's philosophy of sushi.

This music has to be played on the taste buds of the customer. It is a kind of co-creation. Jiro needs your palate to be uncontaminated with starters, beer, tea, etc. so that he can control the taste and flavour experience. He does not want strong perfumes to interfere with the flavour he is so diligently trying to present to your taste buds. He has designed containers to ensure that the rice is kept at a specific temperature. Rice has to be served at body temperature; the temperature of the fish is as crucial as its freshness. Jiro has found out the precise temperatures at which the flavours are accentuated. Timing is very crucial, if the customer arrives late, the same sushi may taste different if it cools down below the optimal temperature band. Allowing walk-ins without reservations would be too disruptive. Not showing up after reservation is nothing short of an insult.[5] He serves each and every item at the perfect moment of deliciousness to every customer, and the last thing he wants to see is the fool taking pictures of his creation while the temperature of the sushi keeps dropping. The pace of the meal would be disrupted if everyone being served is not synchronized, that's why he adapts the sushi size to the gender of the customer. Coordinating the timing of twenty items for a single customer is difficult enough, coordinating it for ten customers at a time is a challenge fit for Jiro. The bottleneck to adding a chair is not the cost of the chair, it is the risk that the complexity would be so high that

[5] In 2019, Michelin announced that it would stop reviewing Sukiyabashi Jiro as it had stopped taking reservations from the general public, opting to only accept reservations from a hotel concierge. The restaurant was forced to take this step due to no-shows from overseas guests. While it may seem that Sukiyabashi Jiro is becoming exclusive, a no-show does disrupt the composition planned for the day. Unlike a concert, Jiro does not have the option to continue his performance without a listener.

conducting the orchestra would become unmanageable. A half-eaten item is like a half-played musical note, jarring to Jiro's aesthetics of the music he is delivering. Unnecessary banter among customers is as annoying and distracting as that in a music hall while the performance is on. How dare you interfere with Jiro's music. Suddenly, Jiro's idiosyncratic dictates start making sense. Understand this clearly—Jiro cares for his music. You are just a *means* to his creation.

Jiro watches his customers intently to understand if all the notes were played right, whether the customer experienced the intricacies of the various notes, relished the overall theme of the composition. Not all customers are alike in their capability to differentiate between the very fine flavours and tastes. Jiro values those who can, his creations are more appreciated by the cognoscenti, the ones with a sensitive palate and keen sense of smell. The true worth of Jiro is apparent to food critics like Yamamoto and celebrated peers like Joël Robuchon. The symphony that Jiro creates is wasted on the lay public whose only qualification to be served by Jiro is the paying capacity. Perhaps he finds more joy in serving his music to people who can discern its quality than the moneybags who just want bragging rights to have been served by the legend.

The 30,000 yen that you paid is not for the umami, it is for experiencing this music on your taste buds.

There is a difference between an Artist, a Conductor and a Composer. Jiro is a Composer. Jiro is the original sushi shokunin who showed that you can compose music with a twenty-item tasting menu. Others can recreate his compositions or compose their own pieces, but there would be only one Jiro Ono who showed the way.

Yoshikazu is a Conductor. He is an Artist in his own right, a Conductor who has played the compositions of the master with aplomb, perfected them, perhaps even interpreting them once in a while. But Yoshikazu is not a Composer. Sushi does not come in his dreams. When he joined the restaurant at age nineteen, he hated it and for the first two years he wanted to run away. What does Yoshikazu dream of? Fast cars. He is crazy about speed. His dream of being a fighter pilot was dashed by poor eyesight, his next-best dream of being a Formula 1 race driver was dashed by lack of a sponsor. He proudly shows off his Audi car that can do 300 kmph. Sukiyabashi Jiro is a *means* for him to fulfil his childhood dream. His reason for being where he is now is simple; the eldest son in Japanese society is meant to take up his father's position. He feels duty bound to continue his father's tradition; he does what he thinks is expected of him. He is not driven by dreams of the sushi kind. Perhaps the same applies to his younger brother. Takashi had felt that only one among the brothers would eventually succeed Jiro Ono as the head chef in Sukiyabashi Jiro. Takashi felt he was not an inferior Conductor to Yoshikazu just because he was younger. Competitiveness drove Takashi to leave and open the Roppongi Hills branch, not dreams.

Jiro dreams of sushi. Why does he not retire, why does he continue to come to work at such advanced age? Surely it is not for the money. In his own words, 'Shokunin try to get the highest quality fish and apply their technique to it. We don't care about money.' But does he care about the customer? Do you think he cares about the customer any more than as a means to an end? Does he, like Howard Roark, intend to have customers so that he can continue composing music on their taste buds? What brings him to the restaurant every day is the dream of the composition that he would play today; the improvisation that he would do given the variability of the best fish supply in the market today, and perhaps the slim hope that he would discover in one of the customers a palate which can experience the music in its entirety. The tuna begs him to do justice. The music begs him to do justice. The palate begs him to do justice. How can the master stay at home?

I would be truthful to you, my friend. Sometimes I do harbour delusions of grandeur, delusions of being a shokunin. Teachers are craftsmen, they craft men (and women). That is my aspiration—to be a teacher. Do you think I care about you? I do, but perhaps I care more for the beauty that I want to describe to you. Your mind is just the means for me to bring the beauty to realization. Just like Jiro has twenty items, I offer twenty sessions in my Elephants and Cheetahs elective. Case studies are carefully selected and sequenced to bring forth the tune that I want to play. The McDonald's case begs me to do justice to McDonald's, Jiro's documentary begs me to do justice to Jiro. And like Jiro, I enter each class with bated breath with the hope that one among the class would be able to grasp her beauty in the entirety. The eyes light up at the moment of enlightenment, there is no faking it. And that to me is true caring for a student. Hope springs eternal. That's why I wrote this book. Perhaps you, my friend, would fall in love with my beloved. Jiro dreams of sushi, I dream of *our* beloved.

But these are not the most important things for you, better refocus on yourself. Do you have dreams? Answer the most pertinent question.

Forget Jiro—what do *you* dream of?

APPENDIX B: COURSE OUTLINE

Indian Institute of Management Ahmedabad

Elephants and Cheetahs: Systems, Strategy and Bottlenecks

PGP Elective
Slot IX–X, 2019–20

Instructor: Professor Saral Mukherjee,
Wing 13, tel: 4929, saralm@iima.ac.in

Course Description and Objectives

'Elephants and Cheetahs: Systems, Strategy and Bottlenecks' is an unconventional treatment of Operations Strategy. It presents the dimensions of competition in the Operations domain through the lens of the natural world and systems thinking. The fundamental premise of the course is that systems are not just a collection of interconnected parts— the whole is greater than the sum of parts. A well-designed system is thus like a living entity with its own structural characteristics, peculiarities, capabilities, constraints and vulnerabilities.

The course builds on the core OM courses taught in first year and would be beneficial for participants who are planning a career in management consulting or general management roles. The relationships between the Firm Level Strategy and Operations Strategy are explored and the interlinkages between Marketing, HR and Operations Strategy are highlighted, leading up to a balanced scorecard approach to tracking organizational performance.

SESSION PLAN

Module 1: Understanding Systems

Session 1:	*Topic*:	What is a system?
	Reading:	1. Introduction (Autopoiesis and Cognition)
		2. Chapter 1 (Autopoiesis and Cognition)
		3. System Typologies in the Light of Autopoiesis
Session 2:	*Topic*:	System Structure, Behaviour and Typologies
	Reading:	1. Chapter 4: Structure and Behaviour of Complex Systems (Business Dynamics)
		2. The Second Cybernetics
Session 3:	*Topic*:	System Constraints and Bottlenecks
	Reading:	1. Variety, Constraint, and the Law of Requisite Variety
		2. On Being the Right Size

Module 2: Operations Strategy

Session 4:	*Topic:*	Operations Strategy
	Case:	The Morrison Company
	Reading:	The Strategic Power of Saying No
Session 5:	*Topic:*	Operations Strategy: Cost Leadership
	Case:	McDonald's Corporation (Abridged)
	Reading:	1. The Rise and Fall of Mass Production (The Machine that Changed the World)
		2. The McDonaldization of Society
Session 6:	*Topic:*	Operations Strategy: Cost Leadership vs. Cost Cutting
	Case:	Kanpur Confectioneries Private Limited (B)
Session 7:	*Topic:*	Operations Strategy: Time Responsiveness
	Case:	Crocs (A): Revolutionizing an Industry's Supply Chain Model for Competitive Advantage
Session 8:	*Topic:*	Operations Strategy: Superior Quality
	Video:	1. Jiro Dreams of Sushi
		2. Begin Japanology: Conveyor Belt Sushi
	Reading:	Competing on the Eight Dimensions of Quality
Session 9:	*Topic:*	Operations Strategy: Flexibility
	Case:	Stermon Mills Incorporated

Reading:	Agile Product Development: Managing Development Flexibility in Uncertain Environments
Session 10:	*Topic*:	Operations Strategy: Risk Minimization
	Case:	Boeing 767: From Concept to Production
Session 11:	*Topic*:	Operations Strategy: Convenience
	Case:	Commerce Bank
	Reading:	Understanding Service Convenience
Session 12:	*Topic*:	Operations Strategy: Superior Design
	Case:	Design Thinking and Innovation at Apple
	Readings:	Enlightened Experimentation: The New Imperative for Innovation
Session 13:	*Topic*:	Operations Strategy: Imitation
	Case:	Rocket Internet: Rise of the German Silicon Valley?
	Readings:	1. Reverse Engineering, Learning, and Innovation
		2. Imitation Is More Valuable than Innovation
Session 14:	*Topic*:	Operations Strategy: Collaboration
	Case:	Wikipedia: Project Esperanza
	Readings:	1. The Collective Intelligence Genome

2. Swarm Intelligence: A Whole New Way to Think About Business
3. New Principles of a Swarm Business

Module 3: System Evolution

Session 15: *Topic*: Evolution and Clockspeed
Case: Shimano and The High-End Road Bike Industry
Readings: Chapter 4: The Secret of Life (Clockspeed)

Session 16: *Topic*: Resilience and Growth
Case: Toyota: The Accelerator Crisis
Readings: 1. What I learned from Taiichi Ohno (The Birth of Lean)
2. The Rise of Lean Production (The Machine that Changed the World)

Session 17: *Topic*: Resilience and Innovation
Case: Managing Innovation at Nypro Inc. (A)

Module 4: System Performance

Session 18: *Topic*: Focused Factory
Case: Managing Orthopaedics at Rittenhouse Medical Center
Readings: 1. Using the Balanced Scorecard as a Strategic Management System
2. All Kinds of Dilemmas, but Just a Few Types

Session 19: *Topic*:   Evaluating System Performance:
                            Non-profits
                 Case: 1. Greenpeace
                            2. World Wildlife Fund for Nature
                            (WWF)
                 Readings: All Kinds of Dilemmas, but Just a
                            Few Types

Session 20: *Topic*:   Comprehensive Case
                 Case: 1. Benetton (A)
                            2. Zara: Fast Fashion

Bibliography

Ashby, W.R. (1968). Variety, Constraint, and the Law of Requisite Variety. In W. Buckley, *Modern Systems Research for the Behavioral Scientist*. Chicago: Aldine Publishing Co.

Babbage, C. (1832). *On the Economy of Machinery and Manufactures*. Cambridge University Press.

Berry, L.L., Seiders, K., and Grewal, D. (2002, July). Understanding Service Convenience. *Journal of Marketing*, 66(3), 1–17.

Brooks Jr., F.P. (1975). *The Mythical Man-Month*. Addison-Wesley.

Camus, A. (2005). *The Myth of Sisyphus*. (J. O'Brien, Trans.) London: Penguin Books.

Cohen, W.M., and Levinthal, D.A. (1990, March). Absorptive Capacity: A New Perspective on Learning and Innovation. *Administrative Science Quarterly*, 35(1), 128–152.

Crosby, P.B. (1979). *Quality Is Free: The Art of Making Quality Certain*. New York: McGraw-Hill.

Deming, W. (1982). *Out of the Crisis*. MIT Press.

Drucker, P. (1954). *The Practice of Management*. New York: Harper & Brothers.

Engels, F. (1845). *The Condition of the Working Class in England* (Reissue Edition [2009] ed.). (D. McLellan, ed.) Oxford: Oxford University Press.

Erlenkotter, D. (1990). Ford Whitman Harris and the Economic Order Quantity Model. *Operations Research, 38*(6), 937–46.

Fine, C.H. (1999). *Clockspeed: Winning Industry Control in the Age of Temporary Advantage*. Reading, Massachusetts, USA: Perseus Books.

Ford, H., and Crowther, S. (1922). *My Life and Work*. Garden City.

Forrester, J.W. (1961). *Industrial Dynamics*. Cambridge, Mass.: MIT Press.

Friedman, M. (1970, 13 September). The Social Responsibility of Business Is to Increase Its Profits. *New York Times Magazine*.

Garvin, D.A. (1987, November–December). Competing on the Eight Dimensions of Quality. *Harvard Business Review*.

Gelb, D. (Director). (2011). *Jiro Dreams of Sushi* [Motion Picture]. Magnolia Pictures. Retrieved from Netflix.

Gerwin, D. (1993). Manufacturing Flexibility: A Strategic Perspective. *Management Science, 39*(4), 395–410.

Ghemawat, P., and Nueno, J.L. (2006). ZARA: Fast Fashion (Harvard Business School Case 9-703497).

Gilbreth, Jr., F.B., and Carey, E.G. (1948). *Cheaper by the Dozen*. New York: Thomas Y. Crowell Company.

Haldane, J.B. (1926, March). On Being the Right Size. *Harper's Magazine*.

Harvey, D. (1982). *The Limits to Capital*. Oxford: Basil Blackwell.

International Labour Office. (1992). *Introduction to Work Study* (4th [revised] ed.). (G. Kanawaty, ed.) Geneva: International Labour Office.

Ishiguro, K. (1989). *The Remains of the Day*. Faber and Faber.

Iyer, A.V., and Bergen, M.E. (1997). Quick Response in Manufacturer-Retailer Channels. *Management Science, 43*(4), 559–70.

Juran, J.M., and Gryna, F.M. (1993). *Quality Planning and Analysis*. McGraw-Hill.

Kafka, F. (1915). *The Metamorphosis*.

Lee, H.L., Padmanabhan, V., and Whang, S. (1997). The Bullwhip Effect in Supply Chains. *Sloan Management Review*, 93–102.

Lee, H.L., Padmanabhan, V., and Whang, S. (2004). Information Distortion in a Supply Chain: The Bullwhip Effect. *Management Science, 50*(12), 1875–86.

Levi-Strauss, C. (1966). *The Savage Mind*. University of Chicago Press.

Levitt, T. (1960). Marketing Myopia. *Harvard Business Review*.

Luhmann, N. (2013). *Introduction to Systems Theory*. (D. Baecker, ed., and P. Gilgen, trans.) Malden, USA: Polity Press.

Makridakis, S., Hogarth, R.M., and Gaba, A. (2010). Why Forecasts Fail. What to Do Instead. *MIT Sloan Management Review, 51*(2), 83–90.

Maruyama, M. (1963, June). The Second Cybernetics: Deviation-Amplifying Mutual Causal Processes. *American Scientist, 51*(2), 164–79.

Maturana, H.R., and Varela, F.J. (1980). *Autopoiesis and Cognition: The Realization of the Living*. Dordrecht, Holland: D. Reidel.

McAfee, A., Dessain, V., and Sjoman, A. (2004). Zara: IT for Fast Fashion (Harvard Business School Case Study 604081).

Metcalfe, B. (2013). Metcalfe's Law after 40 Years of Ethernet. *Computer, 46*(12), 26–31.

Mingers, J. (1997). Systems Typologies in the Light of Autopoiesis: A Reconceptualization of Boulding's Hierarchy, and a Typology of Self-Referential Systems. *Systems Research and Behavioral Science, 14*, 303–13.

Mintzberg, H. (1989). *Mintzberg on Management: Inside Our Strange World of Organizations*. New York: Free Press.

Olhager, J., Rudberg, M., and Wikner, J. (2001). Long-term Capacity Management: Linking the Perspectives from Manufacturing Strategy and Sales and Operations Planning. *International Journal of Production Economics, 69*(2), 215–25.

O'Reilly III, C.A., and Tushman, M.L. (2004, April). The Ambidextrous Organization. *Harvard Business Review*.

Porter, M.E. (1980). *Competitive Strategy: Techniques for Analysing Industries and Competitors*. Free Press.

Reed, D.P. (2001, February). The Law of the Pack. *Harvard Business Review*.

Ridgway, V.F. (1956). Dysfunctional Consequences of Performance Measurements. *Administrative Science Quarterly, 1*(2), 240–47.

Ritzer, G. (2014). *The McDonaldization of Society* (8th ed.). Sage Publications.

Schopenhauer, A. (1969). *The World as Will and Representation* (Vol. 1). (E. Payne, trans.) Dover Publications.

Service, T. (2011, October 25). Riccardo Chailly on Beethoven: 'It's a Long Way from the First to the Ninth'. *Guardian*. Retrieved 26 April 2019, from https://www.theguardian.com/music/2011/oct/25/beethoven-cycle-riccardo-chailly.

Simon, H.A. (1996). *The Sciences of the Artificial* (3rd ed.). MIT Press.

Skinner, W. (1974, May–June). The Focussed Factory. *Harvard Business Review*.

Smith, A. (1776). *The Wealth of Nations*. Bantam Dell.

Taleb, N.N. (2008). *The Black Swan: The Impact of the Highly Improbable*. London: Penguin.

Tanaka, M. (2009). What I Learned from Taiichi Ohno. In K. Shimokawa, and T. Fujimoto, *The Birth of Lean*. The Lean Enterprise Institute.

Taylor, F.W. (1903). *Shop Management*. American Society of Mechanical Engineers.

Taylor, F.W. (1911). *The Principles of Scientific Management*. Harper & Brothers.

Thayer, A.W. (1921). *The Life of Ludwig van Beethoven* (Vol. I). (H.E. Krehbiel, trans.) New York: The Beethoven Association.

Thomke, S. (2001, February). Enlightened Experimentation: The New Imperative for Innovation. *Harvard Business Review*.

Upton, D. (2005). McDonald's Corporation (Abridged). (Harvard Business School Case 9-603-041).

Upton, D.M. (1995, July–August). What Really Makes Factories Flexible? *Harvard Business Review*, 74–84.

von Hippel, E. (1986, July). Lead Users: A Source of Novel Product Concepts. *Management Science, 32*(7), 773–907.

Weick, K.E. (1993). The Collapse of Sensemaking in Organizations: The Mann Gulch Disaster. *Administrative Science Quarterly, 38,* 628–652.

Wheelwright, S.C., and Hayes, R.H. (1985, January–February). Competing Through Manufacturing. *Harvard Business Review.*

Wilson, A., Lowe, J., Roskilly, K. et al. (2013). Locomotion Dynamics of Hunting in Wild Cheetahs. *Nature,* 498, 185–89.

Womack, J.P., Jones, D.T., and Roos, D. (1990). *The Machine That Changed the World.* New York: Free Press.

Zahra, S.A., and George, G. (2002, April). Absorptive Capacity: A Review, Reconceptualization, and Extension. *The Academy of Management Review, 27* (2), 185–203.